Merry Ch

Cape May Point

The Illustrated History: 1875 to the Present

Joe J. Jordan

Schiffer Publishing Ltd

4880 Lower Valley Road, Atglen, PA 19310 USA

Dedication

To the countless visitors and residents who have an enduring affection for Cape May Point.

Library of Congress Cataloging-in-Publication Data

Jordan, Joe J.
    Cape May Point : the illustrated history : 1875 to the present / by Joe J. Jordan.
        p. cm.
    ISBN 0-7643-1830-6
1. Cape May Point (N.J.)--History. 2. Cape May Point (N.J.)--History--Pictorial works. I. Title.
F144.C24J67 2003
974.9'98--dc21
                    2003005243

Designed by Ellen J. (Sue) Taltoan
Type set in Seagull HvBT/Aldine 721 BT

ISBN: 0-7643-1830-6
Printed in China

Published by Schiffer Publishing Ltd.
4880 Lower Valley Road
Atglen, PA 19310
Phone: (610) 593-1777; Fax: (610) 593-2002
E-mail: Info@schifferbooks.com
Please visit our web site catalog at
www.schifferbooks.com
We are always looking for people to write books on new and related subjects. If you have an idea for a book, please contact us at the above address.

This book may be purchased from the publisher.
Include $3.95 for shipping.
Please try your bookstore first.
You may write for a free catalog.

In Europe, Schiffer books are distributed by
Bushwood Books
6 Marksbury Avenue
Kew Gardens
Surrey TW9 4JF England
Phone: 44 (0) 20 8392 8585
Fax: 44 (0) 20 8392 9876
E-mail: Bushwd@aol.com
Free postage in the UK. Europe: air mail at cost.

Contents

Acknowledgments

A very special acknowledgement is due my wife, Sarah, whom I thank profusely for tolerating, over the past four years, the neglect, the deprivation, and the disruptions to our everyday life that have resulted from my concentration on the preparation of this book. I hope she will forgive me; it has required a much larger effort than I had anticipated.

I must also acknowledge the thorough contribution to research on the history of Cape May Point that Donelda Fazakas has undertaken, over a period of many years. I visited her in Florida and was impressed with the work she had accomplished. She has been most gracious to me, and I had considered suggesting a joint authorship for this book. However, the distance to her current residence in Florida, and the difficulties we would have faced in communicating and coordinating our efforts, made such a collaboration impractical.

Some sixty individuals and organizations have provided me with assistance, in diverse ways, for which I am most grateful.

For valuable advice from professional authors, my thanks to Michael Kelly, Margaret Buckholtz, Irv Yevish, and William Allen Zulker, and for excellent counsel on publishing negotiations, my appreciation to Patricia Harper.

The institutions or companies and their staff who have provided essential information and materials include: Suzette Baird, of the Presbyterian Children's Village; Bruce Laverty, of The Athenaeum of Philadelphia; Msgr. Ryan, Pastor of Our Lady Star of the Sea; Sr. St. Michele, of the Sisters of the Immaculate Heart of Mary; Chris Stanwood, archivist at the Philadelphia College of Physicians; Sr. Nora Frost, of the Deaconess Community of the Evangelical Lutheran Church in America; Ione E. Williams, librarian of the Cape May County Historical Society; Jim Campbell, historian, and Pat Pocher, curator, both of the Greater Cape May Historical Society; Mayor Malcolm Fraser, for the use of the Cape May Point photo archives; Susan Avedisian, Editor of the Cape May Star and Wave; Christopher Densmore, of the Society of Friends Historical Library; Jeffrey Gebert and Susan Lucas, of the US Army Corps of Engineers, Philadelphia; Bernie Moore, formerly of the New Jersey State Division of Coastal Engineering; Dean Kromer, of the Cape May Point State Park; Linda Landon, of Breakwaters International Inc; and to Gary and Courtney Romberger, of the West Cape Café.

In Cape May Point, I am grateful to several Taxpayer Association members: to Dorothy Loftus, for collecting various materials and photographs of historical value; to Tony Keiser for safeguarding the collection and bringing it to my attention; and to Peggy Veith, for providing the back copies of the association newsletters, many of which contain important historical data.

Many photographs have come from the private collections of the following residents or visitors to Cape May Point: William W. Dickhart, III, Robert W. Elwell, Sr., Dick Hall, H. Gerald MacDonald, John Mather, Jack and Elizabeth McBride, Marie A. Richards, David Rutherford, E. Roberta Rutherford, Sandy Strine, and Joan Viguers. I am grateful to all and especially to professional photographer, Hugh Hales-Tooke, for a flattering portrait.

I've enjoyed the conversations with, and want to thank, all those who have provided me with interesting and often amusing anecdotes that illuminate the Cape May Point of their youth: Peggy Dickhart, Robert Grubb, Dick Hall, John Mather, Pete Piatras, David Rutherford, and Rudolph K. Schmidt.

I am indebted beyond measure to Trudy Tektiv for a professional job of copyediting, for wise suggestions, for arduous research, and many kind words during the final months of writing. Assistance in many forms has been most helpful from: Neal Blank, for proper language usage and thoughtful editing; Olivera Berce, of Wallace, Roberts, and Todd for AutoCAD map preparation; to Joe Nietubicz for scanning services and help with my software problems; Margaret Rosenberg Lonergan, for an elusive brochure on the Cape House Hotel; Bruce Graham, of Van-Note Harvey Associates, for an autoCAD map disk of Cape May Point; Eileen Kirk for documents on the Weatherby development, for photos, and for advise on hand-colored photographs; Marvin Hume, for information on Sunset Beach; Gary McGinley for information on the old Hughes Brothers Lumber Yard; Nick De Credico and Trudy Cohen for providing photographic equipment; Edith B. Thompson for information on her lakeside cottage, which had been the Cape May Country Club; Anne Hart and Reverend John G. Huber for certain historic data; Lilian Malcolm, for childhood memories as a resident at Sunny Corner; and to Dick Cook for his tales of the Point's Native Americans.

My gratitude to the authors and publishers who have granted permission to quote from their books and articles: Maryjane Briant, managing editor of The Press of Atlantic City, for Richard Degener's piece on Lake Lily; Michele Gisbert, of Rutgers University Press, for Jeffrey Dorwart's *History of Cape May County*; Connie Considine Kelly, author of *"Atlantus" and The History of Concrete Ships*; and to Elizabeth O. Strang, for permission to quote from her father's story about a famous swim across Delaware Bay.

I apologize to all of you who deserve my gratitude for your contributions, if I have inadvertently omitted your name.

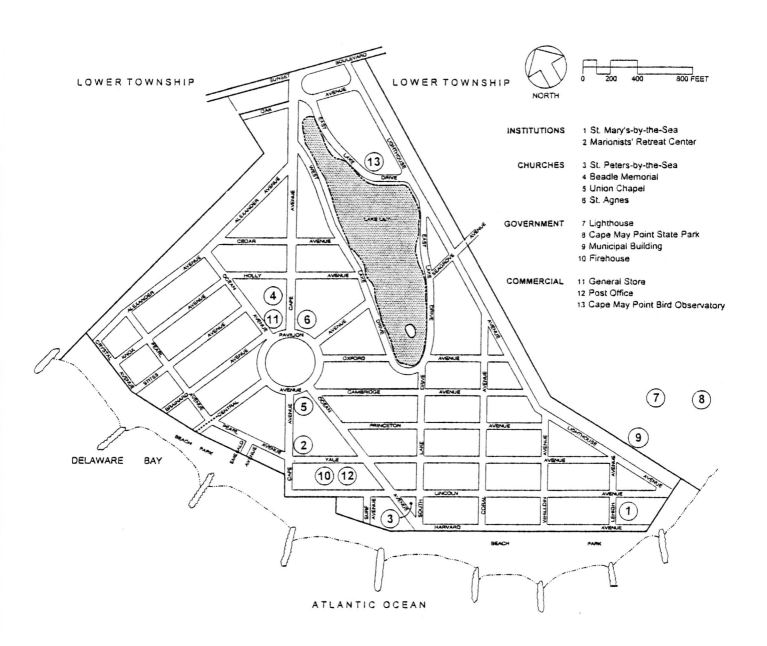

Cape May Point 2003

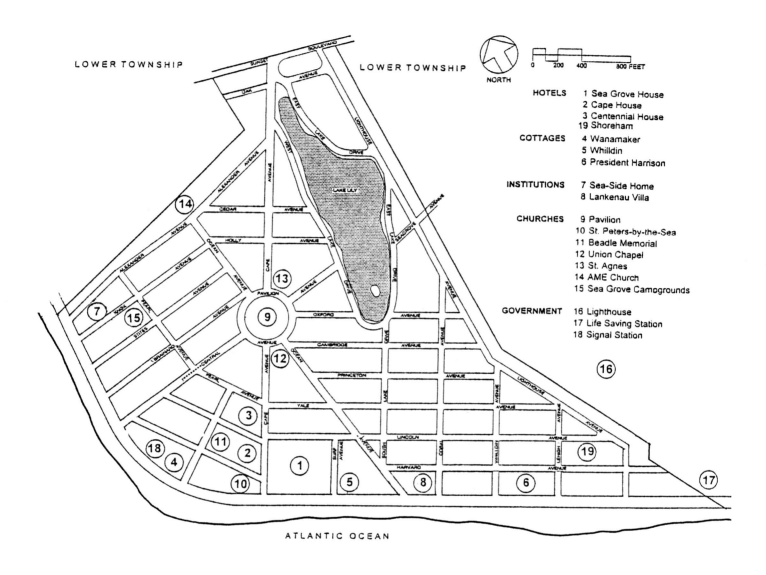

Cape May Point 1878-1900

Introduction

My curiosity is the motivator behind this book. Why, I have asked myself for thirty years, is my parents' Cape Avenue cottage (and today my home) identical to the one next door, to the one across the street, and to the one built behind the one across the street?

An 1877 birds-eye view of Sea Grove depicts all four houses in place. Yet an 1877 map contradicts, showing only the two across the street, together with their owners' names, while our lot and my neighbor's are shown as the only vacant building lots owned by the Sea Grove Association.

This puzzle led me to research early deeds at the County Records Office, and that task led to more research on early tax records, followed soon by even more research, from the County library's microfilm collection of early newspapers, into other aspects of Sea Grove's beginnings. As I started to organize and interpret my findings, I sensed that others might share my interest in the full history of Cape May Point. Today, I still don't have the answer to my original question – I have a book instead.

The book is divided into four parts. The first traces the Point's development in the nineteenth century, the second covers the early twentieth century, the third brings events up to today, and the fourth tells the stories of the Point's neighbors along the coast, from South Cape May to Higbees Beach.

The twenty-two chapters group similar topics together thematically – charitable institutions or noteworthy storms, for example. Within each chapter, headlines announce the topics of the little stories related to that chapters theme. There are over a hundred of such tales – taken together they reveal the history of Cape May Point and of its fascinating neighbors.

Insofar as possible, the book is based on primary sources, such as accounts in local newspapers, minutes of borough meetings, tax and deed records, and historical archives. This helps, but does not insure, accuracy. News accounts are not always correct, archived photographs are sometimes misidentified, tax records are missing from county files, and some old microfilmed materials are illegible. I too am fallible, but I have tried not to make assertions for which I have no evidence. Readers who find factual errors are encouraged to report them to me, so that the record can be corrected in any future edition.

Part 1

The Early Years

1875-1900

Chapter 1

A Righteous Resort

Early Jersey Seashore Developments

Since the beginning of the nineteenth century, Cape May was *the* shore resort for Philadelphia, Baltimore, and Washington. It offered easy access down the Delaware Bay – first by schooner, and then by steamship. Further up the coast, New Yorkers had their Long Branch (also dependent on access by ship) with even earlier beginnings in the late 1700s. Together, their seventy-five-year growth had been slow and steady, driven by the relative speed and comfort of travel by boat over travel by land. Geography was their *raison d'être*.

By mid-century there was little choice for seaside vacationers. As early as 1845, Long Beach Island had occasional visitors who could be put up at a small hotel in Harvey Cedars. Ten years later the Ashley boarding house at Barnegat Light tended to the needs of the few fishermen who found their way across the Barnegat Bay.

The arrival of the railroads changed all that. In 1854, Atlantic City became the latest seaside entry, served by the new *Camden and Atlantic Railroad*. From hot and humid Philadelphia to the cool bathing beaches of the Atlantic Ocean in little more than an hour? Fantastic! Philadelphians responded immediately and Atlantic City boomed. Like Cape May and Long Branch, it soon had boundless sybaritic pleasures to offer eager vacationers.

(c.1878) The 300 room Hotel Engleside in Long Branch, NJ, was a more imposing edifice than its counterpart in Sea Grove, the Sea Grove House. *Courtesy of the Cape May County Library.*

(c.1878) Residence of Dr. T. G. Chattle. Few cottages in Cape May could match the grandeur of this luxurious home in Long Branch, NJ. Cape May and Long Branch were the resort destinations of the well to do in the early nineteenth century. *Courtesy of the Cape May County Library.*

Beach Haven and Surf City were born in the early 1870s, when a rail spur from Tuckerton brought Philadelphians to the shore of Barnegat Bay, and then by Pharo's steamer across the bay to the barrier island. Meanwhile, New Yorkers were drifting to the upper shores of New Jersey and within ten years had established small resort communities at Sea Girt, Ocean Grove, Asbury Park, Monmouth Beach, and Belmar. These tended to be modest start-ups; the speculative ventures of a few real estate entrepreneurs. The land was dirt cheap to acquire, and a quick and tidy profit could be realized if all went well.

Speculation in real estate was not the only driving force behind the emerging seaside resorts. There were those who recoiled from the worldly pleasures to be found in Long Branch, Cape May, or Atlantic City. They were dismayed by the disrespect for the Sabbath, by excessive gambling or public drunkenness. This was the age of evangelism, with religious fervor near its peak. Religious revivals and camp meetings had been going on for more than a century in America.

Reverend William B. Osborn, a Methodist preacher, had started an ambitious camp meeting resort on the coast in North Jersey. He named it Ocean Grove, and it was to be a place for physical and spiritual renewal, with the accent on *spiritual*. The rules were strict: no bathing on Sunday, no vehicles on the streets on Sunday, and no liquor within a mile at any time. Temperance reigned.

During this period camp meetings were common throughout rural New Jersey, but Ocean Grove was the first to be established as a permanent seaside resort. These meetings were religious revivals and their roots can be traced to the "Great Awakening" in the early 1700s. Usually established by Methodist, Baptist, and sometimes by Presbyterian ministers, they drew participants together for emotional preaching and communal prayer.

Over time, some grew from simple tent campgrounds to more permanent cabin settlements. Oak Bluffs, on the island of Martha's Vineyard in Massachusetts, and Ocean Grove in New Jersey are splendid examples of camp meeting communities that have thrived to this day. These two communities were comparable to what Alexander Whilldin envisioned as a new seashore resort for God-fearing Christians.

Alexander Whilldin – Sea Grove's Founding Father

Alexander Whilldin was a religious man, a deeply committed Presbyterian. A Presiding Elder of the church for thirty years, he immersed himself in their charitable institutions. The American Sunday School Union, the Presbyterian Hospital, the Philadelphia Tract Society, the Presbyterian Board of Publication, and the Union Temporary Home for Children all profited from his largess and tireless service. He viewed Cape May's high life with disdain.

Though born in Philadelphia, Whilldin came from an old Cape May County family, his father a sea captain lost at sea when Alexander was only four. He grew up near Cape May Court House on the homestead farm, but at the age of sixteen, he returned to Philadelphia to pursue a life in commerce. It became a very successful life.

After but eight years as a junior store clerk, he opened his own firm with a partner who provided the initial capital. He was then twenty-four. The next year the partner was gone and his business as a commission merchant in cotton and wool thrived. By 1875 he had amassed considerable wealth. Edward S. Wheeler in his 1876 history of South Jersey

(c.1875) Portrait of Alexander Whilldin, who created Sea Grove in 1875 as a "moral and religious seaside home." A wealthy merchant in Philadelphia, Whilldin was from an old and prominent Cape May County family. *Courtesy of the Cape May County Historical Society.*

12

Scheyichbi and the Strand described Whilldin as, "…prudent, sound in judgment, courteous, self-reliant, industrious, and of indomitable energy and persistence."

For fifty years, each Cape May season found Whilldin escaping from business for relaxing sojourns at the shore. He observed "with regret, the increase of a bad fashion which renders the season for rest and health-giving resort to nature but a wearying round of dissipation."

During these visits, Whilldin had thought about a different kind of place – perhaps not a fundamentally religious community like Ocean Grove, but a place that in his words would become a "moral and religious seaside home." Fortunately Alexander Whilldin had the means to achieve his mission. He owned all the land that was to become Sea Grove! His wife of almost forty years was a Stites, and the property had been in her family since 1712. Now nearing seventy, Whilldin decided to act. With the agreement of his wife, Jane, with whom he said, "they had laid the matter before God" he took the first decisive steps by the formation of The West Cape May Land Company in 1872, and The Sea Grove Association in 1875.

(c.1875) Whilldin built his cottage, "Land's End," on a double lot at the corner of Beach Avenue and Surf Street, adjacent to the Sea Grove House. Like most of the original beachfront cottages, it was a victim of the erosion that has plagued the Point from the beginning. It did not survive the storm of 1936. *Courtesy of the Cape May County Historical Society.*

Whilldin had thought about a different kind of place – perhaps not a fundamentally religious community like Ocean Grove, but a place that, in his words, would become a "moral and religious seaside home."

John Wanamaker – Sea Grove's Famous Co-Founder

In addition to Alexander Whilldin, two other Philadelphians, retail merchant John Wanamaker, and architect James Sidney, were to have a powerful influence on the development of Sea Grove. Whilldin provided Sea Grove's foundation – with his vision and his property; the influential Wanamaker contributed to its fame; the talented Sidney supplied this new seaside resort with its charming form.

Through his business contacts as a wool and cotton merchant, Alexander Whilldin knew John Wanamaker, the astonishingly successful department store retailer in Philadelphia, who was to become the most influential stockholder in the Sea Grove Association. Besides their mercantile interests, both were stalwart Presbyterians devoted to the various charitable institutions of the church. Their paths could have crossed in many ways. Whilldin had diverse business interests as President of the American Life Insurance Company and as a Vice-President of the Corn Exchange Bank. Wanamaker, though thirty years his junior, was already a prosperous businessman with an eye on a future career in politics. He shared with Whilldin a passionate devotion to Presbyterian causes.

A product of one of the early Huguenot families from France, who generations before had settled in Penn's colony, John Wanamaker was born on July 11, 1838. His childhood

(c.1860) Portrait of John Wanamaker, Sea Grove's co-founder. In 1875, at the age of thirty-seven, he was already an astoundingly successful retail merchant in Philadelphia. *Courtesy of the Cape May County Historical Society.*

14

(c.1875) The Wanamaker cottage, originally located on Beach Avenue at the northeast corner of Emerald Avenue, next to the Signal Tower. In 1916, it was moved to the northeast corner of Cape and Yale Avenues, and became the summer home of the Philadelphia Presbyterian Orphanage. *Courtesy of the Cape May County Historical Society.*

in the Grays Ferry area of southeast Philadelphia was marked by relative poverty. Following short stints with the clothing firms of Troutman and Hayes, and with Barclay Lippincott, at sixteen he went to work at Tower Hall at 518 Market Street, considered the best clothing store in the city.

During three years of arduous work, he applied himself fervently and learned much about the clothing business – the buying, selling, advertising, and financing of a successful enterprise. Still, the young Wanamaker was to consider other career paths – architect, journalist, doctor, and clergyman. His mother favored the ministry, and it is somewhat surprising that he turned his back on this path. His grandfather had been a lay preacher in the Methodist Church and his father the superintendent of the first Sunday school John had attended. His religion gradually became more his life than a part of his life. Nevertheless, his final decision was merchant, and what a merchant he was to become!

The man who exerted the most influence on Wanamaker's religious vision was John Chambers, the best-known preacher in Philadelphia, who presided over the First Independent Church at Broad and Sansom Streets. John took to heart the teachings of this mentor about the importance of evangelism, the sacredness of the Sabbath, and a view of alcohol as Satan's ally.

At the age of eighteen he became a Sunday school teacher, mustering his own class from the kids in his neighborhood. At twenty, in a career shift, he took a new position as the first full-time secretary of the Philadelphia YMCA, which had been formed only five years earlier. Within a year, he had raised membership from less than a hundred to several thousand, and had placed forty teachers in various Sunday schools. He served as the head of the Philadelphia YMCA for over twenty years, a period in which he was building his mighty retail business.

His initial success with the YMCA and later success in his retail business were overshadowed in his mind by his founding of the Bethany Mission Sunday School in Philadelphia. In February 1858, at the age of nineteen, Wanamaker held the first Sunday meeting over a shop at 2135 South Street with twenty-seven children attending. By mid-July, attendance had risen to over three hundred. Three months later a cornerstone was laid for the new Bethany Chapel – John Wanamaker's first building enterprise, and in January 1859 it was formally dedicated. In time, Bethany became the largest Sunday school in the country, and Wanamaker remained its superintendent throughout his life. It was his singular passion as revealed in his own writings:

Is Bethany the glory or the tragedy of my life? At times I feel that I starved and cheated myself, however, and that I starved and cheated those dear to me by driving so hard all day Sunday, by never being willing to leave it, to change, to modify. I have always been happy in Bethany. I might have done other things with greater effect. But if you are happy? Why people think my Bethany work is either virtue or pose, I cannot imagine. I have just always liked it. And there isn't anything else, not business certainly, that I have just always liked and have gotten always satisfaction and blessing, not worry, out of.

Considering the importance Wanamaker placed on his religious activities for the Presbyterian Church, and the significance of Sea Grove as a largely Presbyterian effort, it is surprising that in all of the biographies of this man there is little mention of his imposing summer cottage there, and no mention of its eventual donation to the Presbyterian Orphanage as a summer home for children.

Stites Beach

Today, it's hard to imagine the wild place that Cape May Point was in 1875, the year it was founded by Philadelphia textile merchant Alexander Whilldin. At that time it wasn't called Cape May Point, or even Sea Grove – it was a wilderness known as Stites Beach or Barren Beach.

Fifteen-foot dunes lined the beaches. Covered with native beach grass, the dunes were a natural by-product of wind-blown sand. Waves of goldenrod, poison ivy, bayberry and beach plum blanketed the undulating sandhills. Gradually the shrubs of gave way to growths of oak and red cedar, often twisted and wrenched into fantasy shapes by the persistent winds from the sea.

Further back were the pin oaks, pitch pines, holly and sassafras. A few sweet and sour gums and an occasional red maple crowded into these woods, forming an almost impenetrable barrier, a thick underbrush of poison ivy mingled with blueberry, huckleberry and greenbrier.

The Indians were gone now. Few white men had any reason to go there. The place was hardly known except to the occasional local hunter. The local newspaper, *Star of the Cape*, called it "…a desert wilderness of trees, brush, brambles, and sand." and "…a dense growth of timber, woody copse, and briar tangles, with a sea front of sand hills and inhabited by rabbits and other wild game." Such was the site that Alexander Whilldin decided to develop as a new seaside resort. He would name it Sea Grove.

(c.1875) Cape May Point as it appeared in 1875 when it was known as Stites Beach after the Stites family who owned the land. Almost forty years earlier, Alexander Whilldin had married Jane Stites, who had inherited the property that was to become Sea Grove. *Courtesy of the Borough of Cape May Point.*

16

The Sea Grove Association

With the presentation of an application to the New Jersey legislature for a charter of incorporation under the name of the Sea Grove Association, Whilldin set out to develop the family tract into a Christian resort. On February 4, 1875, he, John Wanamaker, and James Gass, of Philadelphia County, joined with Downs Edmunds and Dr. Virgil M.D.Marcy, of Cape May County, as the incorporators.

Whilldin's relationship with Wanamaker was probably a mixture of commerce and religion. Whilldin was a prominent wool merchant and it seems likely that the Wanamaker store would have purchased its products for their retail business. Both were zealous Presbyterians, active in many of their religion's charitable causes.

Downs Edmunds, an eminent member of one of the old Cape May County families, had significant family connections with Alexander Whilldin. He had been living on the Whilldin farm for twenty-six years when the Sea Grove Association was incorporated, and one of his daughters married a Stites.

Dr. Virgil Marcy's mother was an Edmunds, which confirms another connection among the group Whilldin had assembled to form the Sea Grove Association. Marcy was a respected Physician in Cape May where he had a large practice for fifty years. The true bond that the incorporators shared was their religion. All appear to have worshiped at "Old Brick," the Cold Spring Presbyterian Church.

The formation of the Sea Grove Association provided the legal right to create a new community under New Jersey law. Long before that action was taken, the serious planning had been underway. J.C. Sidney had already been engaged as the architect, surveyor, and planner. Early winter saw his drawings very near complete.

(c.1880) The architect, James Sidney, designed this rustic timber gateway to mark the entrance to Sea Grove where Cape Avenue intersected the Cape Island Turnpike, known today as Sunset Boulevard. *Courtesy of Robert W. Elwell, Sr.*

James C. Sidney – Sea Grove's Architect

The circumstances leading to the selection of James Charles Sidney as the architect and planner of Sea Grove are not known. We do know that he was born in England around 1819 and had started his architectural practice in Philadelphia in his late twenties. He would have been about fifty-five years of age when he drew the first plans for the new resort.

His career was not confined to architecture. In the 1849 Philadelphia Directory he was listed as a "Civil Engineer" and the following year he formed a partnership with James Neff as "Sidney and Neff - Engineers and Architects." Together they created master plans for two cemeteries: one in Troy, New York, and Oakland Cemetery in Chester County, Pennsylvania.

Several years prior, in the early 1840s, Sidney had been employed as a cartographer by the Library Company of Philadelphia. This training probably accounts for his later employment by the firm of Robert Pearsall Smith, one of America's largest map publishers. Here he produced several notable maps of the Philadelphia region. In an interruption to his architectural career he moved to New York with that company and spent two years assisting in their mapping of New York State.

A decade later he created a new firm with Andrew Adams and described their practice as "Rural Architects, Engineers, and Surveyors – particular attention paid to building and laying out of county seats, cemeteries and public grounds. Surveys and plans made for every kind of building or work requiring knowledge of engineering."

The most significant commission of the Sidney and Adams firm was their master plan for Fairmount Park, adopted in 1859. A contemporary issue of *The Gardener's Monthly* characterized Sidney as "the best landscape-gardener, perhaps, in the country."

After fifteen years of practice under three short-lived partnerships, Sidney continued his career as a proprietorship. He shifted emphasis to institutional architecture, designing, in two years, nineteen public schools in Philadelphia. His professional career seems to have been guided more by circumstance than by design. Was he an architect, or a civil engineer, or a landscape architect, or a surveyor, or a cartographer?

He was for certain an architect, having signed the application for a charter for the Pennsylvania Society of Architects and become a member of the American Institute of Architects in 1870. As for the other fields, he may not have received professional certification, but he gained knowledge in civil engineering, landscape planning, surveying, and map making, and put it to good use in his plans for Sea Grove.

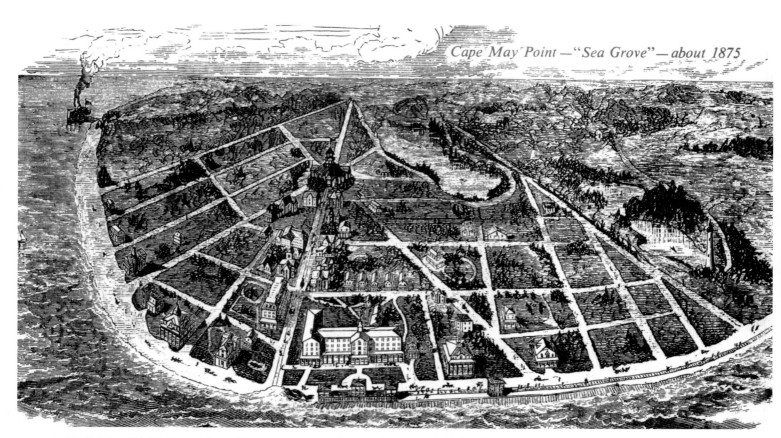

Cape May Point — "Sea Grove" — about 1875

(c.1875) A fanciful bird's-eye view of Seagrove as it may have looked around 1877 – from a promotional brochure published by the Sea Grove Association. The Sea Grove Hotel in the center foreground was lost to the sea in 1936, but the five identical cottages just behind it, originally known as "Walker's Row," and later as the "Five Sisters," remain today on Lincoln Avenue between Cape and Ocean Avenues. *Courtesy of the Cape May County Historical Society.*

Sidney's Imposing Plan

If Sea Grove were to become the "moral and religious seaside home" envisioned by Alexander Whilldin, how should the town be laid out?

J. C. Sidney's design must have been inspired by the religious camp meetings of the period. A typical camp meeting was formed around a central grove in the woods where the religious activities were held. Surrounding the grove, the faithful pitched tents for their families' comfort during the weeklong religious retreats. As the fame and permanence of the camp meeting became assured, small cabins often replaced these tents.

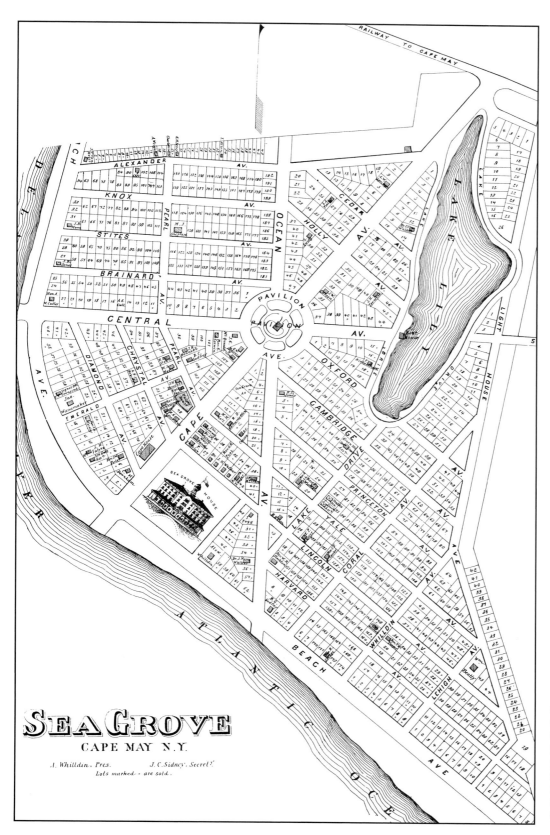

(c.1877) Original map of Sea Grove, prepared by the Sea Grove Association. It shows the lot subdivision and purportedly indicates the ownership of the cottages that had been built or were under construction in 1877. *Courtesy of the Author.*

Frequently, within a few years of its founding, an auditorium would be built in the middle of the grove as a permanent shelter for the evangelical services. Its plan was ordinarily circular in shape although it might take the form of an octagon or other regular polyhedron. Was this not the same design concept Sidney employed for Sea Grove?

Indeed, the most striking characteristic of Sidney's town plan was the pavilion circle, a large round park. In the center, Sidney placed the impressive open-air pavilion where two thousand could worship. This was quite an ambitious gesture when we consider that, were it to be there today, it could accommodate almost all the Cape May Point summer residents at a single service! Practicality aside, it announced loud and clear that this was the heart and soul of the community, a Christian community with public worship as its cornerstone.

The 250-acre site was to provide a total of 981 building lots. Most were at least five thousand square feet in area. Some building sites were as much as twenty-five feet above sea level, but the low land between the lake and the ocean was to be filled and the final street pattern emerged relatively level.

To assure visitors of the prominence of this new community, there were to be no streets, only *avenues* (with but two exceptions: Surf Street, probably because it was to be used as a service drive to the Sea Grove Hotel, and Lake Drive). The three main thoroughfares, Cape, Ocean, and Central, radiated out from the Pavilion Park like the spokes of a wheel. The street plan was quite logical. Cape Avenue was its "Main Street" because it was the point of entry from the Cape Island Turnpike (now Sunset Boulevard). The turnpike brought in visitors from the steamship landing on the bay or from the railroad depot in Cape May. Cape Avenue extended from the turnpike to the point of land where ocean and bay intersect and where the first hotel, the Sea Grove House, was soon to be opened.

The other two radial streets also terminated at the shoreline; Ocean Avenue, running north-south, ends at the ocean beach, while Central Avenue, running east west, terminates at the bay beach. Another prominent street, Beach Avenue, ran along the shoreline to provide beachfront lots where the wealthy could build their impressive summer homes. Lighthouse Avenue became the perimeter-street to the east and Alexander Avenue became its counterpart to the west. Another feature road was Lake Drive, completely encircling Lake Lily and offering a pleasant track where nouveau-riche drivers could display their fine livery.

Interspersed among these key roads was a rectangular grid of residential streets. Some of these are gone today, victims of the northeast storms and hurricanes that gobbled up the shoreline. Those that remain bear their original names.

The avenues between Cape and Central were named for precious stones: Diamond, Emerald, Chrystal, and Pearl. Between Central and Alexander, prominent Presbyterian ministers were honored: Brainard, Knox, and Alexander. From Cape to Lighthouse celebrated universities appear: Harvard, Yale, Princeton, Cambridge, and Oxford. The quadrant farthest from the shore (and since less valuable for development, it remained in its wild wooded state the longest) was appropriately named for the dominant trees to be found there: Cedar, Holly, and Oak. It's hardly surprising that the names of the founding families were included – Whilldin and Stites Avenues.

The Rush to Open Sea Grove

Today it would be impossible to build as much as the Sea Grove contractors were able to complete in the first half of 1875. How they managed to clear and grade the land, lay out the streets and lots, and then build the pavilion, hotel, and cottages in a few short months is astounding. Granted our present-day Department of Environmental Protection was not there to demand a wetlands survey, or was a CAFRA permit required by the State of New Jersey. There were no bureaucratic regulations to deal with. This was during the heydays of the industrial revolution when legislative restrictions were few and Yankee can-do got the job done. Labor was cheap and sufficient manpower not difficult to assemble. Yet the task facing Whilldin and Sidney was formidable. Let us imagine how they addressed the challenge:

In early January 1875, P. McAdams and Company of Philadelphia, a leading railroad contractor, is put in overall charge of the work. Sidney has already prepared the plans and specifications and is receiving proposals in February from more than a dozen contractors for the grading of the roads – three and a half miles of new streets.

Italians, Poles, Germans, and Irish, hundreds of laborers from all over the region, are chopping down the trees and cutting their way through the dense underbrush. Dawn to dusk is their workday and the Sabbath is their rest-day. Trees are felled with ax and saw, brush and vines with machete and scythe. For power tools they have only their horse and wagon teams to haul the cuttings away. The Italian workmen board at the cheaper rooming houses in Cape May, walking the beach or the turnpike twice to earn their daily bread. Soon they find this too troublesome and decide to camp in Sea Grove as the others have done from the beginning. There are three camps. The Italians make do with canvas tents. The other two are little better, just shacks and shanties sufficient for basic shelter. Like today's migrant farm workers, each camp cooks its own food and takes care of its essential needs.

Eighty-hour workweeks, with non-union labor desperate to earn its two dollars each day, produce surprising progress. By mid-March Cape Avenue is graded and other prominent streets will follow in May. The street work is assigned to half a dozen contractors, some local, some, like J. B. Moore, from as far away as Philadelphia. No bulldozers, just teams of horses and an army of laborers work the ground, even leveling the sand dunes to create a roadbed for Beach Avenue. As the dunes are swept away by men in a folly that will take over a hundred years to remedy, so will Beach Avenue be condemned to losing its fight for survival.

The sea was and always will be the victor. At the time it seemed like the bright thing to do. With the dunes leveled, from the center of the Pavilion Park, and looking down the broad avenues named Cape, Ocean and Central, the visual majesty of ocean and bay was striking. So the protective dunes went and with them all hope of a stable coastline. At times, with gale force winds gnawing away the shoreline, it seemed that Sea Grove itself could be erased from memory. Too much of it has been.

(c.1878) The Hughes Brothers Lumber Yard furnished most of the building materials for the new resort community. Located on the north side of the Cape Island Turnpike (now Sunset Boulevard) directly across from the Cape Avenue entrance, it was close to the Steamship Landing at today's Sunset Beach. The house on the right is still there today. *Courtesy of the Cape May County Historical Society.*

Sea Grove's avenues were not all created equal. Cape and Beach could boast a hundred-foot right-of-way, the proper venue for showing off the quality of your family's livery. Next came the diagonals, Ocean and Central, with an impressive eighty-foot width. The remainder were laid out at fifty feet, still comfortable for carriages on residential streets. Excellent Manumuskin gravel, brought in by wagon or rail from the extensive deposits in the Pine Barrens, was the material of choice for the roadbeds. Often this was dressed with a finish cover of crushed seashells, a road construction still in limited use today.

The initial infrastructure of the community was simply the street system. There were no storm sewers, no water mains or gas lines, no waste lines, no electric service poles or phone lines. There were no curbs and a few narrow boardwalks laid on a gravel base sufficed for sidewalks. All the more sophisticated urban amenities would come later, some much later. No sooner had Cape Avenue been made passable in March, than the Sea Grove Association started work on two key features: the new hotel for the corporal comfort and the pavilion for the spiritual comfort of Sea Grove's early visitors. Both would reach completion, sufficient for occupancy, in time for the formal opening ceremonies in June, 1875.

Meanwhile the sale of lots was getting off to a good start. At the bargain end, 50 by 100 foot lots on the smaller streets went for as little as seventy-five dollars. Ocean and Central Avenue lots were bought for two hundred and fifty dollars, and the prestigious ocean front parcels along Beach Avenue cost five hundred dollars. It was not unusual for cottagers to buy two adjacent lots to allow for a larger house and grounds. John Wanamaker bought three.

The association encouraged the ministry to settle in and ensure the spiritual purity of the community by offering them free lots – the only stipulation was that they build a house within a year. The ministers responded; Protestant clergy built ten percent of the first cottages. Reverend Adolph Spaeth was able to build the beautiful Rosemere Cottage on Yale Avenue for $1,100. Many two-story cottages with three bedrooms were being put up for a similar amount. Ownership of several lots by the ministers was common enough with Reverend Stockton, an Episcopalian, acquiring the most. And so Sea Grove's religious foundation was assured, and the ministers profited handsomely.

It appears that the two contemporary Cape May newspapers, the *Cape May Ocean Wave* and the *Star of the Cape*, were regularly being fed information on the real estate sales at the new resort; what we would call today "news releases." Each paper reported what it was told, so the picture we have from that time may be a rosier one than investigative reporting would have produced. By March, ten lots were sold, by April, almost sixty, by May, another twenty-three, and by June, in time for the official opening, twenty-seven cottages had been built. The total number of lots sold had zoomed to 225. That approaches a twenty-five percent sellout – not bad for the first six months' effort! However, two more years of marketing only added forty-four additional sales. From twenty-five percent sales in six months to only five percent sales over the next two years is a substantial let down. An omen, perhaps?

Gingerbread Cottages

Most of the early cottages were modest in size by today's standards. A few showplaces, like the cottages of Alexander Whilldin, John Wanamaker, and President Benjamin Harrison were being built for the wealthy. James Sidney designed an elegant beachfront cottage for Benjamin G. Godfrey on a double lot at the corner of Ocean Avenue and Beach Avenue. Jeremiah H. Townsend, a Cape May contractor, erected this for $3,000. The house was of an unusual shape, as was the siding, which was made from beaded, matched, narrow boards angled in different directions, some up and some down, and others horizontal, the joints battened with plain boards. Starting in the Fall of 1875, this house took six months to build, attesting to the unique design and the richness of its materials and finishes. The typical three-bedroom house was often built in two months!

How could they build so quickly and economically? When talking about house construction, how often have we heard "they don't build them like they used to!" The observation is true enough, and we can be thankful for that. Today's house is to its nineteenth century counterpart as today car is to Ford's Model T.

The Point's early cottages were largely second homes for summer vacationers. They didn't have heat and air conditioning, electricity, gas, or phone. Bathrooms had a split personality – tub and sink inside, toilet in the outhouse. Kerosene was the fuel for the lamps and cooking stove, ice was for the icebox.

Foundations for the model cottage were really simple. Typically they were brick piers set six to eight feet apart instead of the continuous foundation wall so common today. The narrow piers even lacked spread footings since the sandy soil could easily support the light wood frame construction above. A heavy perimeter beam carried the stud frame of the exterior bearing walls. Room width was often limited to twelve feet, an economical span for the floor joists.

The outer walls had white cedar or white pine clapboard siding nailed directly to the studs. The interior finish was plaster on wood lath. Today we would add sheathing between the siding and studs, building paper, plus a vapor barrier and insulating material. Sub-floors were uncommon; most houses had random width yellow pine board nailed directly to the floor joists. The same applied to the roofs, which had a steep pitch, but again no sheathing boards on the rafters. The hand split cedar shingles made a first class roof with a life span of fifty to a hundred years.

The key man was the carpenter-builder who put together almost everything but the plastering and painting. Few cottages had an architect; most house plans and decorative details came from pattern books or from the skill and experience of the builder.

Today's interest in natural habitats and native plants was not the fashion in Sea Grove. The mission then was to tame the unruly wilderness into a more pristine setting for the vacationing gentry. Each property had its lawn and flowerbeds and often a picket fence staked out the property lines. Evidence of this remains today. The houses along Cape,

(c.1910) This impressive cottage, known affectionately as the "Gray Ghost" had been built on Beach Avenue by A. G. Crowell. It appears in this photograph as it looked shortly after it was moved to its present location on the northwest corner of Cape and Pearl Avenues. *Courtesy of the Cape May County Historical Society.*

(c.1890) This cottage, on Lincoln Avenue, has not survived. The tracks in the foreground carried the cars of the *Delaware Bay, Cape May, and Sewells Point Railroad* that connected the Point with the Steamboat Landing at Sunset Beach and with Cape May City. *Courtesy of the Cape May County Historical Society.*

Ocean, and Central Avenues, from the beach to the circle, often have kept their well tended lawns, while those properties developed in more recent times have opted for the natural landscape, preserving what they found and adding plants native to the region. It is this variety, each authentic in its own way, which contributes much to the beguiling appeal of Cape May Point today.

Of the houses built over Sea Grove's first decade, we are very fortunate that several dozen survive today. Those no longer with us were most often casualties of the advancing sea. However, many beachfront homes were moved to safer locations as the receding shoreline made their fate clear. Accurate information on which of these houses have been moved to their present location as well as evidence of their original setting is difficult to come by. Fires have claimed others, but with the exception of major fires in 1886 and 1908, the losses have not been severe.

All have been altered in some fashion over the years. Few have retained the cedar shingle roofs they started with, and most have replaced these with less costly asphalt shingles. Unfortunately, when it came time to repaint, many owners chose instead to use asbestos siding to cover the original clapboard siding. This change in siding texture, from the narrower shadow lines of clapboard to the much wider and fainter lines of the shingles, is aesthetically displeasing.

One of the identifying characteristics of the early houses is the form of their double hung windows. Almost all of these have a vertical mullion in the center of the top and bottom sash, creating a distinctive window with four rectangular panes of glass. This style went out of fashion with the demise of the Victorian era.

Houses were often planned as simple rectangles with fairly steep gable roofs and deep eaves. Larger cottages added a wing for an el shape or two wings in a cruciform plan. Virtually all had open porches facing the street, some wrapping around the sides. Gingerbread was in fashion as the hall-

(c.2002) The charming gingerbread cottage, "Rosemere," was built by Adolph Spaeth, an important Lutheran Theologian, as his summer home on the north side of Yale Avenue between Ocean and Lake Avenues. *Courtesy of the Author.*

mark of the Victorian cottage. Its extensive design variations did much to create diversity of style among the early cottages.

Most of the open porches are now screened-in, homage to our insect friends, including the ubiquitous mosquito and voracious fly. Others have been closed in to add an extra room. Still others have so many additions and alterations that it takes an experienced eye to imagine the original form.

(c.2002) One of the five identical cottages that Dr. J. Newton Walker built on Lincoln Avenue across from the Sea Grove House. Each has been altered over the years, as have almost all of the nineteenth century houses that have survived. *Courtesy of the Author.*

The Wanamaker Cottage

Among the first to put up one of the largest cottages was John Wanamaker. He bought three prime lots on Beach Avenue at the northwest corner of Emerald Avenue. There he had Laver and Knoedler, the Norristown contractors who were building the Sea Grove Hotel, construct his seaside villa. The impressive design was in the Italianate style, a simple three-story rectangle, forty-six by forty feet, with a ten-foot-wide two-story piazza entirely surrounding it. He named it *Lilenmyn Villa.*

Work started in April, and within four months it was completed and ready by July for the first summer season. Surprisingly, when we consider Wanamaker's prominence, the first news report on its use by the Wanamaker family didn't appear until June of 1881 in the *Star of the Cape* newspaper. Who was occupying it during that six-year period?

Adding to this mystery is a report in May of 1875 that John Wanamaker had engaged James Sidney to design a boarding house for the entertainment of ministers free of charge. The building was to contain forty rooms for as many visitors. Since the Wanamaker cottage had no more than thirteen bedrooms it could not be the boarding house Wanamaker had in mind. Could he have scaled back his ambitious venture to house forty clergymen, to the more modest number of thirteen? This is doubtful; a villa for a rich man and a boarding house for ministers are hardly compatible uses.

Unfortunately the location Wanamaker had chosen for his summer residence was the most prone to erosion in all of Cape May Point. For years the ocean waters were held back by the construction of bulkheads or jetties, but the sea was to have its way. Several years after the house's completion, Wanamaker had Downs Edmunds build a brick wall with a flagstone cap to surround his property. High tides in 1892 swept away much of it and seriously threatened the entire property.

The Wanamaker family continued to occupy it until 1896, but three years later they presented it to the trustees of the Presbyterian Sea-Side Home. The *Cape May Wave* observed, "The building is three stories in height and contains thirteen large sleeping rooms, spacious dining room, reception room, sitting room, parlor, besides butler's pantry and all the necessary accessories to an up-to-date seaside summer cottage. Surrounding the entire building are double porches, which afford abundant shade."

It was moved back a little further from the coast but still on Wanamaker's land. It fearlessly stood its ground until 1916, when E. W. Springer moved it to the southeast corner of Cape and Yale. It operated for many years as an orphanage for Presbyterian children and was renamed "Sunny Corner."

(c.2002) John Wanamaker's cottage as it appears today. Its exterior appearance has changed very little since it was built as the Wanamaker summer home in 1875. Today it is owned by an order of Catholic Brothers, who operate a year around retreat program. *Courtesy of the Author.*

The Harrison Cottage

This cottage, probably the largest ever built in Cape May Point, is noteworthy for a number of reasons – including a major scandal, which became national news. This was the first and last time that the Point ever achieved such notoriety.

John Wanamaker had been a very big contributor to the Republican Party. His largess brought him a cabinet post under President Benjamin Harrison. During the early summer of 1889 the Wanamakers were entertaining the Harrisons at their Beach Avenue cottage. Mrs. Harrison was visiting with her father, her brother, and two grandchildren.

The Wanamakers had decorated their cottage to display an elaborate "Welcome!" to their distinguished visitors. The Point residents and visitors, of course, were beside themselves in anticipation of President Harrison's arrival on John Wanamaker's yacht *Restless* the following week. As it turned out, accompanied by General Sewell, he arrived by train in one of the Pennsylvania Railroads magnificent parlor cars.

Following a week of constant entertainment by Cape May's elite, the President's wife took a real liking to the area. As a consequence, a few gentlemen of influence decided it would be a splendid thing if Mrs. Harrison and her husband, the President, were to vacation at the Point every season. If they had their own cottage, of course they would! Why not present them with a handsome beachfront property that could become the Summer White House? John Wanamaker was to be the gift giver.

They bought up four lots fronting on Beach Avenue and Harvard Avenue scarcely a block from the new Shoreham Hotel. For $10,000, they erected an impressive twenty-room villa. It stood alone – the only house on the entire block. In style, it was similar to the houses of Whilldin or Wanamaker, but it was a bit larger and more ornate than either of them.

President Harrison wisely refused to accept such a remarkable gift from his Postmaster General. He understood the motive behind the offer and saw the potential political damage that would follow his acceptance of the property. On the other hand it was an offer that was hard to refuse! Perhaps it could be given to Mrs. Harrison instead of to the President?

In June of 1990, in a White House ceremony, Caroline Lavinia Scott Harrison graciously accepted this thoughtful gift from William H. McKean, editor of the *Philadelphia Ledger*, who was accompanied by her friend John Wanamaker. McKean explained that the presentation was on behalf of a number of subscribers whose names were not to be divulged. An anonymous gift!

The influential political humor magazine *Puck* chided Harrison on August 6, 1890:

> And the press opened fire. To his utter amazement Mr. Harrison received his first lesson in official etiquette, the very existence of which he had hitherto been ignorant. He learned that men in high office should not accept valuable presents unless they wished to lay themselves open to the suspicion of bribe taking. He learned that a high official is held responsible for valuable presents accepted by his wife. He learned that the more or less valuable present that his wife had accepted, and for the acceptance of which he was held responsible, was given with the ulterior purpose of increasing the fame of Cape May Point, and of facilitating the sale of real estate at that sweet seaside spot, and that some of the men who gave it were speculating in that same real estate.

The men referred to in the *Puck* article had formed a syndicate to raise the money for the enterprise. The incorporators included Anthony J. Drexel, George W. Childs, General William Sewell, John Wanamaker, and Anson H. Hamilton. *Puck* got it right – Sewell, as the Director of the West Jersey Railroad, was interested in more passenger traffic and Hamilton was a speculator who had amassed considerable property in the Point.

President Harrison weathered the storm and kept the property. For the next few years the local newspapers continued to chronicle the arrivals and departures of the Harrisons, reporting in great detail every move of the President's family and their socially prominent entourage. It was BIG NEWS for the Point but it was not to last too long. In 1896, John Wanamaker purchased the Harrison House for the use of his own family. His first cottage, on the corner of Beach and Emerald Avenues, had been constantly assaulted by storms and beach erosion. By 1898, he turned it over to the trustees of the Sea-Side Home, one of the Point's early Presbyterian institutions.

(c.1895) John Wanamaker led a small syndicate that built this imposing cottage as a present to President Benjamin Harrison, hoping this would become the summer White House. Such a costly gift created a national scandal. The Wanamakers reclaimed it several years later, finally turning it over to the Society for the Prevention of Cruelty to Children, a charitable institution. *Courtesy of the Cape May County Historical Society.*

The Merchants

In 1994, the only Cape May Point store still in operation was Harriet's General Store at the northwest corner of Cape and Pavilion Avenues. That year, the local zoning ordinance had undergone many fundamental changes. The Point was to become a community of single-family dwellings, with no commercial activities permitted. Existing uses that did not conform to the new purely residential zoning were permitted to continue operating under a "grandfather clause." Harriet's and its successors would have no threat of competition from other stores.

There would be no more shops, no more hotels, and no more boarding houses. These commercial enterprises had been the backbone of Sea Grove. Businesses that had been essential in its formative days lost their usefulness over time. By the first decade of the twentieth century all the hotels would be gone. Before the start of the Second World War the boarding houses would also be gone and so would the little stores that had sprung to life season after season since Sea Grove first welcomed vacationers in 1875.

If you were looking for meats, groceries, or general provisions in the brand new Sea Grove you had two choices: M.H. Golt at the corner of Cape and Yale (where the Marianist's Wanamaker Cottage now stands) or R. D. Edmunds and Son right next door on Yale Avenue. Golt proved to be the more astute businessman – his sales had quadrupled in his first two years. By 1877, he had taken over the Edmunds store and enlarged it several times before offering it for sale in 1881 as his health was failing.

From 1875 to 1900, thirty stores had opened, but not many survived for more than a few years. The grocery business seemed to have the most appeal, if not always the most endurance. Henry C. Jacoby opened his store in 1879, and it operated for another twelve years. He was soon followed by C. Simpson and Son, and by William Keeler, both in 1881, when M. H. Golt retired from the grocery business.

Only a year later, E. Hoffer and Company joined the competition to sell both groceries and meats. From 1888 to 1898, Mrs. Rebecca Jacobs, D. B. Oliver, the young Springer brothers, and the Miller brothers all opened grocery stores in the Point. Oliver, Springers, and Millers offered meats as well as groceries. How they survived at all in this tiny community is a mystery. The real survivor was the Springer family whose store opened in 1897 and was a fixture in the Point for decades.

Not surprisingly, seafood was another staple available in the early days. Fish were so plentiful in the ocean and bay that it was a poor angler indeed who came home empty handed. Nevertheless, the hotels, boarding houses, and cottages provided a large market for seafood. John W. Corson, Jr. opened the first fish market in 1878. He also sold poultry, although some residents were soon raising their own chickens. In some parts of the Point only heavy sleepers were oblivious to the roosters proclamation of dawn's arrival.

For the 1886 season Mark Williams opened what we would call today a raw bar, selling fresh clams and oysters. At that time there was a railroad station on Lincoln Avenue near Cape, and Joseph Sims figured the railroad would generate a lot of traffic, so in 1890 he opened his oyster stand at the stop across from the Carlton Hotel.

(c.1915) Amnon Wright's store on the northwest side of Cape Avenue between Pavilion and Cape Avenues sold "Country Produce, Fresh and Salt Meats". Next door was his boarding house, Wright's Villa. It was remodeled into a three unit condo in the 1990s. *Courtesy of E. Roberta Rutherford.*

(c.1910) Mayor Springer's store was the right place for groceries. The scores of bottles on display look very much like demon rum. The Point was not always a dry town. His store became Gerew's in the 1920s and today the US Post Office occupies this space. *Courtesy of the Cape May County Historical Society.*

(c.1950) What is today the Cape May Point General Store at the corner of Cape and Pavilion Avenues, was in the 1940s, McCullough's, in the 1950s, it was Kreigers, and in the 1970s it was operated by Ed Berghaus. It's been many years since you could fill a kerosene can with fuel for your cooking range. *Courtesy of the Borough of Cape May Point.*

Kids flock to the General Store for candy and toys, and for teenagers, it's where the action is. *Courtesy of the Author.*

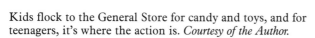

Shops carrying essentially one item were obviously less common. Dr. J. N. Walker, Sea Grove's most important early developer, opened the first pharmacy in 1876. Ever attentive to the desires of his customers and alert to the profits they could deliver, Dr. Walker's drug store was attached to his emporium for hot and cold seawater baths, a popular health benefit at shore resorts. Ocean bathing was thought to be beneficial to one's health. Many anecdotes in the local papers testified to the almost miraculous cures brought about by a sojourn at the seashore. Seawater baths were the solution for the frail or sickly visitor for whom ocean bathing could be intimidating.

Gentlemen smoked cigars, and Sea Grove catered to gentlemen. Charles Deralison set up his cigar shop in 1878 and T. M. Barker opened a competing one four years later. Gentlemen also drank. After 1881 they could do so in public. That was the year the Sea Grove Association sold all of its holdings and removed all of the deed restrictions – including the sale of alcoholic beverages. The new borough commissioners immediately licensed the sale of liquor. Two years later the *Star of the Cape* observed, "for the first time in several years the Point is *without* a saloon. The proprietor of the Club House is moving to Cape May City but another party is interested in starting the same line of business."

A few durable items were available in the Point but Cape May City had much more to offer. Dry goods could be obtained at Mrs. Jacobs's grocery store and millinery at Mrs. Hawkins shop. Markley's Shoe Store, displaying the current fashions in footwear, catered to both ladies and gentlemen. One of the earliest and only stores to sell house furnishings was J. H. Benezet and Brother, a branch of its much larger store in Cape May City.

Cape Avenue could have been called "Main Street" because of the concentration of shops to be found there. No zoning code restricted or directed their location. They were most often opened in one of the two story cottages, although a few had been built as store buildings.

In 1890, all five of Cape May Point's stores were to be found on Cape between the Pavilion Circle and Beach Avenue. Ten years later, at the turn of the century, Cape still had four of them, but now Yale and Ocean had each gained two, and Lincoln one. This was the peak period here of commercial development. By the end of the First World War the hotels were gone, the number of cottages had doubled, and the number of shops was back to five. Today, there is one.

Other Commercial Enterprises 1875-1900

Dr. J. Newton Walker saw Sea Grove as *The Promised Land* – not in the biblical sense but in the mercantile sense. He was an entrepreneur in a hurry, and this was his turf. Walker Row was his first enterprise, five identical cottages on Lincoln Avenue directly across from the Sea Grove Hotel. They still stand, each somewhat altered from its original form, and known in recent years as "the five sisters." Built for Walker by J. H. Townsend, they opened for the Point's first season.

By the fall of 1875, Dr. Walker was planning his next two ventures. His commodious drug store, with its hot and cold seawater baths, was constructed the next year right on the grounds of the Sea Grove Hotel and just across the street from his Walker Row. Without skipping a beat he was off to his third undertaking – an icehouse on the shores of Lake Lily.

Mining ice from lakes during the winter months was still a viable business in the late 1800s. A good cold winter could produce a profitable harvest from the sixteen-acre fresh-water lake. This time Walker partnered with a man named C. Simpson. They built a sizable frame structure with thick cork slabs in the walls and roof to provide insulation. It could hold a thousand tons of ice – enough to last through the year.

Good winters would fill the icehouse to capacity. A mild winter meant importing ice from the upper Delaware or the Kennebec Rivers where it was shipped by rail to Sea Grove. Whether the Knickerbocker Ice Company, with offices on Washington Street in Cape May, was a partner or competitor is uncertain. It is known that Knickerbocker delivered ice to Sea Grove and stored ice in Walker's ice house. Local delivery was provided by an attractive horse drawn ice wagon.

By the end of the century, mining lake ice was no longer good business. The old icehouse, however, was to find a new role as the center of Cape May Point's social life. Its patron was Dr. Randolph Hazzard, a Pittsburgh physician who had a grand vision of rebirth for the resort community. His story is to be found in a later chapter.

As part of the initial development, the Sea Grove Association had constructed livery stables on two lots at the northeast corner of Lake Drive and Yale Avenue to accommodate the horses and carriages of the residents. The operation of the stables was probably leased to a local manager. By 1881 Anson H. Hamilton had acquired the property and enlarged the facilities to serve the growing number of cottagers.

Livery stables would rent a horse to people who did not own one. Even buggies, wagons, and sleighs could be hired there. Throughout the nineteenth century, they served as a gathering place for the men, a spot where they could chat with their neighbors or watch the blacksmith at work. By the time of the First World War, most of the buildings had been removed, as cars were replacing horses for local transportation.

An essential enterprise for Sea Grove was a convenient source of lumber and building supplies for the hotels and cottages that were constantly under construction. A Philadelphia contractor, Smith E. Hughes, saw this opportunity and opened the first lumberyard in 1875 on the Cape Island Turnpike (now Sunset Boulevard) at the end of Cape Avenue. The location was ideal – his materials would come in at the steamship landing (now Sunset Beach) and be delivered to the job site by wagon, down the Turnpike and along Cape Avenue.

The Sea Grove Lumber Yard helped build Sea Grove. Under the management of his brother, Wesley G. Hughes, it provided a full line of building materials delivering to Cape May as well as to the Point.

Gold leaf was a popular product during this period and a number of shops were operating in Cape May. There is a street in West Cape May, off Broadway just north of Sunset Boulevard, called Goldbeaters Alley. It is probable that George Reeves had the only goldbeating business in Cape May Point (location unknown). In 1881, he moved it to Cape May to take advantage of more convenient shipping facilities to Philadelphia. This short-lived venture may have been the only industry ever located in the Point.

(c.1876) The Hughes Brothers, Edward and Wesley, operated Sea Grove's first lumber yard in Lower Township just across the street from the Cape Avenue Rustic Entrance. *Courtesy of the Author.*

(c.1885) Wesley Hughes was in charge of the lumber yard after Sea Grove became Cape May Point. The Hughes brothers may have been relatives of Smith E. Hughes, a Germantown, Pennsylvania contractor, who had built the Sea Grove House. *Courtesy of the Author.*

Chapter 2
By Land or Sea

Getting There

If you are a Philadelphian traveling to any one of the south Jersey seaside resorts, you are "going down the shore." Today there's nothing to it; just hop in your car and within an hour or two you're at the beach. In the 1800s it was a different matter.

Early visitors to Sea Grove had two choices – railroad or steamer. Actually there was a third choice: the stagecoach. But it was more a punishment than a choice, and had few takers. The route from Philadelphia zigged and zagged through dusty roads between the stage stops. Gravel road-beds needed regular scraping, and they didn't get it. Each rain produced new potholes, which spread like a cancer. The trip was harrowing. Three days of suffocating dust in a quaking carriage was not for weaklings.

In 1875, the fastest trip to Sea Grove from Philadelphia was by rail. During the season, an express train could get you to Cape May in less than two and a half hours. There were four trains a day, but two were locals with a four-hour run. Even off-season, there were two trains daily.

The Philadelphia train left from the Market Street wharf, crossing the Delaware by ferry to Camden. In Cape May it arrived at the stunning Grant Street Station on the beachfront, newly opened in 1875. The short ride to Sea Grove along the Cape Island Turnpike (now Sunset Boulevard) was also by train – but powered by horse rather than steam.

The whole train journey was three hours; by stage it was three days. Instead of the stagecoach dust, the trains introduced cinders. Open windows insured a cool ride and an ample supply of coal dust. The alternative was the steamer.

Since 1822, steamship travel to the Cape had been possible. By 1875 the service had become regular and comfortable, though not quite as swift as the train. Even so, it had other inducements to offer. The ride down the river was leisurely. It was clean. Tall stacks carried the steam engine's soot far from the passenger deck.

There was entertainment from the time she left the Walnut Street Wharf in Philadelphia till she docked at the steamboat landing on Sunset Beach. With crisp summer breezes, fresh oysters and beer, musical interludes, dancing on the deck – the appeal of the steamers is obvious.

(c.1840s) Possibly the Delaware Bay pilot boat of Wilmon Whilldin, who developed early steamship service to Cape Island, with landings at Higbee's Beach and at Sunset Beach. *Courtesy of the Cape May County Library.*

The Delaware Steamers

Though steamship travel might have been the preferred choice by some, one visitor in 1846 complained that the trip from the steamboat landing to Cape May was so disagreeable that the cost of this part of the journey should have been *deducted from*, rather than *included in*, the fare from Philadelphia. All this had changed by the time Sea Grove was receiving its first visitors.

In 1875, the Iron side-wheeler *Richard Stockton*, would anchor close offshore at the steamboat pier to discharge its passengers, some with their horses and carriage, all with baggage or steamer trunks. The Cape May Passenger Railway Company's horse-cars met the boat and delivered speedy service to Sea Grove or to Cape May City. The open-air cars seated eleven on each side and the double-deckers ten per side. After a bracing ride along the Cape Island Turnpike, you had arrived at the shore. The rail fare was five cents.

A number of boats had been put in service to Cape May from the time Captain Wilmon Whilldin launched his *Delaware* in 1816. They offered various degrees of comfort and often competed on the basis of speed. None, however, can compare to the majestic *Republic*. Its maiden voyage in March of 1878 set new records. It was bigger. It was faster. It was to the steamer packets what the *Queen Mary* was to ocean liners. That first trip took six hours: the return a bit over five.

Almost the length of a football field, its three decks could carry twenty-five hundred passengers, and often did. It had a dining salon. It had staterooms. It had luxury. The fare was a dollar; kids sailed for half. It was the Dreamboat of its day. It was called the *Palace Steamer Republic*. There were theatrical performances. There was dancing. There were concerts by its "celebrated band." Further attractions came in the form of "Commodore Doyle," a midget comedian who mixed with the passengers. But the days of steamboat travel were numbered. The railroad would be the clear winner. The *Republic* retired in 1903.

(c.1860s) The steam powered side-wheeler *Robert Morris* was one of several lines operating in the Delaware and Chesapeake bays. This one sailed out of Baltimore. *Courtesy of the Borough of Cape May Point.*

(c.1890s) The *Palace Steamer Republic* was able to carry twenty-five hundred passengers. With theatrical performances, concerts, and dancing aboard, it was a luxurious way to travel to Cape May Point, from 1878 to 1903. *Courtesy of H. Gerald MacDonald*

The West Jersey

Railroads transformed America. They accelerated development along the New Jersey seashore. By 1875 Sea Grove visitors could profit from their expansion. The trains were cheap. They were fast. They were frequent. They also made passengers some offers that were hard to refuse.

A free rail pass was one such tempting offer. To encourage building in Sea Grove, the Association had cut this deal with the railroad: the cottage owner could travel free for one, two, or three years, depending on the dollar amount invested in construction. When Sea Grove was under construction, the railroad scheduled a series of excursion trains to lure prospects there. The ride was free.

On a cold April day in 1875, 240 curious folk traveled the three hours by train to Cape May and the twenty-minute carriage ride to the newly opened Sea Grove House. They got a free meal and an enthusiastic sales pitch. They were being offered the opportunity of a lifetime, a chance to "get in on the ground floor." The railroad was not motivated by Christian charity. It was investing in its future.

Railroad travel to the Cape became viable in 1863 when the *Glassboro and Millville Railroad Company* was granted rights to extend its tracks to Cape May. This cemented the link with Philadelphia. The line became the *West Jersey Railroad* in 1868 and was later managed by the *Pennsylvania Railroad*.

New railroads were the speculation of choice for greedy investors. Communities like Cape May, eager (or starving?) for growth, joined the rail mania. Even Sea Grove was not immune. Why not create a more direct route to Philadelphia than the West Jersey offered? By 1878, serious planning began. Cape May wanted tourists and south Jersey farmers wanted big-city outlets for their crops. They dreamed of a connection linking Cape May with Philadelphia *and* New York! The *Star of the Cape* newspaper endorsed the plan and reported regularly on progress.

Engineers laid out a route following the bayshore to the village of Town Bank, and from there inland to link up with communities to the north. Grading of the roadbed was started but opposition was already developing in the legislature. The West Jersey didn't welcome competition.

A new railroad company, *The Philadelphia and Seashore Company*, didn't get very far. Bankruptcy struck before it was able to send forth a train. Its tracks were acquired by the *West Jersey Railroad* and later sold to the new competitor, *The South Jersey Railroad*. The final route adopted by the South Jersey line bore little resemblance to the many schemes that had preceded it. It never got near Town Bank or the shores of the Delaware Bay. But it did get to Cape May.

Its inaugural run in June of 1894 was welcomed in Cape May like the Second Coming! Schools closed, bells pealed, bunting flew, and dignitaries lined up to do their thing. The six hundred passengers stepped off to the blare of brass bands. Cape May was ecstatic. After almost twenty years of anxiety and frustration, its savior, a competitive railroad, had arrived.

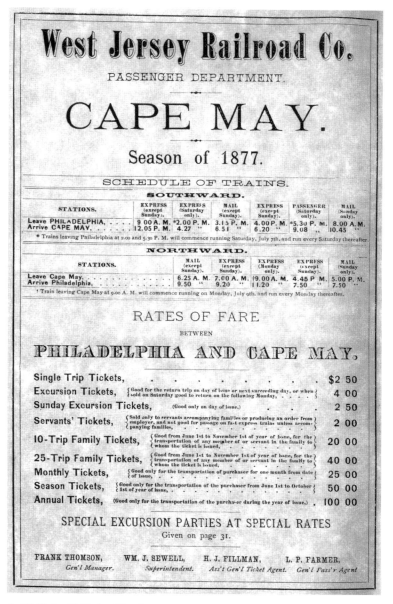

(c.1877) In 1868 the *West Jersey Railroad* offered the first direct connection between Philadelphia and Cape Island. At less than two and one half hours, the trip was considerably faster than that offered by the steamships. *Courtesy of the Borough of Cape May Point.*

Railroad travel to the Cape became viable in 1863 when the Glassboro and Millville Railroad Company was granted rights to extend its tracks to Cape May.

WEST JERSEY RAILROAD DEPOT, CAPE MAY.

(c.1890) The summer depot of the *West Jersey Railroad* brought vacationers right to the beachfront in Cape May City. A ten-minute ride along the coast on the *Delaware Bay, Cape May, and Sewells Point* line took them to Cape May Point. *Courtesy of the Borough of Cape May Point.*

The Carriage Trade

The visitor to Sea Grove had several choices for lodging. The visit might be for a week, a month, or the full season. The vacationers could stay at one of the three hotels on Cape Avenue, the Sea Grove House, the Cape House, or the Centennial House, at any number of boarding houses, at a rental cottage, or in their own cottage. To a great extent the choice of lodging determined the choice of local conveyance.

Those who built or bought their own home were affluent, though generally not wealthy. For the most part it was a comfortable middle class, a professional or merchant class, who settled in. They had their horses and carriages and stables. If not, there was a large livery stable where a horse or team and carriage could be hired and cared for.

The carriage, like the horse-less carriage to follow, was more than a convenience – it was a statement of status. One drove along Beach Avenue or around Lake Lily to be seen and perhaps envied. For those who missed this spectacle, the newspaper would report on the fine team that doctor so-and-so was driving.

Wagons hauled the hucksters' vegetables and the stores' provisions. The horse-drawn colorful public omnibus could take you to the Court House or to Cape May. You really didn't need a carriage. The Point was and still is a walking village. If you had to get to the train station or to the steamboat landing, there was the trolley.

(c.1895) Taxis were available for those who did not choose to travel by public transit. This horse and carriage often made the trip between Cape May City and Cape May Point. The sign on the carriage reads "S. Garrison, Jeweler." *Courtesy of H. Gerald MacDonald.*

(c.1901) A private carriage, possibly belonging to John Lankenau, is departing for a ride in front of the Lankenau Villa. *Courtesy of the Deaconess Community of the Evangelical Lutheran Church in America.*

Trolley Days

When Sea Grove first opened in 1875, the first public conveyance for group travel from the railroad station in Cape May or from the steamboat landing in Lower Township, was the horse-car railroad. In 1875, the *Cape May City Passenger Railroad Company* opened business with Alexander Whilldin as President. The horse-drawn cars were open to the weather. Double-deckers were known as Observatory Cars (though the route offered little to observe). From the steamboat landing at Sunset Beach, track ran down Cape Island Turnpike (Sunset Boulevard) to Cape Avenue, down Cape and around the circle to the Sea Grove Hotel, then back along Cape to the turnpike and off to the Cape May railroad depot. The fare was fifteen cents. Ten percent went to the Turnpike Company for the track right-of-way.

By the 1879 season, railroad horsepower was out and steam power was in. The owners of the steamship *Republic* wanted a better route to take their passengers to Cape May. Their *Delaware Bay and Cape May Railroad Company* took over from the defunct *Cape May and Sea Grove Horse-car Railroad*. Now the cars ran along the beachfront from the steamboat landing to Sea Grove and then on to Cape May City. The Point got its own tracks from Lighthouse Avenue down Lincoln to Cape, then along Chrystal to Alexander Avenue. The train ambled along at ten miles an hour, clanging its bell on the stretch between Ocean and Central Avenues.

Within a few years the line became the *Delaware Bay, Cape May, and Sewells Point Railroad*. New tracks connected Cape May with Sewells Point at the far end of Poverty Beach. The ride was fantastic. It was fast. So fast that by 1882 residents were complaining about the great speed of trains passing through Cape May Point.

Speed was hardly the real problem – storms were. The sea constantly assaulted the stretch along the South Cape May Meadows, from Cape May Point to Cape May City. Northeasters regularly flooded the meadows. Even ordinary high tides became a problem. The roadbed was raised and supported by pilings over the low places. Still every storm brought out a large force of workmen to repair the new damage.

The switch from steam to electricity came along by 1892. The electric trolley had arrived at last! Poles and wires went up. Now Cape May Point had a real modern service that lasted through 1916.

(c.1885) The first locomotive, the "Bay and Ocean," of the *Delaware Bay and Cape May Railroad*, operated prior to the electric trolleys of the early 1900s, transporting passengers along the beach through South Cape May from Cape May City to the Point. *Courtesy of H. Gerald MacDonald.*

(c.1910)The electric trolley, with its open summer cars, just arriving in Cape May City from the Point. This service was operating from 1892 to 1916. *Courtesy of H. Gerald MacDonald.*

(c.1910) The trolley is leaving Lincoln Avenue in Cape May Point and passing the lighthouse on its way along the beachfront through South Cape May's Mount Vernon Avenue. *Courtesy of H. Gerald MacDonald.*

Chapter 3

A Christian Community

The Pavilion – 1875

J. C. Sidney's architectural design for the Pavilion, Sea Grove's first and ultimately its most impressive house of worship, recalls the large chapels built at some of the contemporary camp meeting sites, such as at Oak Bluffs in Massachusetts, or at Pitman Grove or Ocean Grove in New Jersey. A circular rather than a rectangular plan, supporting a wide roof and a lofty central tower, characterized these amphitheaters.

By February 11, 1875, the builder's proposals to construct the Pavilion were due. The contract went to Smith E. Hughes of Philadelphia and the cornerstone was laid just eight days later. Within a month, the building's structural wood frame was raised. All sides were open to the sea or land breezes, for it was mostly to be used during the summer season. However, the pious craving of this community was not to be deprived by the onset of winter. As late as November, Reverend Williamson would come over from Cape May for the Sunday divine service, so a portion of the house under the central dome was heated to accommodate the faithful.

The surface under the pavilion was paved, since it was designed to accommodate up to 2000 souls for religious worship or public meetings. A central steeple, both bell and watchtower, reached a height of eighty-five feet, offering a spectacular view over the cottage rooftops and out to the bay and ocean. Curious visitors, who might be of a mind to purchase a lot, were escorted up the tower as part of the sales pitch. So Sidney's pavilion fulfilled a third need – it was a fine marketing tool!

During Sea Grove's early days, the Pavilion was the only place for worship and the favored location for public gatherings.

By June 1875, regular Sunday services were being held there with Reverend Dr. Alfred E. Nevins preaching in the morning and Reverend Mr. Miller in the afternoon. The Pavilion's builder, S. E. Hughes, a Methodist from Germantown, Pennsylvania, organized a Sunday School with decided success. It is not surprising that Mr. Simpson, the superintendent in 1877, arranged for both Wanamaker and Whilldin to address the Sunday school. *The Star of the Cape* reported that, "The meetings at Sea Grove have exerted a good influence among those who have not heretofore been awakened upon the subject of religion. Some have already professed to have experienced a change of heart."

A year earlier, in the summer of 1876, Alexander Whilldin had sponsored a weeklong National Sunday School Conference in the Pavilion. He brought in ministers from New Jersey, New York, Pennsylvania, Ohio, and Indiana. Eminent Sunday School workers came from around the country to take part in the teachings. The Pavilion was indeed supporting Whilldin's goal to:

"furnish a Moral and Religious Seaside Home for the glory of God and the welfare of Man, where he may be refreshed and invigorated body and soul, and better fitted for the highest and noblest duties of life."

The Pavilion could be considered the first church to go up in Sea Grove but its six-year life was certainly a short one. By 1881, the Sea Grove Association was bankrupt and it was sold to the highest bidder. Its value as a tabernacle brought nothing; its timber fetched $400. The steeple found a new home atop the Congress Garage in Cape May City

It had served well during the first years of Sea Grove as a religious meetinghouse for the whole community. In the decade after 1880 each congregation would build its own church – five in all. One might have expected the Presbyterians to lead off, but the Episcopalians came in first with the charming building they named Saint Peter's-by-the-Sea.

A central steeple, both bell and watchtower, reached a height of eighty-five feet, offering a spectacular view over the cottage rooftops and out to the bay and ocean.

(c.1878) The Pavilion was the center of religious life in Sea Grove for six years. In 1876, Alexander Whilldin sponsored a weeklong National Sunday School Conference here. The Pavilion seated 1500-2000, and Sunday school workers came from around the country to participate in the services. *Courtesy of the Cape May County Historical Society.*

(c.1875) This engraving shows the Pavilion designed in the rustic style favored by its architect, James Sidney. The central steeple, both bell and watchtower, reached a height of 85 feet, offering a spectacular view over the rooftops out to the ocean and bay. *Courtesy of the Cape May County Historical Society.*

Saint Peter's-by-the-Sea – 1880

This diminutive chapel is certainly the most photographed building in Cape May Point. It sits on its little triangular plot like a crown jewel, safeguarded by its white picket fence. The simple form, the crisp grays and whites of its stick-style architecture, account for its universal appeal.

The origin of Saint Peter's remains in doubt, with two contradictory accounts. The *Cape May Ocean Wave* in 1875 reported that that the officers of the Sea Grove Association were donating a 100 by 100-foot lot for the erection of an Episcopal Church, partially to correct the impression that Sea Grove was a Presbyterian resort rather than a Christian one open to all denominations. Plans for the building were being prepared by J. C. Sidney as a gift to the congregation.

A second and more popular story is based on one of the original minister's notes. He wrote "during the summer of 1879 the possibility of building a chapel was talked of, and it was suggested that a fine yellow pine frame for sale at the Centennial Buildings might be made available for the purpose," A parishioner recalled that the frame had been purchased in Philadelphia, disassembled for shipment, and then reassembled on the lot adjacent to Reverend Stockton's cottage on the corner of Harvard Avenue and Lake Drive. In 1880, The *Cape May Wave* confirmed that this was one of the Centennial buildings.

Based on this chronicle, the completed structure was then moved to Cape Avenue just back from Beach Avenue and across from the Sea Grove House. It remained at this prominent location for twenty-three years. The constant assault by the sea on Beach Avenue properties made it advisable to move it to its present site on the little triangular block bounded by Lincoln, Lake, and Ocean Avenues in 1903. At that time the open front porch was added.

Over the years, various improvements have been made but none have compromised the beauty of the original structure. In 1881, M. H. Golt, a local merchant, donated the organ. A year later the splendid belfry was added. Pews were installed for the 1888 season and a pulpit and lectern provided in 1891. Subsequent additions include the sacristy in 1899, choir stalls in 1948, the choir vesting room in 1953, a lavatory and storage room in 1965, and a new alter in 1966.

Although the church was not entirely completed, opening services were held on Sunday, July 25, 1880 to standing room only, with the Bishop and seven clergy in the chancel. It has remained a summer church with services held every season since that day.

(c.1885) The first home of Saint Peter's-by-the-Sea was at this prominent location on Cape Avenue at Beach Avenue across the street from the Carlton Hotel. At the far left in the background can be seen the tower of the Beadle Memorial Presbyterian Church when it was first built near Beach Avenue a block away from the Wanamaker Cottage. *Courtesy of the Cape May County Historical Society.*

(c.2002) This diminutive chapel is certainly the most photographed building in Cape May Point. The simple form, the crisp grays and whites of its stick style architecture, account for its universal appeal. *Courtesy of the Author.*

Below:
(c.1955) In August, 1955, the 75th anniversary of Saint Peter's-by-the-Sea was celebrated with a number of distinguished ministers present. At this time the new Hammond organ was dedicated with Mrs. Sidney Mather performing at the keyboard. *Courtesy of John A. Mather.*

(c.2002) In 1903, the church was moved to its present location on a small triangular lot bounded by Ocean, Lake, and Lincoln Avenues. Sunday services during the season have been continuous since it opened in 1882. *Courtesy of the Author.*

Beadle Memorial Presbyterian Church – 1882

Cape May Point's second church has an unusual floor plan remarkably different from the simple nave of Saint Peter's. Isaac Purcell, a prominent Philadelphia architect who had studied with Samuel Sloan, designed it in 1882. The dramatic interior framing is somewhat similar to that of the 1898 Cape Island Presbyterian Church in Cape May, also designed by Purcell. The Beadle Memorial church, because of the stick style overlay of its exterior walls, bears a certain resemblance to Saint Peter's-by-the-Sea.

Mr. and Mrs. J. Morgan Jennison solicited funds for the erection of the church and by March of 1882 they had managed to raise $1,200. A contract was signed with Frank Tweed, a Philadelphia contractor. He agreed to finish the work in only five weeks at a cost of $2,200. To ensure its timely opening for summer services, the contract called for a penalty payment of $15 per day for late completion.

The church's unusual name honors Reverend Elias R. Beadle, pastor of the First Presbyterian Church at 21st and Walnut Streets in Philadelphia. The personal connections here are interesting. Reverend Beadle was the Philadelphia pastor of the Wanamaker family, and a summer vacationer in Cape May Point. More importantly, he was the father of Mrs. Jennison, the principal fund-raiser. Could John Wanamaker have been one of the major donors?

Like Saint Peter's-by-the-Sea, this church has been moved from site to site. Its first home was at the corner of Diamond and Emerald Avenues, one block back from the beach. By 1920 this had become a precarious beachfront property. The church was moved to the west side of Pearl Avenue, between Emerald and Cape Avenues, and remained safely there for forty-five years.

The great 1962 storm convinced the congregation that another move was worth considering. This would be more complicated than the previous one. The Point had grown

(c.2002) The Beadle Memorial Presbyterian Church. The church's unusual name honors Reverend Elias R. Beadle, who was at the First Presbyterian Church in Philadelphia, and the pastor of the Wanamaker family. *Courtesy of the Author.*

considerably since 1920 and there were many obstacles along the five-block route it would take to its current location.

With the help of the Army Corps of Engineers, the New Jersey Department of Conservation, and the telephone and electric companies, the details of the operation were decided upon. One day in late November, the overhead phone lines and electric lines were lowered to the ground so the steeple could clear. The moving contractor jacked up the light frame structure and ever so slowly rolled it up Pearl to Cape, took a left on Cape, traveled halfway around Pavilion Circle, then right on Cape a few hundred feet to its new (and current) home. All went well – the church was secured to its new foundation, utility lines were restored and everybody went home. On July 3, 1966 the church was rededicated in a joyful opening service.

(c.1925) The Beadle Memorial Presbyterian Church was first built near Beach Avenue, then moved to Pearl Avenue Between Cape and Central Avenues where it is seen here in the left background. The cottage in the foreground is on the corner of Cape and Pearl Avenues, across from the "Gray Ghost." *Courtesy of the Borough of Cape May Point.*

Union Chapel – 1885

The only newspaper record on the opening of the Union Chapel at the corner of Cape and Pavilion Avenues, appears in the *Star of the Cape* on July 10, 1885, in the following account:

> The report of the building committee of the new Baptist church was read on Sunday evening to the assembled congregation, accepted and the committee discharged. The church is owned by the Baptist Association, but is open to all denominations, while subject to their control. The expense of building it was heavy, but it is probable that it will soon be free of debt.

It was a picturesque little church designed in the carpenter gothic style so fashionable at that time. The chapel lacked the ornate gingerbread trim of Saint Peter's and the architectural sophistication of the Beadle Memorial. It didn't need these features.

A steep gabled roof crowned the simple rectangular plan. From the gable end facing Cape Avenue, a slender bell tower rose about thirty feet and then was capped by a plain tall steeple. At the base the bell tower flared out a foot or so to form the entrance vestibule. Like the familiar children's game of interlocking fingers it was saying "here is the church and here is the steeple…" It was the very model of a proper village church.

It survived for seventy-three years but its history is a checkered one. When Edith Mather (author of *The Gingerbread Church* and significant researcher of Cape May Point history) moved to the Point in 1910 she found that the chapel had been closed up for many years. She thought this unacceptable, and soon had enlisted local laymen to conduct services and start a Sunday school.

Over the years, the church continued operation in this fashion with a number of local residents offering religious preaching and teaching together with music to accompany the service. They served as volunteers without compensation. Among them were Miss Sallie Wright, her friend Mrs. Mansell, Mr. and Mrs. Robert Douglas, and Blanche Willard – names familiar to many residents of Cape May Point today.

1958 saw a resumption of the Sea Grove Conference that continued for half a dozen years. Tragedy struck in the win-

(c.1900) The original Union Chapel shown here at the southeast corner of Cape and Pavilion Avenues was destroyed by fire in 1968. The current church at the same location was dedicated a year later. *Courtesy of the Deaconess Community of the Evangelical Lutheran Church in America.*

ter of 1968 when heavy winds damaged the electrical wiring, setting fire to the chapel. The ensuing blaze defied all efforts of the volunteer firefighters. The damage was so severe that the church could not be saved.

There was no interruption in divine services while a new church was being rebuilt with donations coming from virtually every summer visitor and resident of Cape May Point. The fire hall hosted Sunday evening service and Mrs. Douglas's cottage held the Sunday school. The present church was dedicated in 1969. It retained the simple form and may have been built on the foundations of its predecessor.

Once again in 1979 the Conference resumed with Rev. Harvey Warner, pastor of the Community Church in Green Creek, presiding. Rev. Dr. Donald A. Theobald, a Cape May Point resident, who conducted services year-round, followed Warner's tenure.

Like the familiar children's game of interlocking fingers it was saying "here is the church and here is the steeple…"

Saint Agnes Roman Catholic Church – 1885

A year after the Presbyterians had completed the Beadle Memorial Church, the Roman Catholics took the first step in caring for the Catholic residents of the Point. On August 29, 1883, The Bishop of Trenton, the Most Reverend Michael J. O'Farrell, bought three lots at the northeast corner of Cape and Pavilion Avenues. They had been owned by Colonel Anson H. Hamilton, hotel manager of the Carlton, the Cape House, and the Shoreham for many years.

The new Catholic Church was to be named Saint Agnes and reportedly had the same design as Saint Mary's, an earlier Catholic Church in Cape May, which has been replaced by the present Our Lady Star of the Sea. Saint Agnes' stucco exterior suggests a masonry building, but it is actually a frame structure. It bears the characteristics of the carpenter gothic style much favored for church design at that time.

It lacks a bell tower or steeple but the large cross atop the steep gable roof proudly announces its denomination. Its most attractive feature is the array of slender gothic casement windows of brilliant leaded glass. Surprisingly, these sash are quite new, although they are fitted to the original wood frames.

Construction got underway in 1883 but progressed slowly. In stark contrast to the five-week construction schedule achieved by the Beadle Memorial church, Saint Agnes wasn't completed in time for the 1884 summer season. The first Mass was not said until 1885, but since then services have been held continuously during the summer season except for an eleven-year hiatus that started in 1920. At that time the parishioners were dependent for Mass on the church in Cape May or on two local Catholic institutions – Villa Maria-by-the-Sea (the former Carlton hotel) and Saint Mary's-by-the-Sea (the former Shoreham hotel). Both were summer vacation homes for Catholic nuns and they welcomed Catholic laity to their services.

(c.2002) Saint Agnes Roman Catholic Church opened for Mass in 1885. Its design is almost identical to Saint Mary's, an earlier Catholic Church in Cape May that has been replaced by the present Our Lady Star of the Sea. *Courtesy of the Author.*

The Quakers – 1886

The Quakers never established a Friends' Meeting House in Cape May Point, but they did hold regular worship services there during the summer months at the Thomas Hilliard cottage on Beach Avenue. The first of these was convened in 1886 and held each year until 1905. Services were scheduled on the first Sunday of the month during July, August, and September.

The Quakers had been influential in Cape May County society since the latter part of the seventeenth century. Among the enduring names of the earliest Cape May County settlers, the Townsends and Spicers were members of the Society of Friends. The first Meeting House was built at Beesley's Point around 1716, and then, less than a dozen years later, relocated to Seaville (in Upper Township on old Route 9, just above present-day Sea Isle City).

The meetings in the Point were under the control of the Salem Quarterly Meeting of Hicksite Friends. They appointed David B. Bullock, John R. Zerns, and William T. Hilliard to have the care of these summer meetings. It was reported in the October 14, 1897 issue of the *Friend's Intelligencer*:

> On a high piece of ground overlooking the meeting of bay and ocean, stands the cottage of Thomas Hilliard, at Cape May Point, where Friends have met in summers past, and still meet to worship God. Last First-day…we attended for the first time this meeting of ten or twelve gathered together 'in His name' and listened to an original reading by a young woman Friend, and a few words by an elderly man Friend.

After the death of Thomas Hilliard the cottage remained unoccupied until 1923 when the Richards family purchased it from the Hilliard family estate. In 1930 someone wrote this uncharitable critique of the Richards' landscaping:

> It is now owned by Professor Richards of the University of Pennsylvania, whose fancy of prohibiting the use of a lawnmower or shears, has given the property the general aspect of sad neglect and decay. The stern and persistent approach of the rough breakers, though warded off by a long line of piling, is rapidly wearing out the sandy foundation of the house, which is still kept in its Quaker dress of blue-gray trimmed with white. The absence of a lawn, where there is ample space for one, a space now occupied by a neglected growth of rough lengthy seagrasses, intermingled with woodbine, honeysuckle, and prickly pear, is very noticeable to the visitor…

The great September storm of 1936 brought the ocean to its doorstep and severely damaged a portion of the foundation. Professor Horace Richards and his sister, Marie, had it moved back two blocks to a safe haven, on lots that their grandparents had purchased from the Sea Grove Association sixty years earlier. Some years later, as the large cottage became a burden to maintain, they sold the old Hilliard cottage and built a smaller house next door, once again on their grandparents' lots. Since her brother's death, it seems that Marie Richards is the only person in Cape May Point living on land purchased by her family from the Sea Grove Association in the 1870s. The Hilliard Cottage remains today at the corner of Lincoln and Coral Avenues, in fine condition, one of the proud remnants of the early Sea Grove cottages.

(c.1890) The Quakers never established a Friends Meeting House in Cape May Point, but they did hold regular worship services at the Thomas Hilliard cottage on Beach Avenue. *Courtesy of Marie G. Richards.*

FRIENDS MEETING, AT THIS COTTAGE AT 11 O'CLOCK A.M. — TO DAY. —

1886-1905

(c.1936) The great September storm of 1936 brought the Ocean to the doorstep of the old Hilliard cottage, which had been acquired by the Richards family in 1923, following the death of Thomas Hilliard. *Courtesy of Marie G. Richards.*

47

The African Methodist Episcopal Church

The first mention of this church appeared in the *Star of the Cape* on December 12, 1878:

> The quarterly meeting of the A.M.E. Church was held hereon last Sunday. Rev. Mr. Parker, colored, presiding elder, was present and preached an interesting and edifying sermon. The colored people here are trying to raise funds to erect for themselves a small church, as they have no place in which to hold services. They express themselves very thankful to Mr. Simpson for the use of the pavilion building in which to hold services last Sabbath.

They did build a small chapel on Alexander Avenue where most, if not all of the African-American community resided in this very segregated town. Most were part of the large service community that worked in the dining rooms and kitchens or served as chambermaids in the hotels and/or boarding houses.

The church was a modest structure and no photographs of it have been found. It was destroyed in a fire in the 1920s. No one was injured, but two local white youths bragged privately about being the arsonists. No one was charged.

The Sea Grove Camp Meeting Association – 1885

No religious group has left reminders of its former presence in cape May Point more conspicuously than the United Brethren in Christ. The row of diminutive cabins still lining the south side of Knox Avenue west of Pearl are the remnants of the camp meeting grove they established here in 1885.

The designation "The Sea Grove Association" should not be confused with what sounds like its counterpart, "The Sea Grove Camp Meeting Association." The former was the 1875 organization that Alexander Whilldin created to develop Sea Grove. The latter was an 1885 organization established by ministers and laymen of the Church of the United Brethren in Christ to purchase and develop several parcels of vacant land in Cape May Point as a permanent camp meeting site. After acquiring the property in 1882 they set about the construction that would transform the land into a self-contained little village of tents, cabins and communal buildings, often referred to as "the camp grounds" or as "the grove."

The campground proper consisted of the block bounded by Knox, Pearl, Stites, and Chrystal Avenues. This made a grove of 200 by 250-feet, which they enclosed with a picket fence. Tiny parcels, fifteen by twenty-four feet, had been staked out for the erection of tents. The pavilion, for the all-important worship services, occupied the very center of the lot. A third of the block, that portion fronting on Pearl Avenue, had been kept open to seat those attending the pavilion service.

A dining hall for communal meals occupied two lots across the street from the grove at the northeast corner of Stites and Pearl Avenues. This building is there today having undergone many changes before finally being remodeled into condominium apartments. To accommodate transients, A. W. Springer, a Cape May Point contractor, constructed two eight-bedroom cottages.

The accommodations were Spartan, but very cheap. A twelve by twelve foot tent with a wood floor could be rented two months for ten dollars. Furnishings were extra. In this 144 square-foot space, a family of six might have a stove with cooking utensils, dishes, a table and dining chairs, and cots for all. This would add seven dollars to the two-month bill. Not a bad price for a summer vacation in Cape May Point!

Although lodgings were available throughout the season, the religious camp meeting activities were usually confined to August. The length of the programs varied – some for a week, some for ten days. The fourth meeting in 1891 was scheduled during July and August for a full seventeen days! They were a biennial affair, and they were not intended for the *bon vivant* as their newsletter makes clear:

> The place is beautiful for situation, and has the advantages of the Sea-shore, without the objectionable features of many other places, where sin and folly reign supreme. There is not a saloon or licensed place for the sale of liquors in the borough and the absence of the saloon is a strong point in favor of this resort.

Their literature boasted of the easy accessibility by land or sea. The *Delaware Bay and Cape May* railroad tracks passed down Chrystal Avenue, right by the camp meeting grounds. This local connected in Cape May with the *West Jersey Railroad*, making a trip from Philadelphia a simple matter. Prospects were reminded that they could also take the steamer *Republic* down from Philadelphia to the steamboat landing on the bay a few hundred yards up the beach and also accessible by the local rail line.

As in many of the other camp meeting sites, the tents were gradually replaced with pint-sized cottages. They were little more than unwinterized wooden tents. A 1917 map shows them cheek by jowl along Knox Avenue with two other clusters radiating out from the rear of the pavilion. We do not know when the camp meetings ceased or when the Sea Grove Camp Meeting Association gave up its active management of the property.

It has been reported that, in the 1930s, Harry Dilks, then mayor of Cape May Point, purchased the entire church property from the Association. The dining hall became his residence and he moved the center cabins out along Knox and Stites Avenues on twenty-five by one hundred-foot lots. Several have changed little to this day. Others have been delightfully altered and added to, making the strip along Knox one of the special features of the Point.

(c.2002) One of the tiny cottages still remaining on Knox Avenue is a reminder of the Camp Meeting Grounds established by the United Brethren in Christ in 1885. *Courtesy of the Author.*

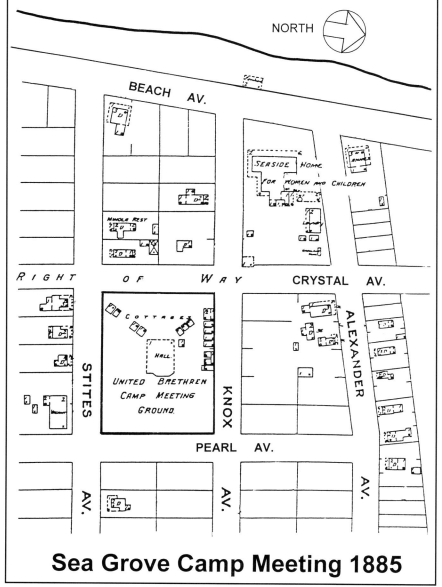

Sea Grove Camp Meeting 1885

Chapter 4
Inns for the Gentry

Lodgings and Diversions

With the arrival of its second summer season in 1876, Sea Grove could offer visitors a choice of three hotels. The best accommodations were found at the Sea Grove House, followed by the Cape House and the Centennial House. The latter two resembled boarding houses more than hotels. Scarcely a block separated the three, all clustered along Cape Avenue close by the waterfront. What differentiated them was the extent of entertainment offered and the refinement of the accommodations provided.

Restaurants were rare at that time even in Cape May, so all the lodging facilities offered full meal service.

Many families spent the entire season at the Sea Grove House. It was more a residential establishment than a transient hotel and guests were more likely to spend a month or at least several weeks than they were a long weekend. Toward the end of September they would be gone, but the house would stay open for the winter, providing minimum accommodations to the workmen who would once again toil through the colder months, clearing and grading more of the land, improving the streets, and building the houses.

For most of the nineteenth century, the Sea Grove House (later named the Carlton House or Carlton Hall) was the center of social life in the Point. It was the place to be and to be seen. Social opportunities (how to meet Mrs. so-and-so) were available in the 230-seat dining room, or on the veranda, but especially in the ballroom. The weekly hop, with music by the Payson's orchestra and the Hayes Quartette, was not to be missed.

For the young set there was tennis on the lawn and roller-skating at the beach pavilion. For gentlemen, there was billiards and bowling. And for the whole family, frequent concerts and an endless array of worship services. A performance of *Uncle Tom's Cabin* or a minstrel show featuring the kitchen and dining staffs were occasional treats.

(c.1880s) For most of the nineteenth century the Carlton House was the center of social life in the Point. It was the place to be seen among one's peers, such as these gentlemen sitting proudly on the spacious veranda. *Courtesy of the Cape May County Historial Society.*

(c.1901) The encampment of the Boys' Brigade on the lawn of the Carlton House was a weeklong event that occurred each summer season. *Courtesy of the Deaconess Community of the Evangelical Lutheran Church in America.*

The Sea Grove House

Newspapers of the day called it "Fine," "Grand," and "Commodious." Was Sea Grove's first hotel such an imposing edifice? Probably not. Its architectural style could best be described as "Cape May Plain." Its modest height of four stories was but one more than some of the nearby cottages. The most impressive feature of the new hotel was the size and position of its five-acre site – on the beachfront with a commanding view of ocean and bay. Thirty-six cottages could have been built on that plot. Such a large parcel insured adequate space for bathhouses, stables, greenhouses, other outbuildings and an expansive seafront lawn, promenade, and croquet ground.

To speed things along, the structural wood frame was prepared in Philadelphia, shipped to Sea Grove and assembled on the site. Construction started in March, 1875, and was completed in early June. But by May, the Sea Grove Association was sensing success and dreaming of adding two one-hundred-foot wings to create a 360-foot facade, to surround each of the sleeping floors with verandas and to triple the room capacity to three hundred. A pipe dream as it turned out. Starting on June 20, 1875, formal grand opening ceremonies extended over several days. There were speeches galore, interspersed, of course, with worship services and sermons. Musical entertainment was in the capable hands of, what the newspapers termed, the famous Hayes Quartette.

Early attempts to engage Colonel Henry W. Sawyer as the proprietor fizzled out. He had managed the Ocean House

in Cape May but was at that time in charge of the Clayton House in Wilmington, Delaware. Sawyer went on to operate the Chalfonte Hotel in Cape May. They then settled for A. P. Hildreth, who had recently left the Metropolitan Hotel in Washington, D.C., and was respected in Cape May circles as a competent hotel man.

The Sea Grove House plan, a simple rectangle 160 feet long, put public functions on the first floor and 100 bedrooms on the three floors above. Encircling the ground floor, a spacious veranda or piazza provided the guests with a strategic spot for people-watching and boy-meets-girl encounters. Entrance foyer, parlors, ballroom, dining room and kitchen filled out the first floor. Hotel bedrooms were small and sparsely furnished, not unusual for seaside hotels of the period. Even the elegant Congress Hall, Cape May's finest, had rooms no more than eight and a half feet wide!

There were few amenities for guests, but, unlike the cottages, the hotel could boast of gaslight in every room. The fuel was not piped natural gas, or propane in tanks – it was manufactured on the premises. In a covered pit close by the hotel a large copper tank was filled with gasoline and from it gas was piped to a smaller copper holding tank before being distributed throughout the building. Good drinking water was plentiful and could be found scarcely sixteen feet below the surface. However, it wasn't long before they needed to add a windmill so the well-pump could keep up with the rising demands of the summer visitors.

In the fall, the contractor, Smith E. Hughes, set about further improvements to the hotel. Instead of the two 100-foot additions conceived in the Spring, he constructed a more modest forty by sixty foot wing at the western end, bringing the bed count up to 125, where it remained as long as the future seawalls held back its inevitable demise.

At the same time, a second addition on the back allowed a threefold enlargement of the kitchen, plus a laundry, storeroom, and space for servants dining. The main dining room was enlarged, borrowing space from an existing hallway and parlor, so that 230 guests could be served at one sitting. Sea Grove's prospects seemed bright.

(c.1875) The most impressive feature of Sea Grove's first hotel, the Sea Grove House, was the size and position of its five acre site – on the beachfront with a commanding view of Ocean and Bay. The seafront lawn served as promenade and as grounds for croquet and lawn tennis. *Courtesy of the Cape May County Historical Society.*

Encircling the ground floor, a spacious veranda or piazza provided the guests with a strategic spot for people-watching and boy-meets-girl encounters.

(c.1875) Beach pavilions were common amenities for beachfront hotels. They provided a stage from which to view the beach activities, with a roof to protect the ladies from the unwelcome tanning rays of the sun. One changed into bathing attire in the bathhouses on the lower level. *Courtesy of the Cape May County Historical Society.*

The Cape House and Centennial House

Buoyed by the apparent success of its first season in 1875, the key members of the Sea Grove Association set about providing more accommodations for the following year. On November 1, 1875, Whilldin, Edmunds, Gass, and Marcy, four of the five incorporators of the Association, joined with Dr. John N. Walker, James Edmunds, and the Norristown building contractors, Laver and Knoedler, to incorporate the Cape House Association. They raised $25,000 to construct a new hotel, ninety-five percent of which came from Whilldin, Walker, and the contractors. For the next twenty-five years Dr. Walker was to become a key player and prime speculator in the Sea Grove enterprise.

A few weeks later Whilldin, Walker, and Smith E. Hughes, builder of the Sea Grove House, got together with James Edmunds, and the architect, J. C. Sidney, and incorporated the Union Hall Association. They invested $16,600 toward the construction of a second hotel to serve the hordes of vacationers they envisioned for the following seasons. Once again Whilldin, Walker and the builder put up the majority of the funds.

Both facilities opened for the 1876 season. At first called the Cape May House, but shortly thereafter known as the

Cape House, its ninety rooms rivaled in size its neighbor, the Sea Grove House, with which it shared several design elements. An early engraving shows a simple rectangular structure three stories high surrounded by a tall open piazza. Its mansard roof, probably of slate, is punctuated with gabled dormers set in line with the windows below. This attic level could have served as guestrooms or servants quarters.

The entrance was at the center of the main façade. One approached it from Cape Avenue up a flight of wooden steps. It was located on a very small lot (nine of which could fit on the Sea Grove House property) one block back from the beach. For the opening season, H. H. Wilson, as manager, saw to the needs of its guests.

The Union House, originally called Union Hall and later the Centennial House, went up a block further from the beach, at the corner of Cape and Pearl, where the landmark Crowell cottage (known to locals as the Gray Ghost) now stands. The Centennial House also was a three-story building and just a bit smaller with seventy-six bedrooms, including the unusual feature of a brick exterior wall for the ground floor. The upper floors were of frame construction with an unusual finished siding that resembled a worked molding. A terrible fire took it down in 1888, along with almost a dozen of the neighboring stores and cottages.

Above:
(c.1885) The Centennial House opened in 1876 on the southwest corner of Cape and Pearl Avenues (where the "Gray Ghost" now stands). Twelve years later it fell victim to a disastrous fire that took down almost a dozen of the neighboring stores and cottages. *Courtesy of E. Roberta Rutherford.*

Below:
(c.1880) The 90 room Cape House hotel, located across the street from the Sea Grove House on the west side of Cape Avenue, between Pearl and Diamond Avenues, was completed in time for Sea Groves second season in 1876. *Courtesy of Margaret Rosenberg Lonergan.*

The Shoreham Hotel

In 1890, the area east of Coral Avenue near the lighthouse was devoid of houses. Almost overnight, the construction of two key buildings changed that. One was a charming new hotel, The Shoreham, on the beachfront east of Lehigh Avenue; the other was the now-famous Harrison Cottage.

Although the national press had a field day with the story about Wanamaker's fabulous gift to the Harrisons, in no time a half-dozen huge new homes clustered around these two icons, drawn there like bees to honey. This was now the fashionable end of town.

The Sea Grove House (called the Carlton House in 1890) and the Cape House were still around, but the Centennial House had succumbed to the great fire of 1888. The Shoreham was the new face in town, and a lot of folks were betting on it. In one way their wager was right – it's still standing, though it hasn't been a hotel for over a century.

Sadly, it was an example of really bad timing. There's little doubt that the hotel's developers were counting on the prestige of Harrison's presence to stimulate trade. The hotel's manager, A. H. Hamilton, who practically owned Cape May Point, was a member of the syndicate that had presented the Presidential cottage to Mrs. Harrison.

Above:
(c.1895) When it opened in 1890, the Shoreham Hotel was the last hotel to be constructed in Cape May Point. The Sea Grove House and the Cape House were still open at that time, but the Shoreham is the only hotel structure that has survived to this day. Since 1909 it has been owned by the Sisters of Saint Joseph and converted into their summer retreat house. *Courtesy of the Cape May County Historical Society.*

Below:
(c.1895) The Shoreham Hotel, built in 1890 at the extreme eastern end of Cape May Point, had an immediate influence on the development of this part of the town. In no time a half dozen huge new homes sprung up nearby along Beach and Harvard Avenues. *Courtesy of the Cape May County Historical Society.*

Several nasty problems arose. First, Mrs. Harrison died suddenly in 1892. Then, that same year, Harrison didn't run for a second term. And finally, none of the Harrison family ever returned to their palatial summer home. The district's presidential attraction had vanished. The *coup de grace* was the financial panic of 1897. The hotel barely survived into the twentieth century, and no more hotels were to be built in Cape May Point.

This was not the first hotel proposed at that location. In 1876 the *Cape May Wave* reported:

> A new hotel is proposed to be built at Sea Grove this coming fall. It is to stand on the high ground in front of the lighthouse. In the center will be a space forty feet square, devoted to offices, hall, reception rooms, etc. Running out each side at an angle of forty-five degrees, will be two wings, 120 feet long. On the first floor there will be a parlor and dining room, and above, chambers. It will accommodate about five hundred guests, and will be especially comfortable, as by an arrangement unusual in the general run of hotels, each room will have a view of the ocean, and all the windows will be shaded from the sun.

The floor plan of the Shoreham, finally built fourteen years later, bears a remarkable likeness to this earlier concept. A brochure, published by its owners, offered this modest description:

> The Shoreham is one of the most delightful hotels on the coast. Its admirable construction, facing on three sides its own court yard and garden, gives to all its public rooms fine light, air and space. The lawn extends two hundred feet down to the sea, with nothing in front or on either side to obstruct its ocean view. It is two hundred feet front, and each wing, eastern and western, are two hundred feet, thus giving to over one hundred of its guest rooms a full ocean view. It has 1,200 feet of cool spacious porch, insuring shade and breeze at all hours and in all weather. Its large dining room faces the ocean on one side and the open country on the other. Its ample exchange, in which the office is situated, stretches with a broad corridor on the western side to the spacious parlor and ball room, with windows on three sides. The music room faces this, opening with its wide archway, making, when needed, a good stage for concerts and entertainment.

At the Country Club

Today it is difficult to imagine a country club in Cape May Point. It would seem out of place here. In the 1890s sentiment was different. The drive for social status was very much alive. What better way to establish one's position than membership in a club for one's equals (or betters)?

A physician from Pittsburgh, Dr. Randall T. Hazzard, may have been dreaming such dreams. Why not build his own country club? On Lake drive at the corner of Central Avenue, at considerable expense, he converted an abandoned icehouse into *The Cape May Point Social Club*. With its wide porches commanding a great view of Lake Lily, and its giant parlor furnished with a dazzling fireplace and elegant stairway, it was a splendid transformation. The country club had many aliases. On any day the press might refer to it as the *Lakeside Lodge*, or *Lily Lake Casino*, or the *Lakeside Villa*.

Announcing that its object was "the advancement of social life in Cape May Point," it opened its doors on August 11, 1899 with (what else) a reception and tea. Fittingly, Mr. Hazzard became the first president. H. G. Ferris, a celebrated artist, was elected vice president.

Determined to make the lake and the clubhouse the focal point of social life, Hazzard also built the famous "rustic bridge" overlooking the clumps of lily pads at the north end of the lake. An annual water fete, with the bridge, boats, and clubhouse ablaze with lights, would attract two hundred guests. The venture was a success.

If a country club in the Point seems odd, how about a golf course? The newspaper reported that a number of the members were ready to lay out golf links and tennis courts. The golf course became no more than a putting green on the lawn, but tennis, together with shuffleboard and Ping-Pong, became popular activities. The ladies gathered weekly for euchre and whist, and every month a tea party cemented their social bonds.

Hazzard further sealed his standing in the community with the impressive cottage he built close to the Shoreham Hotel and across from the Harrison property. Convinced of Cape May Point's bright future, he acquired a number of lots nearby and built several cottages on speculation. All this was in 1899. Unfortunately, the Point was about to enter a decline that would persist for half a century.

The ladies gathered weekly for euchre and whist, and every month a tea party cemented their social bonds.

(c.1905) Announcing that its object was "the advancement of social life in Cape May Point," the Cape May Point Social Club (often called the Cape May Point Country Club) opened its doors in 1899 with a reception and tea. Dr. Randall T. Hazzard, a physician from Pittsburgh, had converted the "Lakeside Lodge" from an old ice house that stood on the shore of Lake Lily. *Courtesy of the Cape May County Historical Society.*

(c.1905) The giant parlor, furnished with a dazzling fireplace and elegant stairway, made a splendid clubhouse for the new Cape May Point Social Club. It has changed very little, but most of its long life has been as a private residence. *Courtesy of the Cape May County Historical Society.*

(c.1925) Lake drive, in front of the Cape May Point Country Club, was a narrow country lane in 1925. The cottage in the center background is no longer there. *Courtesy of William W. Dickhart, Jr.*

Inns for the Proletariat

The boarding house offered more modest accommodations at about half the hotel fare. Guests had a private room, though seldom with a private bath. Meals were served family style in the dining room. Usually the parlor and front porch were available for the visitor's comfort. They served a middle class clientele.

From the beginning, Cape May Point had many to choose from. An early Sea Grove brochure listed the following:

> Sea View Cottage, *Miss A. S. White, Proprietor*
> Ocean Cottage, *Mrs. S. J. Colladay, Proprietor*
> Woodbine Cottage, *Mrs. J. Brooks, Proprietor*
> Salem Cottage, *Mr. Amnon Wright, Proprietor*
> Schellenger's Cottage, *Mrs. J. Schellenger,*
> *Proprietor*
> Cape Point Cottage, *Mr. D. F. Lockerby,*
> *Proprietor*

Two of the larger and better-known boarding houses were the Floral Villa and Wright's Villa, sitting side by side on Cape Avenue between Pearl Avenue and the Pavilion Circle. After the Floral Villa ceased offering boarding accommodations, it became the Bell-May Apartments, and today it's a stylish three-unit condominium.

Amnon Wright, the proprietor of Wright's Villa advertised in the *Cape May Star and Wave*:

> Large, airy rooms and good table. For homelike comforts, convenience and location, there is no house possessing superior advantages. The situation is very desirable, being within two minutes walk of the Bathing Ground, Post Office, Music, Hotels, and Stations.

Next door to the boarding house, the sign on his store announced in bold letters "Country Produce, Fresh and Salt Meats." After his death, his wife Sallie continued to operate the boarding house but converted the store into a rental apartment. She was a beloved figure in the Point, a tiny woman who lived to almost a hundred years of age.

Once plentiful, the number of boarding houses gradually diminished with the change in life styles. None remain today in this community which is zoned exclusively for single family homes.

(c.1890) The Ocean House, owned by Dr. J. Newton Walker, was one of a dozen boarding houses that operated in the Point in the nineteenth century. Mrs. S. J. Colladay was the proprietor who provided meals as well as lodging. *Courtesy of the Cape May County Historical Society.*

(c.1890) The Sea View was one of the larger boarding houses in the Point, built around the time that the Shoreham Hotel opened. Later, it became a private residence and has been known for many years as "Brigadune." It is now a restored oceanfront cottage, still in the same location, at 107 Harvard Avenue. *Courtesy of the Cape May County Historical Society.*

Chapter 5

An Era Ends

Bye-bye Sea Grove – Hello Cape May Point

In 1878, just three years into its infancy, Sea Grove had a problem. It was with the Government of the United States. The feds determined that its post office that had been operating since March of 1876 wasn't legitimate. After all, the Sea Grove Association was not a government body; it was a private enterprise, operating rather independently within the Township of Lower.

Facing up to this predicament, the Association successfully petitioned the State Legislature to incorporate as a borough, independent of Lower Township. The taxpayers approved this in an April referendum. Next problem – the postal service objected to the name Sea Grove. Some say they thought Sea Grove's mail would get mixed with Ocean Grove's, since the names were so similar. Cape May Point (a name certainly not to be confused with Cape May City!) was chosen and approved.

Legal issues and confusion persisted. In 1891, the Point had to reincorporate because of some flaw in prior legislation. Again, the townspeople approved the act by referendum and the Point remained an independent borough – but not for long. Five years later, the state's laws on borough formation were found unconstitutional. Cape May Point's borough status was illegitimate. Surrendering its independence at last, on April 8, 1896, it reverted to being a part of Lower Township.

This game of government checkers was little more than an annoyance compared to Sea Grove's real problem – its financial situation. The newspapers of 1878 kept talking about "the hard times". Their advertisements emphasized bargain prices. Lumber and building materials prices tumbled. Labor was cheap because so many were jobless. One of Cape May City's proudest hotels, Congress Hall, went up for sheriff sale.

The building pace in Cape May Point was slowing to a halt. By 1880 the *Cape May Wave* observed that "while 1876 was a promising year, growth since then has not achieved expectations. A certain class affirms that it will never prosper as a temperance resort."

The newspaper further reported on January 29:

As a seaside resort conducted on puritanical principles...Cape May Point appears to have reached the end of its string...There are people wicked enough who account for the failure of Cape May Point because of the strict temperance and anti-amusement provisions of its charter of incorporation. The directors were invested among other exclusive powers of regulation and control, to forbid the sale of intoxicating liquors, to require of property owners any style and character of improvements, etc., and the directors themselves ruled against allowing any place of amusement.

These tremors of 1880 foretold the calamity that struck in 1881. Bankruptcy arrived. A January audit showed the Sea Grove Association's net worth to be less than $30,000! The venture had been financed by a $60,000 mortgage loan with a five-year balloon. Final payment was now due –desperate measures were called for. The property must be sold. As late as March, they couldn't get their asking price and a public auction appeared the only solution.

The Sea Grove Association had to abandon its dream. All the restrictions that had been placed on building lots would be lifted. No longer would a purchaser have to build within three years; a speculator could hold the land indefinitely. Cottage plans would never again need approval from the Association. The fundament prohibition against demon rum would go. All this relief would apply to past as well as to future buyers.

The April auction was painful – except for the speculators. Everything was for sale. The three hotels, the pavilion, the lake, hundreds of lots, seven cottages, and even the beaches were up for grabs. They all sold at a fraction of their worth. A typical lot went for $175. Beachfront properties brought somewhat more. The grandiose pavilion, symbol of this would-be Christian resort, fetched $400 – for its timber! It was a buyers market.

The consummate player here was Dr. J. Newton Walker. Previously in 1877, he had bought thirty lots from the Sea Grove Association. No one else had acquired so much property there. He didn't bid at the auction, but six months later he acquired another ninety-eight in a private purchase. Early on he had built the five-cottage "Walker Row" (often called the Five Sisters) across from the Sea Grove House on Lincoln Avenue. The drug store and seawater bath complex beside the hotel were his. He had sought his fortune in Sea Grove. So had others. All were let down. The timing was wrong. Cape may Point would ultimately enter a long deep sleep.

As a seaside resort conducted on puritanical principles...Cape May Point appears to have reached the end of its string.

The Great Storms

1875 – New Jersey coastal storms are a fact of life – always fascinating and often treacherous. Sea Grove got its share of storms from day one. Just three weeks after Alexander Whilldin had formed the Sea Grove Association on February 4, 1875, a tornado struck. Plans for the new resort were almost complete and work was about to get underway. The *Cape May Ocean Wave* thought the event newsworthy:

head that ran along Beach Avenue in Sea Grove suffered extensive damage. Since the protective dunes had been removed and replaced by this beachfront roadway there was to be trouble ahead and eventual surrender to the mighty Atlantic.

1878 – An October northeaster the previous year had ripped out some of the pilings of the protective seawall. Then in mid-April a violent squall tore through the borough, uprooting trees and causing some outhouses to take flight. Another northeaster in October further damaged the seawall.

(Date unknown) During a cold winter, the ice buildup on Delaware Bay can be quite impressive. At times the bay can be covered with ice almost as far as the eye can see. *Courtesy of the Cape May County Historical Society.*

The vibration of the lighthouse was so great in the tornado last Thursday evening February 26th that the oil in the lamp spilled out of the lamp bowls, they being open topped. It has been frequently told us that a bucketful of water will spill over from this vibration in our howling Cape May gales when placed on the floor of the lantern deck at the top of the lighthouse.

1876 – The next year saw two more storms. The first came mid-September with gale force winds of 65 mph, the worst storm in many years, they said. The beach drive between Sea Grove and Cape May City was hit hard. The surf pounded away at its gravel surface until it became impassable.

Three months later an even more furious November storm finished off what the previous one had started. This time the Signal Station by the beach at Emerald Avenue registered gale force winds at 72 mph. Even the substantial bulk-

1888 – The *Storm of the Century* it was called – the great blizzard of March 1888. Every hamlet along the Atlantic coast shivered from its fury. The snowfall became so deep, transportation ceased – the trains couldn't run. Farms and villages were isolated for days. Cape May Point could do nothing but hunker down and wait out the storm. Those on the land were spared: those at sea were not. Not far from the Point twenty-one ships were lost to the fearsome wind and raging sea.

1889 – The pilings that lined the shore to form a breakwater had been damaged year after year. Sand washed out through the openings as waves crashed over them. A whole block of Beach Avenue was damaged. This early September storm took away the steamboat landing at Sunset Beach before it could be taken down and stored for the winter.

1891 – Trouble did come again only two years later. Repeated storms had consumed much of the beach west of

Cape Avenue where a number of fine cottages had been erected. At the corner of Beach and Emerald the impressive villa of John Wanamaker stood flanked by a protective brick wall and set well back from the street. Next door was the government Signal Station and then the elegant Victorian cottage of A. G. Crowell (since moved twice and now called *The Gray Ghost*). The October northeaster of 1891 not only chewed up Beach Avenue, it tore away the front section of Wanamaker's brick garden wall.

1893 – Two years later the erosion was spreading both east and west. This time the damage consumed the gravel drive in front of the Carlton Hotel (the old Sea Grove House) severely injuring a youth that was passing by. The natives were getting restless. The whole town was screaming for the commissioners to do something to stop this destruction.

1899 – The worst came last, and it was a hurricane. The *Star of the Cape* described some of the mayhem:

> In front of the Point the beach was cut away badly, the brick foundation of Carlton Hall being washed down

and the building barely escaped being precipitated into the sea. Beyond the Hall the beach drive was almost entirely destroyed and the waves washed over the sidewalk.

The steamboat wharf was torn asunder and its parts distributed for two miles along the shore, the water washing up on the porch of the Delaware Bay House (an excursion hotel located by the steamship landing on Sunset Beach)

The local railroads are practically destroyed, the rails being twisted in every conceivable manner, and the track being carried in some instances a hundred yards inland.

Many beachfront owners just gave up. *The Cape May Wave* said, "a number of houses in this place are to be removed to better locations and rebuilt." This statement was prophetic – the house-moving parade continued for the next fifty years. Cape May Point's unceasing efforts to hold back the ocean's rampages are still going on to this day.

(c.1930s or 1940s) The early beachfront cottages were constantly assaulted by coastal storms: The seawall of wood pilings on the right was not enough to protect this house from the encroaching surf. *Courtesy of the Cape May County Historical Society.*

(c.1930s or 1940s) Storm wrecked cottages like this one on Beach Avenue near the Lankenau Villa became hazardous nuisances that were especially attractive to curious children. *Courtesy of the Cape May County Historical Society.*

(c.1930s or 1940s) A late spring pastime for vacationers in the 1930s and 1940s was walking the beaches to see how many cottages had succumbed to the fall and winter storms. *Courtesy of the Cape May County Historical Society.*

Bulkheads and Jetties

The construction of timber bulkheads and jetties has been the favored means of retarding erosion throughout most of Cape May Point's history. In the nineteenth century, they were the sole devices. The contest between storm and structure was unbalanced. The sea as always had the upper hand.

The earliest seawall, built in 1875, was a pretty substantial structure. Two rows of oak pilings, about twenty feet apart, were driven along the beachfront to protect Beach Avenue. On the outer, or ocean side row, the pilings were placed tight against each other. For the inner row they were spaced about five feet apart and braced by timbers to the outer row. Three-inch planking was spiked to heavy top and bottom rails along the outer row to keep sand from washing out behind them. Space between the rows was filled with soil.

For the beachfront between Cape and Central Avenues this elaborate construction proved ineffective. A third row was added two years later with eight-foot pilings embedded six feet into the sand. This time the space between rows was filled with old railroad ties and rocks. As tides continued to cut in, these breastworks needed constant repair. By 1884 they had been extended to protect stretches at either end.

All such bulkheads have an intrinsic flaw. They reflect energy from the waves and remove sand from the beach, steepening the offshore profile. It became clear that they were not the best defense. Some suggested a seawall of granite boulders, but there was no money for such an expensive project.

The use of jetties at that time was rather limited. The first two built in 1875 and 1876 were nothing more than a row of pilings extending out two hundred feet into the sea. Jetties did have their advocates, however. The most vocal was A. H. Hamilton, manager of the severely threatened Carlton House, who, in 1889, had this to say in the *Star of the Cape*:

> It is unquestionably the fact, that only be means of jetties that the safety of our beaches can be assured. I am so thoroughly convinced of this, that I have arranged to throw out about six of them in front of Cape May Point next autumn, to be from one hundred and fifty to two hundred feet in length. This takes it to low water mark and I think is long enough. The cost is trifling compared with the results obtained. A double row of pilings stayed by planks spiked to them lengthwise can be put out the required length for one hundred and fifty dollars. As to results let those who are skeptical, come to the Point and see what have been the effects from a jetty put out when the Point was founded. For four hundred feet on each side, the sand is in hills and the surf makes no impression upon it. When the influence of the jetty is not felt, there is damage done by every storm tide.

Two years later, a new type of jetty construction, named the Hughes Jetty after the man who had patented it, was tried out with some success. One was installed in front of the Wanamaker cottage at Emerald Avenue. There were reports that the new jetty put the high tide mark seventy feet further out to sea. Now the critics complained that it should have been built higher because the beach level had risen so much that parts of the jetty were covered with sand.

(c.1905) The boardwalk in Cape May Point around the turn of the century was supported by a timber bulkhead on the seaward side. The fanciful tower of the original Lankenau Villa can be seen on the right. The ineffective jetty on the left consisted of wood pilings spaced closely together. *Courtesy of the Cape May County Historical Society.*

(c.1930s or 1940s) One of the severe coastal storms totally destroyed the boardwalk along Beach Avenue and it was never rebuilt. *Courtesy of the Cape May County Historical Society.*

(c.1945) The concrete blocks in the left foreground are the remainder of a seawall project of the WPA in the 1930s. Many beaches were filled with a maze of old pilings that had been installed over the years as jetties or bulkheads, but had been overtaken as the sea marched landward. *Courtesy of the Cape May County Historical Society.*

An Era's End

Alexander Whilldin's founding of Sea Grove in 1875 placed it in the forefront of New Jersey's south shore development. By that time the northern coast above Long Beach Island had already seen ten resorts spring to life. The picture differed in the south.

Below Long Beach Island, Cape May and Atlantic City were well established, but the rest of the coastline remained pristine. Sea Grove broke that tradition. Within a dozen years, seven new resorts from Wildwood to Margate were competing with Cape May Point for visitors and for buyers. One of these, Ocean City, was a particular threat to the Point's growth. Founded by a group of Methodist ministers from Pleasantville, it espoused similar goals of temperance and Christian morality. Ocean City was much closer to Philadelphia; it grew rapidly while Sea Grove stumbled into bankruptcy.

It's unlikely that location or religious aspirations were Sea Grove's problem. A weak economic plan appears the probable culprit. The initial investment in what are today called soft and hard costs must have been staggering. Professional fees for advertising, marketing, legal, survey, planning, and design services would not have been too costly. These soft costs were predictable and manageable.

The cost of land clearing, road development, the construction of three hotels, the pavilion, a school, greenhouses, stables, and bathhouses was another matter. These were all built in the first two years. For all this to be paid for, lot sales and cottage construction had to advance rapidly for five years without letup. After a promising start the sales rate fell to a trickle. 1881 brought the financial reckoning – all the Sea Grove Association holdings were sold at auction. It also brought land speculation – an enduring curse that Whilldin had hoped to avoid.

Those attracted to Cape May Point in the last quarter of the nineteenth century were largely from the professional or business world. Doctors, lawyers, and ministers mixed with men who had made their money in manufacturing or in commerce. John Wanamaker, Whilldin's co-founder, was the leading light of this society. The country's most successful retail merchant, Wanamaker was a tireless supporter of Cape May Point. For twenty-five years he was its most conspicuous summer visitor, except during the brief appearance of President Harrison in the early 1890s.

They built their summer homes by the sea or they stayed in one of the three hotels along Cape Avenue. Social life centered on the largest one, Carlton Hall (as the Sea Grove House was renamed after its bankruptcy sale). It wasn't until 1890 that the town's social center began to drift as the area near the lighthouse drew in the Shoreham Hotel and the President's cottage. By the end of the century the Cape May Point Country Club on Lake Lily was making its bid for society's homage. But society was leaving and the town was about to change.

People of lesser means did not generally build the nineteenth century gingerbread cottages. They were more likely to stay in one of the many boarding houses, or to occupy the houses that had been built as rental properties by the more affluent. Most of the twenty-five-foot wide lots along Alexander Avenue had small dwellings where the hotels' waiters and chambermaids lived.

Scarce borough government records and some newspaper accounts tell a bit about Cape May Point's first quarter century. There were few headlines recounting the latest tragedy to befall the community. The biggest single news event was the fire of 1888. It was certainly one of the worst disasters in the Point's history.

Flames were first seen after midnight on a cool November night in 1888. The fire spread rapidly through the four-story Centennial House. Fortunately, the hotel was unoccupied – it had closed for the season. Without a fire company or equipment to fight it, the whole town was in peril. A distress call went out to Cape May, but hours passed before their horse drawn pumper finally arrived. More time was lost in securing additional hoses to reach the only adequate water source, Lake Lily.

The fire had crossed over Pearl Avenue and torn through the store in Mrs. Jacoby's cottage, consuming all her new merchandise. It crossed Cape Avenue too, taking down Fadely's general store. Cape May's support did save the town, but the losses were staggering. The final toll was one large hotel, four residential stores, and ten cottages. Cape May Point would never again see such a firestorm. It was probably arson.

The only serious crime reported was in 1876 – an attempted poisoning. The victim, M. H. Golt, whose store was on the corner of Cape and Yale, drank water that had probably been tainted with a lye solution. He survived and the culprit was caught – a twelve-year old kid. This turned out not to be his first crime. He confessed to having set fire to the local streetcar and to having attempted arson on a newly-built cottage.

The Borough Council took care of governing, but didn't have too much to do. Their biggest task was holding back the ocean – a never-ending challenge. Breastworks were built, repaired, and rebuilt. Nothing really worked. The sea kept gnawing away at the beach and chewing away parts of Beach Avenue. Beachfront protection was expensive, and there wasn't enough money to go around. This problem persisted through most of the twentieth century

(c.1915) In this bird's-eye view from the lighthouse, the cottage built for President Harrison can be seen on the oceanfront at the far left, and the cottage built by Alexander Whilldin in 1875, also on the oceanfront, at the far right. The large building on the waterfront to the right of center is the second Lankenau Villa, a summer home for the Lutheran Deaconesses. The long low building in the foreground is "Long Tom," owned then by William Braun. Today, considerably shortened, it can be seen at 105 Lincoln Avenue. *Courtesy of William W. Dickhart, Jr.*

Those attracted to Cape May Point in the last quarter of the nineteenth century were largely from the professional or business world.

Part 2

Through the Two World Wars

1900-1946

Chapter 6
A Charitable Community

Caring for Others

Charitable seems an appropriate attribute for Cape May Point. It was founded in the spirit of a religious community with the aim of providing a moral environment.

For over one hundred years, it has welcomed more than a dozen charitable organizations. Presbyterians, Lutherans, Catholics, and Episcopalians have each provided summer vacation homes here for their congregations. Some have offered accommodations to their churchwomen; others have served the more needy among their laity. Just two remain – both are Roman Catholic institutions.

Presbyterians were the first group to provide boarding facilities, and the last institution to move out. Both Presbyterians and Lutherans built substantial new quarters for their parishioners. The others occupied former hotels or cottages that had been vacated by their owners.

The golden age of the charitable institutions lasted twenty years, from 1916 when the Presbyterian *Sunny Corner* took in its first orphans, until 1936 when the Immaculata Sisters had to abandon their summer retreat house, Villa Maria-by-the-Sea. By then it was Villa Maria *in* the Sea!

The Sea-Side Home

The model for Cape May Point's Sea-Side Home may have been The Seaside House for Girls, erected in Long Branch in 1874 by the Women's Christian Association of Philadelphia. In any event, the Presbyterians lost no time in asserting their charitable leadership in the new community. Their Presbyterian Orphanage in Philadelphia built the splendid Sea-Side Home that opened in 1879. While the Long Branch facility was meant as an affordable and sheltered lodging place for young working girls, the Sea-Side Home in the Point offered two-week vacations to the children of the orphanage, as well as to children and mothers of limited means from the many Presbyterian congregations.

A graceful two-story veranda surrounding the three and a half story institution offset the enormous scale of its long tri-gabled façade. With its several outbuildings, it occupied the whole block bounded by Beach, Alexander, Pearl, and Knox Avenues. Except for the hotels, it dwarfed the other buildings in the Point. Even the showplace cottages of Wanamaker and Whilldin were diminished by the size of this new arrival.

The first year saw a total of 115 mothers and children. Within five years that number had more than tripled to 366. The youngest was two months and the oldest eighty-three years. For full room and meals the women paid only three dollars a week, plus a dollar and a half for each child.

The Philadelphia orphanage kept sending more and more mothers and children to this enticing summer home. Ten years later, across Alexander Avenue, a three-story annex was added in 1889 to keep up with the increasing number of summer visitors.

Both buildings were on beautiful beachfront sites, but they were constantly menaced by storms. Their bulkheads worked most of the time, but when the real tempest would hit they were helpless against the huge waves. After the ferocious spring northeaster in 1936, things were desperate. The Sea-Side home was about to go seaward.

At this time the borough was planning a series of four new jetties, with federal WPA funding covering most of the costs. The borough would be responsible for the remainder. Alexander Avenue was one of the proposed locations. Mayor Dilks asked the Sea-Side Home to share in the borough's costs since the home would be the major beneficiary of this new beachfront protection. He announced that the Board of Managers agreed and pledged $1,500 as their contribution, which allowed the project to proceed.

A year later the Sea-Side Home Board reneged on its pledge. The jetty work was complete and further erosion had ceased. The borough needed the promised money, but, nevertheless, some taxpayers were upset with the mayor and sympathetic to the Sea-side Home. Things got really testy. At a stormy meeting of the borough commissioners, the mayor resigned, saying, "the taxpayers of the borough of Cape May Point do not seem to approve of my policies in the administration of the borough's business, particularly as to the beach erosion, and I therefore tender my resignation as Mayor of Cape May Point to be effective as of September 17."

All this had been reported in the *Cape May Star and Wave* but the following week's issue told quite a different story. The Sea-Side Home revealed in a scathing letter to the *Cape May Star and Wave* that it had agreed to a payment of only $150, not $1,500. It explained that Mayor Dilks was notified of the board's decision on many occasions. Their board did find it possible to raise their pledge amount from $150 to $200.

The Sea-Side Home survived the onslaught of that 1936 storm, but it seemed only a matter of time before it would be battered again. Time ran out in 1944 when the next big storm sealed its fate. It was demolished three years later. Its charitable service to countless children and mothers had lasted for sixty-eight years.

(c.1885) The Sea-Side Home, erected by the Presbyterians in 1879 on Beach Avenue, between Knox and Alexander Avenues, offered two week vacations to the children of the Presbyterian Orphanage in Philadelphia as well as to children and mothers of limited means from the many Presbyterian congregations. *Courtesy of Robert W. Elwell, Sr.*

Left:
(c.1885) This covered pavilion near Alexander Avenue enabled the mothers and volunteer housemothers to watch over the children of the Sea-Side Home, when the young ones were playing on the beach. *Courtesy of Robert W. Elwell, Sr.*

Sunny Corner

c.1930s – The Last Rendezvous "I guess we were about thirteen or fourteen that summer, and we were getting interested in girls. The Sunny Corner orphanage was a real goldmine when the girls were down for their month's vacation. You couldn't take them out – the housemothers kept a tight rein on them – but we got to know some of them, one way or another.

Late at night, when the lights were out, we used to shinny up the drainpipe to see the ones sleeping on the third floor. There were four of us, Joe Riley, the Rutherford boys, Sunny and Buddy, and myself. We would lie on the porch roof and talk to them through the windows. There was one really pretty blond, Helen Barnum, and we all had a crush on her.

One night we almost got caught. We had been there for a while when we heard their housemother, Mrs. Ranigan, come in bellowing, "What's going on here?" Well, we panicked! As the lights went on, we just jumped from the second floor roof and landed in the big hedge below. We got pretty scratched up and we hightailed it out of there. I think that must have been the end of our nightly trysts at Sunny Corner."

—*Rudy Schmidt*

The second charitable institution established by the Presbyterians was called *Sunny Corner*. It also opened as a summer home for the children from the Presbyterian Orphanage in Philadelphia, located at 58th Street and Kingsessing Avenue. Starting in 1879 the orphaned children had been coming to the Sea-Side Home for vacations, where they shared quarters with other children and their mothers. At Sunny Corner they had a place of their own.

All this was made possible through the generosity of John Wanamaker, who had chaired the board of the Presbyterian Orphanage for many years. Shortly after 1900, he moved his beachfront cottage back from the eroding shoreline and donated it to the Haddock Memorial, a Presbyterian institution in downtown Philadelphia, to be used as a summer home for their children. As serious erosion continued, he had it moved once again to a double-lot site on the northeast corner of Cape and Yale Avenues, where it stands today.

The number of children at the Philadelphia Orphanage had been increasing each year. Their ages ranged from a few months to the older teens. In the early 1900s there were over one hundred at the home. The Wanamaker cottage was large enough to accommodate all of the boys for one month and the girls for the other month. The children were under the care of several volunteer housemothers.

Lillian Malcolm, who was there as a child in the twenties and thirties, still remembers Bill the Lifeguard and John the Cop. Bill Yaeger was a big powerful guy. You could never drown when Bill the Lifeguard was guarding the beach. John, however, was the more colorful figure. He wasn't tall but his impressive uniform made up for his lack of stature. With riding jodhpurs encased in boots laced to the knees, and a Sam Brown belt over a military twill shirt, he made an impressive Officer of the Law. The conspicuous pistol in its leather holster and four-dimpled hat insured his position as a *gendarme* to be reckoned with.

When the children took their daily march to the beach, John the Cop would be at the corner of Cape and Beach Avenue to ensure their safe crossing. He would set up his semaphore signal, commanding traffic to STOP or to GO, depending on the direction he would turn it. The children were out of danger when John the Cop was on duty. They would have been just as safe without him; there were only a few cars in all of Cape May Point.

(c.1920s) The children of "Sunny Corner," the cottage that John Wanamaker had donated to the Presbyterian Orphanage in Philadelphia as their summer vacation home, ranged in age from a few months to the early teens. *Courtesy of the Presbyterian Children's Village.*

Most of the vacationers remember the children as perfectly behaved and immaculately dressed. On each Saturday night trip to Cape May's boardwalk, the boys would be in navy blazers and matching short pants with starched white shirts and ties. The same uniform took them to the Beadle Memorial chapel for weekly services and to the Union Chapel for Sunday School.

Over the years the institution acquired three more contiguous lots to provide room for expansion. The Edwin Gould Cottage on Yale Avenue, adjacent to the cottage Wanamaker had donated, was started in 1927 and completed in 1928 as an additional dormitory for the orphanage. This allowed for the children from four of the eight Philadelphia cottages to come to the Point at one time. The property continued as a summer home for the orphanage for forty-six years. In 1962, ownership was transferred to Gertrude W. Michel of Pennsauken, New Jersey, who concurrently sold it to the Marianist Society, Inc., a non-profit corporation of New York.

(c.1930s) After the Wanamaker cottage had been donated to the Presbyterian Orphanage in Philadelphia, and moved to the northeast corner of Yale and Cape Avenues in 1916, the boys would come down for one month and the girls for the other month. In the center background can be seen the diving board, erected over the steel jetty on "Skeezix Beach" at the end of Cape Avenue. *Courtesy of the Presbyterian Children's Village.*

Villa Lankenau

c.1930s – Villa Lankenau "One of the deaconesses, Sister Marie Koch, had a wonderful potion that was a sure cure for the pains of influenza, or a severe cold. Later we found out the recipe – one-third lemon juice, one-third honey, and one-third whiskey."

—*Peggy Dickhart*

The most striking reminder of the Lutheran's presence in Cape May Point was the majestic Lankenau Villa. It was named after its benefactor, John D. Lankenau, a wealthy banker with the venerable Philadelphia firm of Anthony J. Drexel. In his role as president of the German Hospital in Philadelphia, he saw the need for well-trained nurses who could speak German. In 1884, he arranged passage of seven Lutheran Deaconesses from Germany to become the hospital's principal nursing staff.

Lankenau provided them with commodious quarters in a new building on the hospital grounds known as the Mary J. Drexel Home and Philadelphia Motherhouse of Deaconesses. Dedicated in 1888, it included housing for elderly Lutherans, a hospital for children, and living accommodations for the Deaconesses. John Lankenau clearly saw the value of these well-trained and devoted nurses to the Lutheran community, and gave generously to ensure their comfort and encourage the spread of the deaconate in Philadelphia.

The Lankenau Villa on the southwest corner of Beach and Coral Avenues was his second installation for the Sisters. It is probable that he knew of Cape May Point through his acquaintance with Dr. Adolph Spaeth, a prominent Lutheran minister and theologian. Dr. Spaeth had taken advantage of the Sea Grove Association's generous offer to the clergy of a free building lot. He became one of the Point's pioneers, running down to his cottage each summer from 1875 on.

Lankenau first introduced the Sisters to the Point's attractions in 1888, when he rented Dr. J. N. Walker's Ocean Cottage for their use that summer. Two years later, he built the Lankenau Villa, where the Deaconesses could spend their month's vacation. It was enlarged and made more grandiose by two additions in 1901. Its thirty rooms were lavishly furnished, but its grandeur was short-lived. In the spring of 1908 a terrible fire struck and completely destroyed one of the Point's signature buildings.

The replacement Villa was built on the same site in 1909, with financial aid this time from William A. Braun, a wealthy manufacturer who owned the entire block of lots across the street. The new building was large enough but more straightforward in its design. It lacked decorative features like the three onion dome towers and the triple row of dormers that had made the original building so distinctive.

Mr. Lankenau and the nurses from the German Hospital had been able to continue their summer vacations at the Point with the loss of only one season. However, the incoming sea constantly threatened their setting, and he had to build extensive improvements to the bulkhead in front of his and his neighbors' properties to hold back the ocean. They were successful for many more years, but by 1952, they surrendered to the inevitable and sold it.

Now christened the Chelsea Hotel, it was reported to offer a hundred rooms – and nine lives. It changed hands several more times as the ocean kept up its relentless attacks. By 1960, William Morrow, a Cape May retailer of nuts and candies, was able to purchase it for $600 and a few hundred more in back taxes.

He got only sixty rooms; the ocean had taken the forty in the front half of the building. Why did he buy such a wreck? His joking reply "I like a lot of rooms; I like to entertain people. I always wanted an ancestral home. Now I have it."

Somehow it survived, an ominous relic, providing cheap rooms for the young and adventurous, until the final reckoning came with the great storm of 1962. Like most of the waterfront cottages it was destroyed by the fierce waves of this three-day northeaster.

Although the Lutherans had never built a church of their own, their presence in the Point was unmistakable. The unique dress of their Deaconesses made them stand out in a town that was more familiar with the black and white habits of the Catholic nuns. Many of the Deaconesses attended services at the nearby Episcopal chapel of St Peters-by-the-Sea.

Below:
(c.1901) John Lankenau first introduced the Sisters from Philadelphia's German Hospital, to Cape May Point when he rented Walker's Ocean Cottage for their use in the summer of 1888. Two years later he provided them with quarters in the Lankenau Villa, which he built on Beach Avenue between Lake and Coral Avenues. *Courtesy of the Deaconess Community of the Evangelical Lutheran Church in America.*

(c.1900) John D. Lankenau was a wealthy banker with the venerable Philadelphia firm of Anthony J. Drexel, and a generous contributor to Lutheran charities. *Courtesy of the Deaconess Community of the Evangelical Lutheran Church in America.*

For many years Lutheran services were conducted at the Union Chapel on Cape Avenue. In 1924, William C. Schwebel, a Philadelphia lawyer who had recently built his cottage at the corner of Yale Avenue and Lake Drive, (next door to Lutheran theologian Dr. Spaeth's house, the lovely "*Rosemere*" cottage on Yale Avenue) started to sponsor regular Sunday services in the chapel. Guest pastors were brought in and the Deaconesses were conspicuous among the congregation.

The Deaconess community had started a school in Philadelphia and was bringing their girls to the Point for summer programs. They had taken over the old McClure cottage at the southwest corner of Yale and Ocean Avenues for the children's boarding school. The girls often sang in the choir at the Union Chapel on Sundays. Services continued under Mr. Schwebel's leadership for more than thirty years but were discontinued in 1958.

(c.1895) The Lutheran Deaconesses enjoyed summer vacations at the Lankenau Villa. In 1884, John Lankenau, president of Philadelphia's German Hospital, arranged passage for seven Lutheran Deaconesses from Germany to serve as well-trained nurses who could converse with the hospital's German patients. *Courtesy of the Deaconess Community of the Evangelical Lutheran Church in America.*

Saint Mary's-by-the-Sea

c. 1940s – The Catholic Nuns "*There were hundreds of nuns there and sometimes we'd watch the younger ones play softball on the lawn in the large courtyard. The older ones lined up around the porches that enclosed the court on three sides. The fourth side was the beach where we'd be watching. They all wore full habits at that time – dressed modestly in black robes from head to toe. I remember one of the younger ones, as she stepped up to bat, hiking up her skirt to get a full swing and the older ones roaring with laughter and cheering her on.*"

—Bob Grubb

What did Philadelphia's Fairmount Park have to do with the establishment of Saint Mary's-by-the-Sea in Cape May Point as a summer retreat house for the Sisters of Saint Joseph? The connection is tenuous, but nevertheless, interesting. The story begins in 1898. The park commissioners were interested in adding to their parkland holdings in the upper Wissahickon Valley, and, for $20,000, the sisters agreed to transfer to the Commission part of their land at Mount Saint Joseph.

With this windfall in hand, the next year they were able to build Saint Joseph's Convent, a new summer home in Sea Isle City. To their surprise, within ten years they found it inadequate to accommodate all of the sisters, for their community kept growing. They would need to build an addition and a new, larger chapel – and funds were always short.

While these expansion plans were being considered, they learned of the availability of the old Shoreham Hotel that was now up for sale in Cape May Point. It could be had for $9,000 with all its furniture – far less than the cost of new construction in Sea Isle City. The deal was closed in short order and the Sisters now had more than enough room to provide a place not only for rest and convalescence, but also for their summer retreats and vacations. Father McDermott, pastor of old Saint Mary's Church in Philadelphia, had negotiated the sale and provided the money. At his request it was named Saint Mary's-by-the-Sea.

Its quiet location at the extreme eastern end of Cape May Point made it an ideal spot for the sisters – "well suited for the silence of retreat or for the sister's relaxation after the day's duties." What had been the ballroom of the hotel became the chapel. The addition of a statue of Mary in the courtyard and a crucifix atop the peaked roof announced its new role as a Catholic institution

Four years later they bought a large cottage that could serve as a rectory for the priests who vacationed there during the season. A third purchase in 1923 of the nearby McAvoy cottage, still known today as The Queen of the Sea, filled their needs for the future. Both of these beachfront cottages were moved to their present location on Lehigh Avenue opposite Saint Mary's after the great 1962 storm.

Older residents of the Point remember the days when there would be as many as three hundred sisters there at one time. In the evening hundreds strolled down the empty gravel lanes, as many as six abreast, saying the rosary. Many residents would congregate outside Saint Mary's each evening to listen to the sisters sing the beautiful strains of the *Tantum Ergo* at the Benediction service.

World War II brought a halt to the sister's summer retreats. Early in 1942, at the government's request, the facility was leased as a military barracks for the troops stationed at the encampment now occupied by the Cape May Point State Park. It was returned to the Sisters in the summer of 1946, but for four years the annual retreats had to be held at the motherhouse in Chestnut Hill, which forced a significant reduction in the number of students who could attend their summer school.

The retreats now bring hundreds of visitors from across the country. The sisters can no longer bathe on the beach in front of their property. Long gone is the broad lawn that used to lie between the hotel and the beach. Now there is little more than a high wooden bulkhead and massive granite boulders to hold back every tide. The sisters come here to rest and to pray. Some of their prayers may be to their patron saint, Joseph, asking him to "please, please continue to save this refuge for us."

(c.2002) Saint Mary's-by-the-Sea, the old Shoreham Hotel, was acquired by the Philadelphia Sisters of Saint Joseph in 1909 to be used as a summer retreat house for the Catholic Nuns. Four years later they bought a beachfront cottage across the street from the convent as a rectory for the priests who vacationed there during the summer season. *Courtesy of the Author.*

Villa Maria-by-the-Sea

Four years after the Sisters of Saint Joseph had acquired the Shoreham Hotel for a summer retreat house, the Philadelphia Archdiocese purchased the Carlton Hotel (formerly the Sea Grove House) for the Sisters of the Immaculate Heart of Mary. By April of 1913, negotiations were complete. For only $5,000 the Sisters had a fine summer home. However, ten times that amount was soon spent on repairs of the neglected structure and the erection of a seawall and jetties on the beachfront.

The Sisters moved in that summer with each nun there for two weeks – one week on retreat and one for vacation. The luxurious furnishings of the old hotel were gone, replaced by furniture more appropriate for its new tenants. There would be no more lawn tennis or croquet, no more billiards or bowling, no more Saturday night hops. Still they had the magnificent sunsets viewed from the veranda, daily bathing in the surf, and leisurely walks around the Point just before dusk.

For years, the sea had been coming on strong and something had to be done if Villa Maria were to survive. The hurricane that came in August 1924 showed how vulnerable the property was. A small fortune had already been spent to defend it, but the Sisters were running out of financial resources. Finally during the spring of 1931 the New Jersey legislature was persuaded to come to their rescue. The state

would put up $20,000, the borough and the church each $10,000. This bought several new jetties, not made of wood or of rock but of steel, and at a much lower cost.

Another hurricane visited the Point in September 1933, and the jetties seemed to be effective at diminishing the force of the storm driven waves. If such a furious storm could be weathered perhaps all was well. Unfortunately all was *not* well. A savage northeaster with hurricane force winds came to call three years later. It was one of the three fiercest storms to strike the Point in the twentieth century. Villa Maria was hit hard. The wood pilings and stout planking of its protective bulkhead were snapped and splintered by the crushing waves.

Large holes formed in the front yard. Windows and screens blew out and awnings were ripped to shreds. The Coast Guard ordered occupants of the convent to evacuate fearing the building would soon collapse.

First to come down was the priest house on the Cape Avenue side of the hotel grounds. Its seawall had been badly damaged. Each high tide was bringing the surf under its porch, so great had the erosion become. In December 1936, four local men were hired to remove the now-derelict building. The Sisters stopped paying taxes and abandoned their retreat house. That August, a wrecking firm from Delaware started to pull down the once-proud hotel. In three months it was gone. The battle was over; the Sisters had lost – the sea had won.

(c.1930) Villa Maria-by-the-Sea had been the old Carlton Hotel, purchased by the Philadelphia Archdiocese in 1913 as a summer retreat house for the Sisters of the Immaculate Heart of Mary. The purchase price was only $5,000, but the amount soon spent on repairs for the neglected structure and the erection of a bulkhead and jetties came to ten times that amount. *Courtesy of John A. Mather.*

Chapter 7

A Changed Community

The Little Bungalows

c.1920s – Camp Ground Cottages "Our family of six lived in one of the camp ground cottages. There was no water there, so I had to hike two blocks to the pump at the Sea-side Home and carry back a bucket full for the family's use. Mom cooked on the kerosene stove. Our bathroom was a common privy in the middle of the grove – boys had a one-holer on one side and girls had one on the other. At first we felt embarrassed and went out there sheepishly, but after a while we just strode out proudly waving our toilet paper roll over our heads. There was a pump right close to the privy but I guess we had sense enough not to use it. We came there every summer for about ten years."

—Bob Grubb

Cape May Point's pattern of development in the nineteenth century had been compact and uniform. The town center comprised the triangular area bounded by Central and Ocean Avenues and Beach Drive. Here, clustered around the hotels, most of the early cottages were built. Cape Avenue was "Main Street" with five stores and all three hotels built on each side of this broad avenue.

Cape Avenue was also the dividing line between two halves of the community. Throughout the nineteenth century the ocean side of Cape was favored over the bay side by a margin of two to one. Lots around the southern end of Lake Lily and those near the ocean beach were especially favored. To some, the bay side of Cape Avenue, especially the section between Central and Alexander Avenues, was the "wrong side of the tracks." This is where the hotel's service-workers lived and where the United Brethren put up their camp ground tents in the 1890s.

Almost all of the houses constructed during this period were two or more stories high. They were built in the prevailing Victorian style featured in the builder's journals. Few had architects. Steep roofs, open porches, and gingerbread trim were almost universal. Community style standards, enforced by a design review board, could not have produced a greater homogeneity. The single story house was a rarity – with the exception of a few stores and the one block of cabins created at the campgrounds.

The early twentieth century, from 1900 to the end of World War II, brought on the invasion of the bungalows. Suddenly the previous pattern was reversed – no more two-story cottages, just little one-story bungalows. More than a hundred sprang up during this period. They were very small, little more than a third the size of their predecessors. Few were larger than eight hundred square feet, several as small as three hundred. Most had porches, but now enclosed with screens to provide another room.

Now it was the *bay* side of town that got the lion's share of new houses – by a margin of two to one! The Beach Avenue block was now in the bay, but the section from Chrystal Avenue to Coral Avenue was filling out fast. Few had architectural ambitions; they were built for shelter and economy, not for prestige. Some were called "Frank Rutherford Specials" after the local carpenter-builder who had put up so many of them.

Zoning requirements and building setbacks were nonexistent. Some folks had built to the lot line; some had built in the street right of way. After six little ones had been built around Pavilion Circle, some taxpayers began to take notice. What was the Point coming to? The town had changed; the gentry were largely gone, and with them the community's social aspirations.

(c.2002) The early twentieth century, from 1900 to the end of World War II, brought on the invasion of the one-story bungalows. More than a hundred sprang up during this period. *Courtesy of the Author.*

Dirt Roads and Privies

Each spring the borough truck would come out and, with plow attached, scrape the roads to fill the deep potholes that had formed over the past year. All the streets were still gravel and had been for half a century. Since the heavier traffic of the summer season only lasted ten weeks, a good spring scraping and rolling was all the maintenance they got. By August, a heavy rain could wash out enough gravel to form puddle after puddle down the street. By the time the sun was out and warmed the ground, barefooted kids would be splashing their way down the road, delighting in the feel of the hot muddy water. If the boys could splash some muddy gravel on their buddies, that was the best part of the ritual.

By the mid-1930s, this children's game was dying out – along with the Point's gravel roads. State aid was becoming available for road repairs because the depression-strapped communities couldn't afford to do it alone. Improved road construction was possible. The borough commissioners were tired of the complaints about the ruts in wet weather and the dust in dry. A new surface was in order. Now, after the gravel was scraped and rolled a tank truck would lay down a thin coat of heavy oil. A topcoat of gravel followed this and in time the vehicle traffic would bind the oil and gravel into a tough bituminous surface. That became the standard in Cape May Point until the 1980s, when Macadam paving finally took over. Gravel roads are not a thing of the past, however. They persist throughout rural America, with state highway departments conducting continuous research and establishing new engineering specifications for their construction.

For all but the richest households in Cape May Point, the outhouse was a necessity throughout the nineteenth century. Even after 1900, sanitary sewer lines were slow in coming, so, whether it was called the shanty, the shack, the throne, the necessary or the relief office, almost every one of the little bungalows had to have one. When one of the northeasters or hurricanes reached gale force strength, some of the privies were gone with the wind. By the 1930s, most had been replaced by bathrooms with complete indoor plumbing.

Many properties remained without sanitary sewer lines on their streets, so cesspools and septic tanks were not uncommon. For many years the borough simply pumped its sewage into the South Cape May Meadows. In 1941, the State Department of Health demanded an end to this practice. The commissioner's response was to seek an agreement with Cape May City to have the Point's sewage discharge into Cape May's line on Sunset Boulevard. An annual fee was negotiated for this connection and the US Defense Public Works office built the new force main that was required, with the borough picking up half the cost.

Although the work was completed and approved by the State Health Department in 1944, that was not the end of the controversy. James Woolson, who was in charge of the water and sewer works, had no state certification. After two years of fighting off law suits and fines, while Woolson continued to fail the state exam, the borough got off the hook in 1946 – the engineer succeeded in getting his license.

As for garbage collection, the borough saw no need for this for sixty years. After all, there was a choice of three dumps – two public and one private. One was on Alexander Avenue; the other was off Lighthouse Avenue in what was then referred to as swamplands, not wetlands.

(c.1911) Not all of the roads in Cape May Point were properly maintained and some seem to have been almost impassable. This may have been a portion of Lake Drive. *Courtesy of the Cape May County Historical Society.*

The third, and preferred choice, was your own backyard. Packages and papers got incinerated, garbage and cans, and sometimes even bottles and jars, got buried. Each week a new hole would be dug in the sandy soil to deposit the accumulated waste. The garbage was quickly absorbed, but it took years for the cans to rust away.

There was no bulk-pickup day; if it was too big to bury it went to the dump. In 1943, the commissioners advertised for bids for a garbage collector. Alfred Evans submitted the low bid of $1,250 for annual pickup of garbage, trash, and ash. Still you could take stuff to the city dump, but no garbage, only trash – the town was getting more particular.

(c.1890) The photo caption indicates that this is the road to Lake Lily, so it is probably Seagrove Avenue in Lower Township. *Courtesy of Robert W. Elwell, Sr.*

(c.1910) Mayor Springer's cottage at the southeast corner of Princeton and Ocean Avenues. The privy is made more gracious by the addition of an entrance trellis. *Courtesy of the Cape May County Historical Society.*

Two Forms of Captivity

c.1930s – Gerew's Store "When we got hold of a dime, that could buy us an ice cream soda at Gerew's store. He had a great new soda fountain along one side of the room, and the other side was lined with booths like a real ice cream parlor. It was all modern and every body went there for ice cream and sodas. Next door, where the post office is now, was his grocery store, the only one in the Point. You could go from one side to the other through a large doorway in the center. At that time the post office was on Cambridge."

—*Bob Grubb*

To a lot of young kids, a school is a place of captivity – not a real prison, but the next thing to it.

It wasn't long before Sea Grove had its first place of confinement – an elementary school. The Cape May Point Schoolhouse was not constructed in 1875 when Sea Grove was enjoying its first season, with nothing more than a large hotel, several shops, and a few dozen cottages. There is no mention of it in the extensive press coverage of that year.

It was, however, in operation three years later with George Eldredge as schoolmaster, teacher, and entire staff. Although he was an experienced teacher who had taught for a number of years in Cape May City, his tenure may have been brief. Based on newspaper reports of the period, the Point's school seemed to have a different teacher almost every year.

Surprisingly, it wasn't literally a one-room schoolhouse – it was actually a two-room schoolhouse, because it was two stories high, with grades one through four on the open first floor and grades five through eight on the second. It's doubtful that overcrowding was ever a problem – with few year-round residents there were not many children of school age. Nevertheless, classes continued until 1931, when the Consolidated School in Lower Township took over.

The school building has survived at its original location on Cambridge Avenue, a stone's throw from the lake. The most recent owner has carefully restored it from a duplex apartment to an impressive single-family residence, retaining as many of the historic features as possible.

Cape May Point's second and official place of captivity was the Jailhouse, a truly minimum-security prison that may hold several worlds' records as the smallest jail, with the fewest inmates and the shortest periods of incarceration. Its first recorded appearance is in 1908, although it may date from an earlier time. That was the year that Cape May Point finally separated form Lower Township to become an independent borough with its own police department in the person of Albert B. Schellenger as the first Marshall.

The diminutive building occupied a lot on the northeast side of Pearl Avenue between Cape and Central, next to the Godfrey Cottage and across the street from Emerald Avenue. It's primary function, if one is to believe local gossip, was as a temporary depository for the occasional miscreant whose consumption of too much demon rum, placed him in no position to return to hearth and home. A sleepover in the jailhouse, arranged by the town marshal, would be more an act of mercy than of criminal punishment.

In 1927, the borough saw no further need for the jail and decided to offer it for sale to raise a little cash and to free up the valuable lot on Pearl Avenue for future sale. The one bid received was considered inadequate, and they moved it to a lot behind the present firehouse, where it became a storage building for the Volunteer Fire Company. By 1934 it was still listed in the tax records as the Jail, and as a tax-exempt property owned by the borough.

There it stayed until 1983, when the commissioners offered it to the Historic Cold Spring Village in Middle Township, where it resides today among the many historic buildings that have been assembled in the village. It has been reborn as a children's craft shop to the delight of the thousands of kids who visit there each year.

(c.1930) Cape May Point's Jailhouse may have held several world's records as the smallest jail, with the fewest inmates, and the shortest periods of incarceration. Its original location was on the northeast side of Pearl Avenue between Cape and Central Avenues. *Courtesy of the Cape May County Historical Society.*

(c.1890) Cape May Point's first and only school building has survived at it's original location on Cambridge Avenue, a stone's throw from the lake. The present owner has restored it from a duplex apartment to an impressive single-family residence. *Courtesy of the Deaconess Community of the Evangelical Lutheran Church in America.*

(c.1900) There was a lot of open land and few houses at the turn of the century in the Point. The schoolhouse is in the background to the right of center. *Courtesy of David Rutherford.*

Volunteer Firemen

The Lankenau Villa fire in the early spring of 1908 was a wakeup call for Cape May Point. Vacationers had not yet arrived, and most of the cottages were still closed for the winter. The fire went unnoticed for several hours before the first call went out. By that time the Villa was beyond salvage, and the fierce northeast wind had carried the flames across Lincoln Avenue to the fifty-room Surf House Hotel.

The crew from the Coast Guard Station joined with the few town residents to form a bucket brigade. But their efforts to contain the blaze were fruitless. As the wind intensified, more cottages were ignited. A panic call went out to Cape May City, and when the trolley raced back it had extra cars full of firemen and equipment. The smoke was so dense it could be seen for miles. Wind from the sea grew even stronger. People were screaming and the firefighters were terrified. Nearby residents rescued what they could, fearful that their place would be next.

When the wind shifted to the northwest, even the memorable oceanfront cottages across from the Shoreham Hotel were at risk. In desperation, hose lines were extended to bring in water from Lake Lily, but the pump was inadequate to carry it that far. More equipment came in from Cape May. The only remaining choice was to save the houses not already claimed by the inferno. The fire had had its way. The final count of severe damage or total destruction was: One 30-room institu-tion, a 50-room hotel, a boarding house, St. Peter's church, and seven of the large nineteenth century cottages.

A special meeting of the taxpayers was called up in July to organize a fire department. New chemical engines and hoses were ordered but had to be stored in the old jailhouse. The home for the man-powered water wagon was an old shed on Yale Avenue that had been a carpenter shop in earlier days. By 1911, they had acquired two fire hose carts with 1,000 feet of hose and four nozzles. Most of the hand-drawn fire apparatus carts were kept outside on an open lot at the northeast corner of Yale and Ocean Avenues. Suspended from a timber frame, an old steel wheel rim from a locomotive served as the fire alarm.

It wasn't until 1922 that the Cape May Point Volunteer Fire Company was formally authorized by borough ordinance. Two years later, it got its real firehouse and first fire truck. The two-story structure on Yale Avenue was completed in 1924. Two years after that, it got its first 400-gallon pumper, a top-of-the-line product from the celebrated American-LaFrance Company. The very next year produced a City Service Hook and Ladder. The Volunteer Fire Department was now in business.

The volunteers had kept fire losses to a minimum. Over the forty years following the great Lankenau Villa fire, it has been said that only three houses were lost: the Buckman cottage in 1917, the Chew cottage on Alexander Avenue in 1940, and the Gallagher cottage on Harvard Avenue in 1946.

(c.1911) Following the great fire of 1908, the borough had acquired two fire hose carts with a 1,000 feet of hose and four nozzles. Most of the hand-drawn fire apparatus carts were kept outside on an open lot at the northeast corner of Yale and Ocean Avenues. Suspended from a timber frame, an old steel wheel rim from a locomotive served as the fire alarm. *Courtesy of Toni Keiser..*

(c.1930s) The volunteer firemen had kept fire losses to a minimum. Over the forty years following the great Lankenau Villa fire, only three houses were recorded lost by fire: the Buckman cottage in 1917, the Chew cottage on Alexander Avenue in 1940, and the Gallagher cottage on Harvard Avenue in 1946. *Courtesy of the Borough of Cape May Point.*

(c.1925)2 In 1924 the recently organized Cape May Point Volunteer Fire Company got its first real firehouse and first fire truck. Two years later it had its first 400-gallon pumper. *Courtesy of H. Gerald MacDonald.*

The Upper Chamber

Managing the borough affairs was a pretty simple operation for the first half of the twentieth century. Extensive state and county regulations had not yet been introduced and each community was free to govern itself without the watchful eye of big brother. Just about anything could be built up until 1936 when the first ordinance to require a building permit was passed.

Carpenter shops and lumberyards, stables and gas stations, stores and street stands – all were tolerated. Even when a building permit was finally needed (to raise revenue – not to monitor construction), there was no zoning requirement to limit what could be built where, no height limit or setback requirement. The borough solicitor said the building permit ordinance would not hold up unless it was accompanied by a zoning ordinance, but the commissioners passed it anyway. This laissez-faire policy persisted another twenty years until a planning board was finally appointed in 1955.

Since it was first established as a borough in 1878, Cape May Point never even had a municipal building – its commissioners met at various locations and often in one of their homes. After 1909, they convened above Springer's store and paid rent for the privilege. Springer was the Mayor. When the firehouse was built in 1924, they were able to hold their meetings on the second floor, but again they paid rent to the Cape May Point Volunteer Fire Company.

The Point's annual budgets were modest. In today's money, it came to about $77,000 for the year 1910. A decade later, it had only increased twelve percent. But the following decade saw an almost two hundred percent rise to about $250,000. Most of the money and most of the headaches for the commissioners involved containing beach erosion. Finding the money to build or repair the bulkheads and jetties as well as keeping the streets passable was a full-time job for these part-time officers. The speculators who had bought up a lot of properties lobbied for more protection while the rest of the taxpayers pressured them to hold the line on taxes.

Two other issues arose during this period that attracted some attention. There were boosters in Cape May who thought it would be a dandy idea if Cape May City, and the independent boroughs of West Cape May, South Cape May (both lying on either side of Sunset Boulevard between Cape May Point and Cape May City), and Cape May Point could consolidate as a single municipality. Fortunately, all of the boroughs thought otherwise, and the concept died peacefully.

The second issue that stirred things up was the disappearance of $244.53 (about $3,100 in today's money) in tax funds. Frank W. Hughes was the tax collector, and the money had been in the safe at his house. Hughes was informed of the shortage by the auditors, but Hughes allegedly told the Mayor not to advise the other commissioners of the problem. Subsequently it was revealed that Hughes had simply recommended that the investigation be kept quiet to increase the chances for recovery of the funds. The county prosecutor had already been informed, and they wanted to limit publicity.

The borough sought relief from the insurance company that had furnished the tax collector's indemnity bond. They denied culpability, claiming that they were only insuring Hughes for "the faithful performance of duty" with no provision for the loss of money in his custody. This brought a lawsuit by the borough against the bonding company. Between conflicting statements by the mayor and the tax collector, and the resignation by Hughes of his position so that he could become the Point's postmaster, the citizens had plenty to gossip about for a year or so.

Carpenter shops and lumberyards, stables and gas
stations, stores and street stands – all were tolerated.

Chapter 8
Leisurely Pursuits

At the Beach

Beaches come and beaches go, but in Cape May Point they just go and never come back. The past century and a quarter have robbed the borough of several hundred yards of beach. The Point's location at the tip of the Jersey Cape has made it especially vulnerable to erosion, and the removal of the natural dunes by the Sea Grove Association in 1875 added significantly to the problem.

The first beach for sea bathing, as it was then called, was at the foot of Cape Avenue, in front of the Sea Grove House. Close by Beach Avenue and across from the hotel's broad lawn, where games of lawn tennis or croquet could be enjoyed, was a two-story beach pavilion for the spectators of this lively scene. One hundred feet to the east, a long row of bathhouses permitted those who chose to bathe to change into the appropriate costume, rather than promenade along the strand.

Decorous clothing for bathers was essential in this community where strict moral behavior was expected. The proper attire could be rented at the bathhouse. For most of the nineteenth century, women's bathing costumes formed a total enclosure from head to toe, ensuring that they would not be exposed to the unwelcome rays of the sun, or to lustful glances from any lecherous males who might be on the scene.

All of this changed, of course, as the century and the hotel era came to an end, and public bathhouses were no longer available. The Victorians' view, that no one "of the better sort" would dream of being seen in bathing attire except on the beach, did not survive the nineteenth century. People changed at home as they do today. Most people, that is. In 1938, the Cape May Point commissioners found it necessary to request that the guests at the Sea-Side Home stop changing clothes on the beach. From time to time some of the day-trippers would be guilty of the same transgression.

The Jersey shore beaches are prized more for sunning, bathing, or surfing, than for swimming, and Cape May Point is no exception. But swimming has its enthusiasts, although few can match the zeal of a big fellow from Philadelphia by the name of Durburrow. John Orr, a lifelong resident of the Point, liked to tell the following story about Durburrow's feat that occurred here many years ago:

Around 1910, swimming the choppy waters of the English Channel was a feat that got worldwide news coverage. Challengers came from many countries; most failed, but some persevered to succeed on subsequent tries. For many years an Egyptian man held the record crossing time of ten hours and fifty minutes.

Weren't the waters off Cape May Point pretty much the same as the English Channel? Weren't the infamous rip tides off the Point as treacherous as the channel currents? Durburrow thought so, and decided he would match the achievements of those who had swum the channel.

He teamed up with two locals, John Corson and George Boehm, who operated two commercial fishing piers near Sunset Beach. Every day Durburrow would battle the "rips" and then, for a little rest, would swim beyond to the buoys, where he would climb up, rest awhile, and then return to shore through the forceful rip tide.

Durburrow, Corson, and Boehm met almost daily, discussing surf and wind conditions, trying to determine the best days and the best time to start off. It was clear he needed an early morning start, so at four AM, heavily coated with grease for insulation, and wearing a cap and swimmers' sunglasses, he entered the surf at Cape Avenue.

The route, that had been studied and plotted carefully, called for him to swim a zigzag course, taking advantage of favorable tides, and swimming at a different angle when they were unfavorable. A boat with food and liquids, rowed by George Boehm, led the way. On board, adding to the dead weight, were two passengers, one a representative of the New York Athletic Club, and the other from the Turggemide, a German Athletic Club in Philadelphia. They argued constantly, and when Durburrow came alongside for nourishment, each tried to persuade him to sign up with their club.

At 7:15 that evening, an exhausted Durburrow swam through the surf to the Delaware shore. His swim had taken over fifteen hours and he had swum a forty-mile course, far more than the fourteen-mile route taken by today's ferries. I don't know whether he ever signed up with either club.

The beach at Cape Avenue remained the guarded beach for many years. In the 1930s, it even had a diving board on top of the steel jetty that had been built there in 1931. It was a makeshift affair, and the kids had to swim out pretty far to reach it because it was in deep water. Lifeguards kept a close watch because swimmers in deep water were always at special risk. From year to year, and up through the 1920s, a lifeguard would be chosen each season. Their pay was a dollar a day.

For many years the Point had only one protected beach, although it was not always at the same location. In 1945, the beach in front of the old Lankenau Villa near Coral Avenue was the bathing beach. However, in 1952, taxpayers complained to the borough that there was no lifeguard that year at Coral Beach. Mayor Hughes explained that in previous years there had been many complaints that the bathing beach was too far away, and the commissioners had decided to make the Cape Avenue Beach once again the only protected beach. In time, as the summer population grew, more guards were hired until the borough was able to provide protection at Brainard, Saint Peter's, Coral, and Whilldin beaches.

There are times when no beaches are guarded – times when tragic drownings have occurred. Had a trained lifeguard been present, it's likely that the victim's life would have been spared. Many unfortunate deaths were reported in the newspapers in the late 1800s, when visits to the seashore were becoming quite popular.

However, no guard could have prevented the death of Sadie Nichols, a guest at the Cape House in 1886. When the manager found that she was unable to pay her hotel bill, and she was penniless, he generously offered to cover her fare back to Philadelphia. But lack of funds was not her only problem. She was in deep despair over unspecified illnesses, based on the several suicide notes she left addressed to friends and family. How she drowned is unknown, but her body was found on the beach in front of the Sea-Side Home.

The drowning of ten-year old George Aikin the following year is an even sadder tale. He had just disembarked from the *Republic* at the Steamship Landing. After securing a suit from William O'Donnell's bathhouse, he rushed into the water. But, unable to swim, he stayed close to shore.

He was in no danger until he was enticed by an older man, who had also arrived on the same boat, to venture out further into deep water. Resisting at first, the youngster finally gave in, and soon the two were in deep water – and in deep trouble. Realizing he was in danger, the man abandoned the boy, and cried for help as scores of vacationers watched helplessly from the beach. The bathhouse keeper was able to pull the man to safety but the boy had just disappeared.

It was soon learned that this fellow had been quite intoxicated when he left the boat, and, because of his drunken state, had been refused a bathing suit by O'Donnell. He had then conned a sober friend to rent the suit for him. The boy's body washed ashore the following morning.

The twentieth century saw few such terrible events during the regular summer seasons when lifeguards were assigned to the designated bathing beaches.

While bathing was the main attraction, fishing ran a close second. Surf fishing in the early days was at least as popular as it is today. There were no stone jetties to cast from, but many of the veteran anglers either had their own rowboats, or hired one for the day from the Kidder Hughes fleet at Sunset Beach.

Other opportunities to fish in deeper water presented themselves from time to time. The borough constructed a fishing pier around 1920 with the expectation that the money collected from its fishermen would pay for its cost. It must have been a financial failure because the following year it was demolished, and Springer bought the timber for his carpenter shop. A decade later, in 1931, the enterprising Frank Hughes was granted permission to build one on the beach between Brainard and Central Avenues.

It was around this time that the author's uncle, Samuel Jungkurth, pursued a novel twist on the fishing pier concept. He built a large rectangular fishing deck with a perimeter railing, under which he attached a series of empty 55-gallon oil drums to serve as pontoons. The contraption was floated about a hundred yards off shore in the bay, not far from the concrete ship, and held in place by several lines and anchors.

He planned to use his small outboard motor boat to deliver a few fishermen at a time to this bobbing pier. For a while it seemed like a successful venture, but it wasn't long before the wind and current would slowly turn the floating deck until the anchor lines gradually rubbed together, and the constant friction finally severed them. He never solved that problem and the unique enterprise scarcely lasted one full season.

(c.1878) Close by Beach Avenue, and across from The Sea Grove House's broad lawn, was a two-story beach pavilion for the spectators of the lively beach scene. 100 feet to the east, a long row of bathhouses permitted those who chose to bathe, rather than promenade along the strand, to change into the appropriate costume. *Courtesy of the Cape May County Historical Society.*

(c.1890s) A more modest pavilion over the water was in front of the Carlton House on the bathing beach. *Courtesy of the Cape May County Historical Society.*

(c.1890s) Promenading along the strand, in full Victorian dress, was as common as bathing in the nineteenth century. *Courtesy of the Cape May County Historical Society.*

Lake Lily

More stories have been told or written about Lake Lily than about any other aspect of Cape May Point. Exciting tales persist of Indians and pirates, of heroic exploits in wartime, of events that occurred long before the Sea Grove Association made the lake a centerpiece of their new community's social life in the last quarter of the nineteenth century. Some of these colorful chronicles, that go back centuries, may be apocryphal, but no history of the lake can ignore them.

For countless centuries the lake had been a valuable source of fresh water for the Indian tribes in the region. They relinquished technical ownership when, in 1630, the Dutch West India Company bought a good bit of the land around the New Jersey cape,

The local Kechemeche tribe continued to use the lake for hunting and fishing and especially for fresh water. They seem to have abandoned the area before 1800, but reminders of their presence have been plentiful. An old Indian trail that ran through the woods along Sunset Boulevard has yielded a plethora of artifacts. Current residents David Rutherford and Richard Cook have impressive collections of thousands of arrowheads and stone tools found not far from the lake.

In a story on the lake that appeared in the *Press of Atlantic City* on August 21, 1991, staff writer Richard Degener has this to say about the pirates and their treasure chests:

Legend has it that pirates landed at Cape May Point to take fresh water from Lake Lily and steal provisions from nearby farms. Captain Kidd and Blackbeard, the legend goes, frequented the area and may have left buried treasure behind, treasure that has never been found.

As recently as 1893, a tree near the lake was known as Kidd's tree because he supposedly buried treasure near it. Legend also has it that French and Spanish privateers who raided British and Colonial merchant ships at the mouth of the Delaware Bay landed here to get fresh water from the lake.

The line between legend and fact is murky, but at least one official report fires the imagination. An August 10, 1699 report filed in England indicated Kidd and other pirates did land at the tip of the peninsula with stolen plunder.

Perhaps the most frequently retold yarn of the lake's earlier days is the one about the war of 1812. For several years, British warships guarded the mouth of the Delaware to stop any American vessels that might be headed up to Philadelphia. Anchored for months at a time, not too far from the shore, they were clearly visible to the residents of Cape May County. When stocks ran low they would send ashore an armed barge to replenish their supply of fresh water from Lake Lily.

After watching this repeated procedure, the locals decided to strike a blow for the American cause. They had fresh water from their own wells, they didn't need it from the lake. Why not pollute the lake with salt water? The solution was simple enough, but the execution amounted to backbreaking work.

A half-mile or so to the north, Pond Creek, a small tidal stream, meandered through marshlands and emptied into the bay. A channel connection between it and the lake would turn its fresh water brackish and unfit to drink. With spade and shovel, with pick and hoe, they set about the task. A deep, narrow ditch was dug with these imperfect tools and their countless hours of hard work finally paid off. The salty water from Pond Creek flowed into Lake Lily with each high tide, and the lake was soon too poisoned for drinking! It is said that sections of the old ditch are still discernable although it was filled in ages ago.

The modern history of the lake began in 1875 when Alexander Whilldin's ambitious dream brought it out of its wooded isolation. When Lake Drive was completed and the thick underbrush cleared out, the lake took on a new role. No longer the domain of duck hunters and local anglers, it was transformed into a center for carefree recreation.

The rustic boathouse at the foot of Central Avenue was one of the signature structures designed by Cape May Point's architect, J. C. Sidney. Under the command of A. W. Springer, here were the rowboats and sailboats for hire that are often depicted in early postcards. J. B. Moore had the contract to dredge the lake to insure a minimum depth of several feet and to cut the banks down square so that a boat could be brought to shore anywhere.

To ensure good fishing they stocked the lake with black bass, supplementing the native catfish, eels, perch, and carp that had always been there. Good-sized ones – over three pounds and up to eighteen inches long – had been brought up from the Potomac River at Harper's Ferry in the spring of 1875. A previous attempt to bring in eight hundred mountain trout from the Susquehanna River had ended in disaster. Only two had survived the long train ride.

So now the lake had good fishing and good boating – and lots of customers. Party groups were organized and the boathouse manager had plenty to do. He oversaw and maintained a small fleet of sailboats and rowboats. He arranged and judged the weekly "regattas" that were held for the amateur sailors.

One time a half dozen kids got together for a "tub race." Galvanized washtubs were their vessels, so they must have been pretty young. Screaming and paddling furiously, they were having a great time, as was the large crowd cheering from the shore. Two capsized and had to wade ashore, so the event was entertaining enough to merit press coverage. The lake has never regained the activity that characterized its use in Sea Grove's early days.

Winters opened up a whole new set of opportunities at the lake. Ice-skating was, of course, as popular as it is today, in spite of the occasional accident. During the very first winter young Frank Townsend, son of the Signal Station operator, crashed through thin ice and almost drowned, a feat that would be impossible today, because the lake is so shallow now. When a really cold winter made the ice thick enough to support them, sail-propelled ice boats were launched. If you have ever tried this sport, you may well wonder how they managed to avoid crashing into the shore on such a narrow lake.

Before 1900, good winters also brought out work crews to cut slabs of ice for Walker's icehouse that sat right behind the boathouse at the foot of Central Avenue. By1899, lake-cut ice was no longer competitive and the old barn-like structure was transformed into the Lakeside Lodge and the home of the Cape May Point Country Club.

A prosperous and socially ambitious physician from Allegheny County named Randall T. Hazzard had bought the lake, built the clubhouse, erected the famous but long-gone "rustic bridge" at the north end, and constructed the little island at the south end. Curiously it's always been called Amnon's Island. Perhaps it was the brainchild of Amnon Wright, owner of Wright's Villa and grocery store on Cape Avenue. A quarter century after Sea Grove's founding, Lake Lily was experiencing a renaissance. Ownership of the lake remained in his family for decades and was finally sold by his estate around the beginning of the Great Depression.

In 1930, the lake was acquired by the Ferris family of Philadelphia. Their Cape May Point cottage, which they purchased in 1925 and named "Kechemeche Lodge" after the Indian tribe that had inhabited this region, remains today at the northeast corner of West Lake Drive and Coral Avenue.

Jean Leon Gerome Ferris was well known as a prolific historical painter and illustrator, whose career reached prominence by the turn of the century. He had attended the Pennsylvania Academy of Fine Arts and had continued his studies in Paris. He spent his later years at the Point, continuing to paint in his cottage studio

Ten years after Ferris' death in 1930, his widow, Annette, deeded the lake to the borough of Cape May Point with the following stipulation:

> That it shall be preserved as a lake, for the free use of the public, forever.
>
> That no motorboats shall be permitted upon the lake, and that no building shall be erected thereon, or upon the adjoining land, except for a pavilion or boathouse, if needed for public use.
>
> That no trees or bushes shall be cut or removed until the property has been in the possession of the borough for five years, except to keep the open spaces as they shall exist at the time of my death.

The arrival of the First World War pretty much coincided with the final departure of Cape May Point's social set. The parties on the lake, the annual "Venetian Fetes," the sailboat races – all were gone and the lake was no longer such an attraction for recreation and social life. The boathouse had closed down and only a few private rowboats remained.

The author remembers the lake in the thirties as one of his favorite haunts. When he was fourteen, he had the only sailboat on the lake. It wasn't a real sailboat – it was more like a kayak with a clothes-pole for a mast and bed-sheet for the mainsail. It was eight feet long, with a rudder and a dagger centerboard. He spent a whole summer building it from his own design – a cross between a Chesapeake Bay sneak box and a kayak. The canvas covering was painted a tasteful yellow and black with bold letters fore and aft spelling out its name, *Dinky*. With unbounded pride he would wheel this elegant contraption over to the lake for a few hours of ecstasy whenever the wind was up – but not too far up. It was a bit precarious in fresh weather. None of his friends could sail it because it was designed to float no more than his skinny 75 pounds. When the wind died down completely he had a kayak paddle – another clothes-pole with wood roof shingles at either end – to propel him, often faster than the wind would.

By this time all the real fish were gone. The kids would sometimes catch a sunny, but at three inches long it was a bit of a stretch to call it a fish. Hunting for frogs was another favorite pastime. There were plenty of them sunning themselves on the sandy shore or perched almost invisible on a lily pad. A slingshot or BB gun was the weapon of choice, and the skittish frogs were a real test of a kid's marksmanship.

The boats are gone, the lilies too. They couldn't survive the '62 storm that flooded the lake with salt water. No more picking water lilies and selling a fistful to passing motorists on their way to Sunset Beach. Today even the kids are gone. It's a different lake now, home to ducks, geese, and assorted other waterfowl. One could say *it's now for the birds.*

(c.1885) The rustic boathouse at the foot of Central Avenue was one of the signature structures designed by Cape May Point's architect, J. C. Sidney. *Courtesy of Robert W. Elwell, Sr.*

(c.1880s) The cow led by the children probably came from a nearby farm. The schoolhouse appears in the left background. *Courtesy of Robert W. Elwell, Sr.*

(c.1890s) When Lake Lily was dredged by the Sea Grove Association in 1875, a log and pile bulkhead along the shore enabled the boats to land where they wished. *Courtesy of the Cape May County Historical Society.*

(c.1920s) Jean Leon Gerome Ferris, who owned lake Lily, was well known as a prolific historical painter and illustrator. His Cape May Point summer cottage remains at 602 East Lake Drive. His widow deeded the lake to the borough in 1940. *Courtesy of Emelia Oleson.*

Chapter 9
Getting Around

The Trolley Retires

c.1930s – Selling Water Lilies "In the morning we would go over to the lake and pick water lilies. Then we'd run out to Sunset Boulevard and sell them to passing motorists – ten cents a dozen. That was enough for candy. Gruber's store at the corner of Stites and Chrystal was only a block from our house, and just a penny could buy you five green leaves, or two caramels, or a large tootsie roll. So that dime from the lilies made for my day's stock of candy."

—*Bob Grubb*

It's 1879, and Cape May Point is getting a new steam-driven trolley. Everybody is happy. No more horse manure and no more slow motion, the four-year-old horse-car railway is a thing of the past. From now on it is steam all the way. The tracks are the same, and the cars haven't changed, but the horsepower is now steam-power! Well, the word "power" may convey a bit more than the "Steam Dummy," as the little engine was called, can deliver. This locomotive is scarcely large enough to house the upright wood-burning boiler. Still, it is an improvement.

It's now 1892, and Cape May Point is getting a new electric trolley. Everybody is glad to say goodbye to the old-fashioned steam trolleys. After all, they were jerky, noisy, and dirty – all those coal cinders getting in your eyes and throat. True, the little Steam Dummy had been replaced with a real coal burning locomotive, but look what comes with the electric trolley – a ride that is faster, quieter, cleaner, and altogether agreeable.

Here's what the *Star of the Cape* had to say in 1892:

"The motor used is the improved Westinghouse, and is considered the best in use. The cars are built in Chester and will each seat about forty persons. Six cars are provided with motors, with six other trail cars to attach, and in addition to these, which are opened and curtained, there are three large enclosed cars for use in stormy weather. Each car is lighted by five electric lights, and are models of beauty and comfort. There is no jolting, jerking, or grinding noises to jar the nerves of passengers, but the ride is one of pleasant gliding along without annoyances."

The fare is cheap, schedules are frequent, service is better – everybody is pleased with this brand new ultra-modern local transportation, the electric trolley.

Now it's 1908, and *nobody* is pleased. The schedules are erratic, trolleys don't meet the trains, and the tracks in Cape May Point are downright hazardous. Everybody is complaining. The commissioners fire off a resolution demanding, at a minimum, service every half-hour. They want the tracks to be planked at each intersection so carriages can safely cross the high rails. They get nowhere. Things turn really bad and in 1916, they petition the State Public Utility Commission to compel the trolley line to do something, saying, "...the car service is uncertain and grossly inefficient and the cars are flat-wheeled, unsanitary, and so poorly equipped as to be positively dangerous..."

The following year the court orders the *Delaware Bay, Cape May, and Sewells Point Trolley* to stop running and Cape May Point is without public transit for the first time in forty-two years. Trolley days are gone forever.

The car service is uncertain and grossly inefficient and the cars are flat-wheeled, unsanitary, and so poorly equipped as to be positively dangerous.

(c.1910) The Cape May Point electric trolley tracks ran along the South Cape May Meadows past the borough of South Cape May. Coastal storms could make the trip an exciting adventure. *Courtesy of H. Gerald MacDonald.*

Busmen's Holidays

The commissioners may have won the battle with the trolleys, but the Point lost its only means of public transportation. The train station in Cape May was a good two miles away. They didn't want to be in the transportation business but what other choice did they have? It seems two whole seasons went by before they bought their own buses and hired a driver.

Starting in 1919, you could get to Cape May for fifteen cents, and your bus would come along about every half-hour. They weren't new and the borough had no one to maintain and repair them, so one was often out of service. The following year two brothers, Jim and Harry Woolson, were hired to replace the first operator, H. H. Busse. Only a year later, apparently fed up with the bus problems, the commissioners sold the machines to Belford Ewing and Raymond Bailey, and contracted with them to provide the bus service.

The borough had dispensed with one problem, the buses, but people still needed transportation. In 1929 they begged the *Reading Seashore Lines* to offer bus service to the Point. When they were rebuffed, they went after the *Atlantic City Railroad*, but that line was even less interested.

Meanwhile, Horace Church, who had a service going in Cape May, had been trying to sign up Cape May Point for several years. Possibly for good reason, he couldn't get the franchise. Turning back to local franchising, they hired Edward Cottee and Rhoda Fattis, who called themselves the *Cape May Point Transportation Company*.

The very next year, Cottee was out and Church at last was in. That's when a new round of troubles began. Like his predecessors, he was always promising more than he was delivering. Meeting after meeting failed to produce results, only excuses. The situation came to a head in the fall of 1936, when Church closed down bus service entirely. Finally exasperated, the commissioners appealed to the State Public Utility Commission.

Church fought back, claiming that since he had lost his job as the school bus driver, he couldn't make a profit with the few passengers who rode during the winter. The commissioners countered – why had he been using his private car instead of the bus for the past five years? This was not living up to the terms of his franchise. The PUC commissioners promised to rule on the dispute.

This was during the depression and times were tough for everyone. The Point backed down a little, reducing his mercantile license from $100 to $10, with the stipulation that he spell out his route and schedule and stick to it.

He did neither. The bus stopped running. Excuses galore followed – he was still waiting for the registration tags; his liability insurance policy was running late; it took a month to get the flat tire off the rusted rim!

The Point commissioners were at an impasse. Invitations to bid on the bus franchise went unanswered. Once again they would have to buy their own bus. This time it was to be a station wagon, a classy nine-passenger *Chrysler Town and Country* model. The borough commissioners were divided – $2,435 was a lot of money to put out, to say nothing of the costs for insurance, repairs and maintenance.

Its now 1942, and the transportation saga continues. The country is at war. Why not use the school bus? Remember, it's available all summer and could be used in the winter once school classes are underway. A terrific idea – it would save a bundle and the County School Superintendent agrees. But just a minute – how does the Cape May Point School Board feel about the use of *their* school bus? Oops! Nobody asked them. Their noses are really out of joint. They are at the borough meeting and loaded for bear.

School Board members ask, "Why did the mayor first sound out Senator Scott and the County Superintendent? Why did the School Board have to read about this in the local newspaper? How much does the borough expect to pay for the rental of the bus even if the Board is even willing to consider such an idea?" Oops again! The borough is just hoping to borrow it, not rent it.

The mayor is in a quandary – he's on the School Board and is a borough commissioner. He represents both sides!

The Clerk of the School Board attacks. She thinks the mayor wants the school bus now only because his passion to buy the fancy station wagon is in jeopardy. The mayor denies this and she backs down. But the mayor switches into reverse – it's not a good idea to use the school bus, let's buy the wagon.

The borough commissioners dither about what to do. They can't agree on anything. A savior arrives at last. Wildwood's *Five Mile Beach Railway Company* agrees to run a bus service to the Point but they won't tolerate competition from any taxis. That would put Eddie Hallman's taxi out of business and so a compromise is reached. They will hire Eddie as the bus driver.

It's now 1946, the war is over, and pretty soon there will be plenty of cars and little need for public transit to Cape May City. The transportation crises are over at last.

(c.1920s) The section of Cape May Point west of northern Cape Avenue was heavily wooded and the last portion to be developed. The section east of lake drive had been lowlands that had been filled and was without trees until recent years. *Courtesy of H. Gerald MacDonald.*

The mayor denies this and she backs down. But the mayor switches into reverse – it is not a good idea to use the school bus, let's buy the wagon.

Chapter 10
Stormy Weather

The '36 Nor'easter

"Sisters, you've got to get out, you can't stay here. It's dangerous, this place could go down any minute!" – ominous words from the guards at the Point's Life Saving Station. The waves were pounding the bulkhead and crashing across the little bit of lawn still left in front of the Villa Maria. The flood tide was tearing away at the foundations. The building shuddered under the assault of fierce winds. Windows and screens blew out and awnings were ripped away. If this continued, it might not survive the night.

The Immaculata sisters were not the only ones forced to leave their homes that day. The coast guardsmen worked without letup, fighting one of the worst storms of the twentieth century. Long before dawn on Friday, September 18th, the northeast wind started howling. Within hours, the full force of the tempest was felt. Winds reached eighty miles an hour and mountainous waves lashed the coast. Beachfront cottages had to be evacuated. The venerable Sea-Side Home at Alexander Avenue was in danger and so was the Lankenau Villa. Dr. Richards' cottage lost its porch. Homeowners were worried – fear was palpable.

In front of the Sea-Side Home, men scrambled to remove the wooden forms they had just built to cast concrete boulders for the new jetty. They carted off what timber and equipment they could before the next tide arrived. Beach Avenue was hit hard, especially at Cape Avenue. Trees toppled everywhere.

Up the coast things were even worse. Mount Vernon Avenue, connecting the Point with Cape May City, was flooded out, and the beachfront cottages were helpless against the pounding wind. Twenty-two terrified residents of South Cape May heeded the warnings of the Coast Guard and cleared out. The mayor's house and his neighbor's both surrendered to the force of the gale. Fifteen residents had to be put up at the Coast Guard Station for the night.

The bay area was a graveyard. All the little private boats that had been anchored off the shore tore loose from their moorings and crashed against the piers and bulkheads. Some escaped harm but floated about aimlessly for days after the storm had died. The farmlands suffered too. Cornfields were leveled and other crops destroyed by the floodwaters. Cape May Point would not see another storm this destructive for twenty-six years.

(c.1936) A walk along the beach shows that what were once beachfront cottages are now real *beach houses* with lawns of sand.
Courtesy of the Cape May County Historical Society.

(c.1936) The 1936 Northeaster brought winds of 80 miles an hour and mountainous waves lashed the coast. *Courtesy of the Cape May County Historical Society.*

(c.1936) Homeowners and trash pickers salvaged what furniture and furnishings they could before the complete collapse occurred. *Courtesy of the Cape May County Historical Society.*

The '44 Hurricane

c.1930 – The Tennis Courts "*After trying for several years, my grandmother, Mrs. Arthur Dale, persuaded Mayor Springer to have the borough build some tennis courts for the people in the Point. They built two on the west side of Surf Street (the only street in Cape May Point—the others are all avenues). The surface was oil and gravel—the same as the paving of the streets back then. The backstops were just chicken wire.*

From our house on Ocean Avenue, we could see if a court was open. We made a path from our property through woods of windblown scrub oaks, cedars, and holly to Surf Street. We took our tennis equipment and a broom. We needed the broom to sweep the court of loose stones that made it very slippery.

Balls often went right through the holes in the chicken wire, landing in the weeds where you couldn't find them. But our dog could, and so we never had to buy tennis balls.

We usually played with my mother and sister against my father and me. Once in a while though, I would get to play against Charles Givens. I don't think I ever won, but it was fun – at least for Charles, who eventually married Ada Palmer, the lighthouse keeper's daughter.

Now at least one house has been built over the spot where we used to play on the old courts."

—*John A. Mather*

The hurricane that swept up the Jersey coast in mid-September came as no surprise. The radio and newspapers had been issuing ominous warnings for days before it struck. From the author's U.S. Air Force base in Texas he called his parents in Cape May Point, urging them to get out before the "storm of the century" arrived. "No, no," he was told, "there's nothing to worry about. In the thirty years we've been coming here, we've never had any storm damage. We'll be OK, don't worry about us."

Of course, he did worry, since the news accounts were predicting disaster. As it turned out, his parents were right, the Point was spared this time. So was Wildwood. Cape May City was a different story. It got slammed by the worst storm in its 150-year history.

A single wave of monumental force wiped out two miles of its boardwalk, depositing huge chunks of the timber walkway as far as three blocks inland. Most of it crossed Beach Avenue and ripped into the cottages lining the oceanfront. It used to be the custom for locals to watch the fury of the regular northeast storms from the porch of the Peter Shields Inn, a prominent landmark villa on Beach Avenue. Fortunately there were no such voyeurs this time. The wind had kicked up to ninety miles an hour. Practically the entire town was flooded. As the waters receded they left a desert of sand – up to four feet deep in places – strewn with wreckage. From one end of town to the other, Beach Avenue was impassable.

The fishing pier went and so did much of the convention hall ballroom. In another week it would have been closed for the season. The orchestra's instruments were still on the stage when the giant wave hit. They went out to sea as did all but 30 feet of the ballroom. Cape May was a disaster area. Damages estimates exceeded $1,000,000 – a lot of money in 1944!

Cape May Point, on the other hand, survived with little damage. Cape May's colossal wave never reached the Point. The surf did cross through the South Cape May Meadows, putting Sunset Boulevard under floodwaters and isolating Cape May Point for a day. It suffered the usual erosion, always ending with less beach than it had started with. The long abandoned cottage that John Wanamaker had built for President Harrison became the most conspicuous victim of the storm. It survived, but it had been severely damaged; its days were numbered.

(c.1942) Chrystal Avenue was the second beachfront street to be wiped away by the persistent storms that ravaged the Point in the 1930s and 1940s. The heavy piling bulkhead to the right could not hold back the flood tides. *Courtesy of the Cape May County Historical Society.*

After the Storms

Who can dream up a "Bright Idea" to protect Cape May Point's beaches? This is the game played after each big storm would claim more of the beachfront. Everyone agreed – something must be done!

For the past fifty years, jetties and bulkheads of wood pilings had been the answer. In 1925, the borough commissioners invited sealed bids for the driving of five hundred pilings on the beach between Brainard and Emerald Avenues. The *Cape May Star and Wave* notice described the proposed work:

> The bids are to be for labor only, the piling being provided by the Borough. They are sixteen feet long and must be driven to a depth of ten feet. There will be three jetties or sections each of which will be composed of two parallel rows of piling, the rows being four feet apart, and the piling being driven as close to each other as possible. The jetties will run from the high water mark seaward, and will have approximately 166 pilings in each.

Well, wood jetties may have helped but they didn't seem to do enough. By 1931, the time had come for the first "Bright Idea". Why not build new jetties out of sheet steel piling instead? It would be cheaper and faster. The technology was simple enough. This method had been used for decades as temporary shoring for building excavations. The jetties would be slim and elegant – no more ugly wood pilings leaning this way and that way. And what could be stronger than steel?

There would be twelve of them from Surf Avenue to Brainard, the stretch that had suffered the most destruction. Six bids came in, all very close, and J. N. Terry was awarded the contract – a dozen new jetties for a little under $31,000. What a bargain. What a disaster! Unfortunately, steel rusts. Quickly. Especially in salt water. They didn't last too long, but they left plenty of souvenirs. Cape Avenue beach, once the Point's favorite, has been closed to bathers for many years because of the jetties' hidden sharp steel shards that poke up from the ocean floor.

(c.1940s) Covered porches were often the first things to go, but, with the collapse of this cottage's foundations, it is questionable whether the main structure could be salvaged. *Courtesy of the Cape May County Historical Society.*

(c.1940s) Many homeowners had their houses moved to new locations often several blocks back from the beach. The owner of this disaster did not act in time. *Courtesy of the Cape May County Historical Society.*

(c.1940s) The cottage does not appear to be salvageable, but there is still time to bring out some furniture as friends and neighbors look on. *Courtesy of the Cape May County Historical Society.*

Help from the WPA

The great storm of 1936 had bruised every town along the New Jersey coast. They all needed more beach protection projects and none could afford to provide them. The depression was well under way – town budgets were strained. The "Bright Idea" was to use Roosevelt's WPA money, and Cape May Point grabbed at the opportunity.

Here's how it worked. The feds covered the labor costs and the Point hired the local residents to do the work. Even the disabled could participate, as guards or night watchmen. The scheme was to build jetties or seawalls out of giant concrete blocks. The methodology was simple enough – construct wooden forms on the beach, use the beach sand and a little crushed rock for aggregate, add cement and fresh water, cure the concrete for a few weeks, then lift the blocks from the forms and drop them into place along the beach.

The resulting pile wouldn't be pretty. It was to be nothing more than a wild jumble of odd-shaped concrete blocks randomly dumped in place. But nobody was thinking about aesthetics. The concept was to hold down erosion and put Cape May Point's unemployed to work. Starting in July 1936, up to thirty-six were to be hired for the eight months needed to complete the first project.

Applications for four projects had been submitted to the WPA. Although three sites were eventually approved, only two sections were actually built, one at Cape Avenue to protect the Villa Maria and one at Alexander Avenue to safeguard the Sea-side Home. The Ocean Avenue project in front of the Villa Lankenau never happened.

Work progressed intermittently as government funds were slowly released and government bureaucracy could be dealt with. From time to time frantic requests were made to move the work crews from one site to another depending on which location appeared more vulnerable.

The first project at Alexander Avenue ran over schedule and over budget, leaving a cash shortfall for the borough's twenty-five percent share when the Cape Avenue work finally got underway. Meanwhile the tides were tearing into Beach Avenue down at Brainard as well as up at Ocean Avenues. Unless the commissioners came up with their share of the cost, the WPA would pull the plug. The situation was ominous. Individual taxpayers made voluntary contributions, and the borough went into serious debt to keep the WPA work going.

Were these concrete block piles effective? The ferocious storm that came in September 1936 sealed the fate of the Villa Maria before the WPA work there could get started. The first project, at Alexander Avenue was finished in May 1937. This may have helped the Sea-Side Home, which survived until the next big blow came along seven years later.

Jetty construction at Cape Avenue moved in fits and starts. In 1939, it halted for the better part of the year. Later, crews were moved to Stites Avenue to protect the beachfront there. All of this WPA work stopped in 1942, shut down by the War Department. The effectiveness of these jetties was short-lived. By and by, the concrete blocks, built with beach sand, decomposed into nothing more than – beach sand.

(c.1930s) Franklin Delano Roosevelt's brainchild during the Great Depression was the WPA, which took care of the labor costs, while local men created seawalls of concrete blocks, constructed in wood forms by the beach. *Courtesy of the Cape May County Historical Society.*

(c.1942) The concrete block seawalls and jetties, built under the WPA project, were not very effective in slowing beach erosion. The abandoned Rockwell cottage in the foreground did not survive, nor did the old Whilldin cottage, which can be seen in the background. *Courtesy of the Cape May County Historical Society.*

Desperate Measures

Building bulkheads and jetties year after year had failed to stop beach erosion. Everyone could see this but what else could they do? At the same time they were negotiating with the WPA for more new jetties, the Cape May Point commissioners were entertaining a far different approach. They fired off a letter to the Maritime Exchange in New York City asking for information on obtaining old ships and scows. "CAPE MAY POINT TAKES ACTION TO SAVE ITS BEACH" blared the headline in the January 30, 1936 issue of the *Cape May Star and Wave*:

> Mayor Dilks and Commissioners LeNoir and Bair, of Cape May Point, have a plan, which, they think, if successfully carried out, will result in not only saving their beach but in building it up.
>
> They have applied to the War Department for a permit to sink six steel hulks of vessels along the beach between the concrete hulk sunk, some years ago, near Sunset Boulevard and the Life Saving Station to the east. Between these points are the important structures of the Sea Side Home, Villa Maria, Lankenau Villa and St. Mary's, all of which are menaced by ever-encroaching erosion of the sea.
>
> These hulks can be obtained from Sandy Hook. They are about 416 feet long. It is proposed to anchor them at reasonable distances apart and partially fill them with sand. The plans for the work have been prepared by a Philadelphia engineer named Robinson, and are now in the office of Lt. Col. Lee of the War Department Corps of Engineers, Custom House, Philadelphia.
>
> As the only question about letting Cape May Point have these hulks and sink them as proposed is whether the hulks would adversely affect navigation, it is believed the permit will be granted.

Fortunately this bizarre idea died from natural causes. It wasn't, however, the end of the story. In 1945, Corson, the borough engineer, suggested picking up some old landing barges from the government. They couldn't be too old – the war wasn't over yet. Not to be outdone, the mayor decided to raise the ante. He promised to check out some old destroyers. His plan was to get a junk dealer to buy the hull after the ship was dismantled. If that wouldn't work out, how about getting some of those old concrete ships like the one off Sunset Beach?

It's a rather disturbing vision; a whole fleet of derelict ships lined up along the bathing beaches? It would have made one heck of a tourist attraction. In the end it did nothing but prove the Point's commissioners enjoyed fertile imaginations.

(c.1942) All that remains of one of Cape May Point's landmark buildings, the Whilldin cottage, "Land's End," demonstrates what an apt name he had chosen. *Courtesy of the Cape May County Historical Society.*

The First Half 1900-1946

Profound changes were evident in Cape May Point with the arrival of the twentieth century. The numbers of Protestant gentry who had colonized it soon after Sea Grove opened were thinning out. As its aspirations to become a fashionable (albeit Christian and moral) resort remained unfulfilled, more people of means were leaving. The Point had attracted a few men of wealth or fame – Wanamaker, Whilldin, Harrison, Lankenau, and Hazzard – but by the beginning of the century, they were pretty much gone on to that land of no return.

A new class was coming in – a class without servants, without social pretensions, and without a lot of money. They were not poor and they could afford to build their own house, but it was not a big comfortable cottage with a wrap around veranda and a room for the maid. They built bungalows with a single bedroom and a tiny porch. Lots were plentiful and affordable. Some could be had for back taxes. Never again would the Point see grand Italianate Villas like those of Whilldin, Wanamaker, or Harrison.

The hotels were closing, victims of old age and declining demand. The Immaculata nuns took over the Carlton Hotel – once the proud Sea Grove House and center of the Point's social life for a quarter century. The striking Shoreham Hotel, with its commanding view of the Ocean as far as Cape May, went to the Sisters of Saint Joseph for a summer retreat house. Faith and prayer replaced the popular Saturday night hops in the hotel ballrooms.

Many rented their houses, and full-season leases were commonplace. The bigger Victorian cottages sometimes had their rooms subdivided; that way one bedroom could become two. This either brought in more rent, or more cousins, nephews, and nieces.

Following the First World War, automobiles had replaced carriages. Mother and the kids might spend the whole summer with the family car (only one per family) available for local transportation. Depending on the bus was like depending on the weather. Dad could come down by train on weekends. Eddie's Taxi was at the station just in case Mom was too busy to give him a lift over to Cape May Point.

Things were getting more formal. The commissioners met at the Firehouse instead of in the mayor's parlor. They were starting to pay more attention to the environment. Chickens and pigs were no longer welcome. Neither was hunting. Some folks thought that shooting ducks, hawks and possum ought to be outlawed in Cape May Point. Some thought not, but a hard-fought ordinance finally prohibited such activity.

The most costly civic enterprise remained beach protection. Construction, repair, and replacement of jetties and bulkheads, or the repair of roads damaged by erosion, kept the Point's coffers empty. The battle was never-ending, the solution always elusive. The constant damage was maddening.

By 1946, almost a dozen city blocks had disappeared into the Ocean or Bay. All of Beach Avenue and its boardwalk was a memory. Those cottages that didn't get moved got dunked. In the thirties and forties, as families came down for the season, their first step would be a trip along the beach counting the derelict wrecks or remembering where so-and-so's house had been.

Not as much would change in the next half century. A bit more erosion, a few more cottages lost, but nothing like the way it had been. In time, the biggest changes would be the scarcity of building lots and the sky-high real estate values.

(c.1942) The Whilldin cottage outlasted its next door neighbor, Saint Mary's-by-the-Sea, which had been demolished in 1936 but by 1942 its fate was also sealed. *Courtesy of Dick Hall.*

Part 3

Peace and Prosperity

1947-Present Day

Chapter 11
Shifts in Realty

Goodbye to Charity

The year 1945 marked the beginning of the end for most of Cape May Point's charitable institutions. The August and September storms of 1944 had turned the once-stately Harrison Cottage into an abandoned hulk. It had had many interesting lives. Starting in 1890 as a political gift from Wanamaker and his cronies to President Harrison's wife, that ownership was short-lived. After she died a year later, Harrison soon tired of it, and in 1896, Wanamaker bought it back through a straw party. For some years the Wanamaker family used it, but eventually turned it over to the Pennsylvania Society to Prevent Cruelty to Children.

Abandoned and neglected after the 1944 storms, except by occasional youthful vandals, the institution's summer home was condemned and torn down by the borough in 1945. The second casualty soon followed. That same storm had doomed another of the Point's landmarks, the venerable Sea-Side Home. In spite of the bulkheads, the old wood jetties, the new steel jetties, and finally the WPA concrete jetties, the bay waters won out. In danger of collapse, the old summer home that had delighted so many mothers and children for almost seventy years, had to be torn down as well.

The third storm victim, the Lankenau Villa, summer home for the Lutheran Deaconesses, held out valiantly until 1952. While not the engaging edifice that the first Lankenau Villa was, it still made its mark in the community. Like the other two institutions, it had spent a considerable sum of its own money, fortifying its position in vain hopes for survival. It wasn't destroyed at that time, but the last storm had convinced the sisters that it was time to go. The Lutherans sold it, and it lived on as the Chelsea Hotel until 1962.

The fourth charity to leave town, the Presbyterian Orphanage, was not motivated by fear of the sea, but by changing social conditions. Since 1916, it had occupied the original cottage of John Wanamaker after that building had been moved from its Beach Avenue location to two empty lots at the corner of Cape and Yale Avenues. Adoption of parentless children was replacing the role of orphanages, and the population at Sunny Corner, as the Presbyterians called the home, was dwindling. The year 1959 was the orphanage's last year in Cape May Point.

In 1962 they sold their property through a straw owner to an organization of Catholic Brothers, the Marianist Society, Inc., of New York. Although originally intended as a summer retreat and vacation home for the Brothers, it is currently operated as a boarding house with weekly or weekend rentals for lay groups from the region. Some of these operate as family retreat programs in which the Brothers participate; others are free to organize their own activities without a religious component.

(c.1947) The Sea-Side Home had been fighting the beach erosion that threatened it for almost twenty years. It had been the most important reminder of the Presbyterian prominence in Cape May Point for almost seventy years. It was demolished in 1947. *Courtesy of Dick Hall.*

Dirt Cheap Lots

The rumor persists that, during the great depression, you could buy a full size building lot for 25 bucks. It's only half true. It wasn't *during* the depression – it was *after* the depression. In the decade from 1930 to 1940 many couldn't afford to pay their real estate taxes, and the borough acquired their properties. With economic recovery finally in sight, the commissioners started to unload the lots to realize annual tax income again.

For six years starting in 1940 you really could buy a lot from the borough for 25 dollars. The Second World War kept the number of sales low, but over forty people snapped them up. It was a real estate bonanza! With the exception of true tax-sale lots, which had occasionally been auctioned by the borough for the actual tax owed on them, it was the deal of a lifetime. After all, some of these lots had sold for ten times that amount when Sea Grove opened in 1875.

When the war ended, the commissioners, knowing there would be more buyers, started to raise the sale price. Now the least expensive lot went for 50 dollars, and the more desirable ones for $200. For a decade after the war, these lot prices kept creeping up, but by 1956 the average was merely $225. Only an ocean front lot would go as high as $500, the same sale price that the Sea Grove Association had charged eighty years earlier!

If you had been clairvoyant enough to buy one of these borough lots at the end of World War II, you could sell it in 2003 for 1,000 times what you paid for it. That wouldn't have made you rich, but it certainly would have made you an exceptionally fortunate investor.

(c.1920s) Most building lots in Cape May Point were 50 by 100-feet or larger, except along Alexander Avenue, where 25-foot wide lots were laid out for the service workers in the hotels and boarding houses. *Courtesy of Joan Viguers.*

Design or Discord?

No one could ever say Cape May Point is celebrated for the quality of its architecture. Unfortunately, it has but a few noteworthy buildings, and far too many disappointing ones. Yet the overall aspect can be delightful, thanks to a fine master plan, wise zoning laws, and a spectacular setting safe from peripheral sprawl. The character of its housing stock, past and present, large and little, gorgeous and ghastly, demonstrates a pattern of non-conformity and individual choice. It wasn't always that way.

The Sea Grove Association was, in a sense, a design review board. Although no specific standards had been drafted, each proposed building was to be reviewed by the Association. Few had architects; most were built from pattern books available to the local carpenter-builder. The remarkable similarity of the houses built in the nineteenth century makes them easy to identify today. Each would have a gable or mansard roof, a rectangular, L-shaped, or cruciform floor plan, and a large, open veranda. Invariably two or three stories high, they were sheathed in clapboard or shingles. Victorian gingerbread adorned most, but even the largest avoided ostentation. In 1900 the architecture was surprisingly homogeneous. It was an upper-middle class town, and the buildings reflected its social status.

The second phase of development, from 1900 until the end of World War II, had a similar degree of uniformity. Gone was the gingerbread along with the second story, steep roof and wrap-around veranda. In came the bungalow, one story high, no attic and not much larger than a one car garage. They dominated this period, although a few larger cottages appeared here and there. The bungalows had straightforward plans, simple and economical, without pretence. While the upper-middle class was drifting away, a new middle class was settling in.

Following the war, prosperity was slowly getting underway. Building lots were plentiful and still inexpensive. Newcomers could afford to put up more substantial homes. "Modern architecture" was replacing "traditional" – too often with disheartening results. The Point got its share of A-Frames, split-levels, and unsightly houses. Architectural sensitivity was elusive. The expensive beachfront lots were especially hard hit.

In the seventies and eighties a backlash followed in the form of neo-Victorian. Elaborate fretwork was being added to new houses, perhaps with the hope that they would appear like one of the original nineteenth century cottages. Gingerbread woodwork could be had at the local hardware store, for Victorian-mania was everywhere, not confined to Cape May Point.

This is not to say all the new houses lacked architectural merit. The few that have been worthy additions stand out from the crowd, reminders that good taste survives in Cape May Point. Unlike other New Jersey resorts, the Point has not been devastated by the siege of greedy developers.

All of the speculative building in recent years has been small scale, generally one house at a time. In most cases, they tend to be innocuous boxes of vinyl siding and Anderson windows, different only in size from what is invading the entire nation.

Cape May Point is almost built out. Few lots are available for those who want to build here. This scarcity and high demand have raised land values to unprecedented levels. The old bungalows may soon be gone, replaced by luxurious new homes, victims of that inexorable force, supply and demand. The upper-middle class has returned.

(c.1910) William Braun built this impressive cottage on the northeast corner of Harvard and Coral Avenues. It was demolished in 2001 by a developer to provide two beachfront lots for sale. *Courtesy of the Cape May County Historical Society.*

(c.1890s) This one story house is a rare example of a Victorian Bungalow in Cape May Point. Prior to 1900 almost all of the houses were two-story cottages. *Courtesy of the Cape May County Historical Society.*

Chapter 12

All Together Now

Togetherness

Cape May Point has had its share of civic and social associations. The first was the purely social enterprise organized by Dr. Randall T. Hazzard in 1899 as the Cape May Point Social Club. Its original clubhouse still stands at the corner of Ocean Avenue and Lake Drive. But it's been almost a century since the Point has seen such organized social activities as Mrs. Hazzard arranged. Never again would there be lavish receptions and afternoon teas, parties for the ladies' whist and euchre games, and lawn tennis for their gentlemen. Its duration was short: Dr. Hazzard died in 1905.

In 1936, the Taxpayers' League of Cape May Point was formed. The borough was in financial trouble. It wasn't bringing in enough money to cover its costs. The depression was severe and people couldn't afford to pay their taxes. The commissioners had approval for WPA beachfront improvements but not the funds to pay for the materials and equipment

that represented their share of the project costs. The WPA work was critical – it provided desperately needed employment and vital protection from erosion. Fearing the loss of this government grant, some of the taxpayers formed the Taxpayers' League of Cape May Point to pressure the borough commissioners to act. They were successful. The borough took on additional bonded debt of $10,000, and the League pitched in with enough cash to buy a carload of cement to keep the work moving.

A small sister organization was active in 1938. It called itself the Beach Front Property Owners Association. The members lobbied for new jetties and bulkheads from Ocean Avenue all along the beach to Lighthouse Avenue, a stretch that had already seen Beach Avenue and all its beachfront houses taken by the sea. Neither the borough nor the members of the association had the money that was needed, so the organization soon lost its purpose.

(c.1959) Annual beauty pageants in Cape May Point were an important event in the 1950s and these contestants could hold their own in almost any such event. *Courtesy of the Borough of Cape May Point.*

The Civic Club

It started with an afternoon tea. With Mrs. Charles Makin as hostess, several women met in the spring of 1954 to consider forming a club to enhance civic pride. The borough commissioners had already given their blessing to the idea and the Volunteer Firemen had offered the firehouse hall for their proposed meetings. Invitations went out to all women in the community to attend an organizational meeting at the Fire Hall on the sixth of May. And so was born the Cape May Point Civic Club.

Their first enterprise, decorative planting at the Cape Avenue entrance, was a modest but successful effort. A more ambitious plan to provide playground equipment for Pavilion Circle soon followed. To raise funds to carry out their projects, they sell donated goods at an annual bazaar. With the money raised from the sale and from donations to the club, a portion is set aside for emergency assistance in the community and for an educational award to a graduating senior. Half of the remainder goes to the Volunteer Fire Company, the other half primarily to various non-profit groups.

(c.1900) The rustic bridge erected by Randal Hazzard at the turn of the century, when he owned Lake Lily, is long gone, and so are the lily pads that gave the lake its name. *Courtesy of the Cape May County Historical Society.*

LILY LAKE, CAPE MAY POINT, N.J.

The Taxpayers' Association

1964 – The Taxpayers' League, which had been established in 1936 to deal with urgent beach protection and financial matters, had disbanded before the end of World War II. Twenty years later, the idea of a taxpayers' association resurfaced. The same concerns that bought taxpayers to form an organization in 1936, beachfront protection, motivated them to take action after the 1962 storm.

Roland Henry, whose severely damaged house had to be moved back from the beach, was fed up with the "we don't know what we're going to do" attitude prevalent at the borough meetings. He and Wolf Veith felt that a taxpayers' association could help by working with the cash strapped commissioners to press for federal aid.

An invitation to all property owners brought twenty together for the initial meeting on October third. They found the records of the old league in Cape May Court House, so they didn't have to reinvent the wheel. With a change in name and some editing they were able to put together a new charter, articles of incorporation, and by-laws. Roland Henry became the first president. And so was born the Cape May Point Taxpayers' Association.

1972 – Despite this inauspicious beginning, rapid growth followed, with the membership reaching 340 within the next eight years. The following year, like many new organizations, they found it necessary to update their constitution and by-laws.

1982 – Genevieve Van Bever started the Annual Garden Awards Program that honors the best gardens in the Point with ribbons, and first place is honored with an engraved silver cup. The awards, charmingly presented by Nanine Dowling at the Association's annual meeting, have stimulated the creation of hundreds of attractive new gardens and intense competition among the amateur gardeners.

1986 – The artificial dunes, which had been constructed by the Army Corps of Engineers after the 1962 storm, saved the Point, but who would save the dunes? Without a good cover of vegetation the sand would blow away instead of building up the dunes. A Dune Committee was started. It called on volunteers to plant beds of dune grass each spring and fall. When Dick Miller took over in 1988, he found the spring plantings could not hold up through the summer heat, but the Columbus Day effort was producing durable plants that had no trouble surviving the winter.

Several hours of hard work at the beach, all carefully organized by good leadership, has done a lot to reinforce the line of dunes that have successfully defended Cape May Point from serious storm damage since 1962. Each year additions of Japanese Black Pines, and shrubs of Bayberry, Rosa Ragosa, and Beach Plum have further stabilized the dunes.

Donations from the community pay for the materials. At one time there were no walkways – so people just walked over the dunes to get to the beach. This destructive practice stopped when the wooden walkways and fences were put up and people were forbidden to walk on the dunes.

1989 – Fear and fury accompanied the proposal to improve Pavilion Circle. Since 1891, when the Sea Grove Association sold its pavilion, the circle had become sort of a lost soul. Stripped of its symbolic status as the religious center of this moral, Christian resort, the circle couldn't seem to redis-

cover its *raison d'être*. The intervening years had not been kind. Invaded by electric service poles, and for a time by Cape Avenue itself, it was the neglected orphan of Cape May Point.

Its inhospitable surface, more cactus and weeds than grass, didn't encourage its use for anything more than a short-cut across to the General Store. Many were surprised when the Taxpayers' Association proposed an ambitious restoration. Envisioned was a real public park, a dignified space not unlike a "Village Green."

Sally Sachs had persuaded a prominent landscape architect, Roger Wells, once a partner of her late husband, Skip Sachs, (who was a former commissioner), to develop designs for the improvements. Wells graciously offered to provide his professional services without compensation. A Circle Improvement Committee brainstormed ideas and reviewed seven concept sketches before making a presentation to the community.

Instead of approval by acclamation, there was an outpouring of objections at the public meeting. Proponents proclaimed the design would be beautiful, all costs would be covered by donations, not taxes, the play areas would be unobtrusive, and volunteers would provide the maintenance. The circle could once again become the symbolic center of the Point.

Not everyone agreed with this vision. "Our taxes will go up, the proposed sewage sludge fertilizer will be a health hazard, noisy kids will shatter the peace and quiet – we like it the way it is." Fear of the unknown threatened the pro-

(c.1990s) The Taxpayers' Association sponsored the first annual block party in 1989 at the firehouse, and a small string band had the overflow gang dancing in the street. *Courtesy of the Borough of Cape May Point.*

posal. Some objected to the grassy berms, seeing them as out of character with the relative flatness of the Point. They were unaware that the whole area had had an undulating form of hills and hollows before the Sea Grove Association graded it into its current almost-level profile.

Cooler heads prevailed, and the project was approved in July 1991 by a two-to-one majority. When the borough formally approved the work, Roger Wells prepared the final plans and visited periodically to ensure the landscape construction and plantings adhered to his design. Elizabeth Parsons, a Point resident and trained horticulturist, volunteered to manage the project on a day-to-day basis. The work was completed in a few years.

Volunteer "Bedfellows" recruited by Sally Sachs care for the fifteen beds of shrubs and flowers, which add so much color to the park. Spring and fall "Mulch Days" put more volunteers to work laying down a rich bed of mulch at each of the planting beds. The borough supplies irrigation, grass cutting and fertilizing, but the remainder of the maintenance is provided by the "Bedfellows."

1989 – In a departure from its more serious pursuits, the Taxpayers' Association scheduled the first (soon to become annual) Block Party at the firehouse on September 16th. It was an unstructured affair with no planned program, just a BYOB bash to bring together friends and neighbors. A small string band, mostly volunteers from Philadelphia, played tirelessly and, in no time, had the overflow gang dancing in the street.

The Sunset Beach Sportsmen's Club

This club was formed for camaraderie, not civic commitment. Fishing and boating drew them together and they knew how to party, both privately and publicly. The annual Labor Day weekend was their big event of the year. Starting past noon with organized races and games, it ended with a gigantic beach party at nightfall that would bring out 150 guests.

A five-mile boat race was open to speedboats that could average sixty mph and to outboards that could do almost as well. It was a family affair that day and members brought out the wife and kids. The games on the beach were mostly for women and children, with races like the three-legged, wheelbarrow, or peanut and spoon. Kids had more fun seeing who could blow the biggest balloon or biggest bubblegum bubble. The guys preferred the tug-o-war. It was old-fashioned fun. Except for the main event, the contest for the biggest fish of the season – that was serious business!

The members built the first clubhouse themselves on two lots at Chrystal and Alexander Avenues. Starting in May 1952, they hoped to get in by the July fourth weekend, but bad weather prevailed, and they finally finished up before the big Labor Day events. Within three years, beach erosion was so severe that the clubhouse had to be moved. They petitioned the borough for a site where the old Villa Maria had stood. When that didn't work out they moved to Sunset Beach.

The building is still there, just a hundred yards north of Sunset Boulevard. The big Labor Day parties are a thing of the past but private partying lives on – for members only.

(c.1930s) The author's two cousins and their boyfriends are showing off a typical day's catch from the Delaware bay near Sunset Beach. *Courtesy of the Author.*

Chapter 13
Getting Organized

Bureaucracy Arrives

c.1944s – Mosquito Bites "We were staying for the summer at my great-grandfather's little cottage on Cape Avenue, and each day I had to go over to the post office to pick up the mail. It was just around the corner, next to Gerew's store, not even a block from our house. But before going out, I'd tuck my long pants into my socks, roll a winter cap down over my face, and pull on my gloves. This was my anti-mosquito outfit – that's how bad they were that summer.

I used a different defense when I wanted to bike over to Cape May City. I had to ride along Sunset Boulevard, which seemed to be the mosquitoes' home base. It turned out, that if I kept up a certain speed, they wouldn't bother me. I would pump and pump and never slow down until I reached Congress Hall.

—Joseph Jungkurth*

After the First World War, the state legislature slowly began introducing laws affecting the management and fiscal policies of local governments. These were tough on pint-sized communities like Cape May Point, but the irresistible force of bureaucracy was just getting started. By the 1980s and 1990s, it sometimes seemed as if the Point was governed by the New Jersey legislature rather than by the borough commissioners.

The old-timers had a difficult time dealing with this. Cape May Point had its own way of managing its affairs and they didn't need the State telling them what to do – let alone how and when to do it.

Nevertheless, many of the new regulations were needed to awaken smaller communities to better business practices. Along with the burden of these new directives came a multitude of grants and loans to enable cash-poor towns to cope. Cape May Point responded to the state and federal offers of financial aid like a kid in a candy store. Grant money was snapped up together with favorable loans from every conceivable agency. In the race for funding, Cape May Point often finished first.

From 1875 to 1950, the borough introduced about ten new ordinances during each decade. From 1950 to 1980 the average was up to forty each decade. The real explosion has happened since 1980, when the commissioners were approving a dozen new ordinances each year!

This period saw a complete revamping of the town's infrastructure. Streets and utilities were transformed from a patchwork of crisis repairs to state-of-the-art installations good for the next half century. The town was becoming more sensitive to its valuable heritage. New codes for zoning and building were adopted in time to ensure against runaway development and a diminishment of the natural environment.

(c.1890) The A. G. Crowell cottage on Beach Avenue between Emerald and Central Avenues was moved to the corner of Cape and Pearl Avenues, where it is well known today as the "Gray Ghost." Next-door was the Signal Station, designed by J. C. Sidney, as one of the New Jersey weather stations. *Courtesy of the Cape May County Historical Society.*

Real Police

The Sea Grove Association had taken care of law and order for the first few years, investing that responsibility in a "Committee on Protection of Property." In 1891, the *Cape May Wave* reported:

> William Turner, one of our most intelligent colored men, is serving in the capacity of deputy sheriff. The bigotry is condescending and reflects attitudes of the times. The title deputy sheriff seems to be the name applied to the Point's first police officer. Since then, they have been called everything *but* police officer.

After Cape May Point said goodbye to Lower Township in 1908 and finally became an independent borough, it established a police department and appointed Albert B. Schellenger as its first Marshall. Lawlessness was hardly a major issue at the time, because Schellenger was only on duty from seven PM until midnight. His tour of duty started in July and ended in September.

Following the New Jersey legislature's act of 1922, governing the election of constables, Cape May Point elected John Carmignano as Marshall, but everyone always called

him "John the Cop." By 1946, the borough knew John to be its Constable. His reign seemed to last forever, but John Carmagnano eventually retired in 1953. Next, three policemen got appointed to keep order, joined by three more the following year. The force swelled to ten in 1955.

It would seem now that Cape May Point had more policemen than were necessary, but they weren't real police – they were "special police." That meant they were untrained residents who had been given a badge and paid by the hour – a kind of "Rent-a-Cop." Cape May Point was satisfied with its one police car and no police chief. This informal approach to public safety may have been good for the municipal budget, but it didn't have the same appeal to the county or the state.

The Point did get its police department properly organized, but by 1986, it decided to get out of the police business and let West Cape May handle it under an Inter-local Agreement. For some time this arrangement provided good police service at a lower cost to the community. As expenses rose for police operations, Cape May Point found it was paying an unfair share of West Cape May's police budget. The final resolution came in 2001, when the Point negotiated a new agreement under which Cape May City's police served the Point as well as West Cape May.

(c.1936) Storms in 1933 and 1936 brought the ocean dangerously close to the cottages along Beach Avenue in the vicinity of Ocean Avenue. Neither the Rockwell cottage, nor the Whilldin cottage beside it, survived. *Courtesy of Marie G. Richards.*

High Crimes

Criminals had always been scarce in Cape May Point, so it's understandable that the place did without any real police force for so many years. A little teenage mischief, like shooting out streetlights or breaking into houses abandoned after storm damage, might need attending to.

It was pretty rare to find a reckless driver in Cape May Point, but there was one incident that a lot of people remember. It happened on a winter day in 1991. A fellow from Connecticut was leading police on a high-speed chase through Cape May County. He was hitting 90 mph along Sunset Boulevard, and he didn't slow down much as he spun into Lighthouse Avenue. The pursuit was over when he lost control, flipping eight feet into the air and crashing into the corner house at Lighthouse and Whilldin.

While the Point was almost trouble free, Cape May City was getting more than its share of lawlessness during the 1980s. The *Cape May Star and Wave* was full of stories about every crime short of murder – rape, robbery, muggings, arson, even armed bank robbery. Vandalism and graffiti hardly counted.

Cape May Point's own "Crime of the Century" was a white-collar caper. For years, a borough clerk and tax collector had been embezzling from Cape May Point and from West Cape May, where she was also a borough clerk. This went undetected until, in 1999, the Point's auditors discovered some of her illicit transactions. It took the best part of a year for the accountants to straighten out the books. The crime had cost the Point over $45,000. It cost the former borough clerk six months in jail, community service, fifteen years probation, and eligibility to hold another public office in New Jersey.

(c.1925) The east end of the Point was sparsely developed in the 1920s. The fenced vegetable garden in front of the Braun cottages was owned by William Braun and supplied food for the Deaconesses in the Lankenau Villa across Coral Avenue. *Courtesy of William W. Dickhart, Jr.*

New Setbacks

For years you could pretty much build what you wanted where you wanted it, as long as you owned the land. After the Sea Grove Association disbanded in 1881, there was no public entity to control what was built. Things went on this way for the next seventy-five years.

Starting in 1936, the commissioner in charge of public works was given the responsibility of issuing a permit to construct or to tear down a building. There were but three restrictions: two stories high, a "well finished front," and commissioner approval, which was seldom withheld.

They decided in 1955 that the borough was just too small to be bothered with one of those "building codes." After all, nobody was building anything except houses. Any carpenter knew how to do that. However, they thought a Planning Board might be a good idea. There were no standards for the board's guidance, it simply ruled on what the owner could or could not do.

Ten years went by before a Construction Official was appointed to handle these matters, and the following year the Planning Board was restructured in accordance with New Jersey statutes. The first zoning ordinance was enacted in 1968. For the next six years construction requirements gradually grew tighter with the introduction of, and amendments to, building and zoning codes.

The rush to develop New Jersey's coastal area really took off in the 1980s and 1990s. Cape May Point was feeling the pressure as the quantity of available building lots was rapidly diminishing. Density was a big issue if the character of the community were to be saved.

The borough commission now had a professional planner, Walter Sachs, under whose guidance zoning regulations got a significant rewrite. Floor Area Ratio, Building Height, and Lot Coverage restrictions that he introduced in 1984 kept the Point free of the oversized vacation houses that other resort towns were seeing. The zoning map was redrawn – no more commercial and no more multiple-family dwellings would be permitted. Taxpayers voted overwhelmingly in favor of single-family dwellings only.

(c.1905) An annual water fete, with the famous rustic bridge and the rowboats and sailboats ablaze with lights, would attract 200 guests. The bridge became one of the Point's most notable landmarks. *Courtesy of the Cape May County Historical Society.*

But Not a Drop to Drink

The crisis came in 1970 – Cape May Point's water would soon be undrinkable. Lots of residents said it always had been undrinkable – a comment on the high saline content that had been present for a long time. Even in the 1940s, the saline taste was distinctive – to some, downright repulsive. There was good fresh tasting water at the lighthouse well in the1930s if you didn't mind cranking the hand pump. That's where a lot of folks got their drinking water. Some found the local water so objectionable that they swore they could taste it even in boiled potatoes. For making coffee – forget it!

This wasn't the first time the Point had a problem with water quality. The bacteria count was so high in May 1935 that the State Department of Health filed an injunction. A new pump and chlorinator solved the problem but not before the threat of complete water shutdown had rattled the borough commissioners.

Mayor Malcolm Fraser, in several of his periodic reports called Implementing Municipal Government, wrote this about the Point's water system:

> The original well water source for Cape May Point lay adjacent the lighthouse, beneath the new Municipal Hall. The original steam engine pump delivered water to an elevated wooden water tank, much like an old railroad tank which supplied the locomotives. The first water main was placed along Yale Avenue and the immediate side streets toward the ocean, and ended at the intersection of Pearl and Central Avenues. The last remnant of this venture is the 1898 fire hydrant at the corner of Yale and Whilldin Avenues.
>
> As the borough began to grow in the 1920s, new water mains were laid throughout the northwestern area which housed most of the year-round residents at that time. As the system spread – main lines were 4-inch transite pipe, and branch lines 2-inch max galvanized pipe. Mains and laterals were replaced as they corroded out. The current standard calls for 8-inch mains and 6-inch branch lines.

By 1970, Cape May Point's old well water was close to the maximum salt content allowed by law. To make matters worse, there was a water shortage that summer. Fire insurance rates were rising because the single well did not meet insurance rating standards. Something had to be done.

The commissioners found the available choices to be as unpleasant as the taste of the water. They could install desalinization equipment at their well or hook up to the city of Cape May's water service. The Cape May approach won out and a ten-inch line was laid along Sunset Boulevard to bring in the new supply. Everyone knew that this was just a stopgap – Cape May would soon have the same salt intrusion problem.

From the mid 1980s to the late 1990s the entire water distribution system was reconstructed with 8-inch mains, 6-inch branch lines, and copper laterals to every property in Cape May Point. In 1995 the old tank by the lighthouse was dismantled and a new one built just west of Cape Avenue along Sunset Boulevard. The Point was ready for the twenty-first century with a water system to rival any in the state.

By the mid nineties Cape May City was wrestling with the same problem that had plagued the Point in 1970 – salt water intrusion in its under-ground aquifers. The best solution proved to be a desalinization plant which was completed in the late 1990s. Water costs shot up and the Point had to cough up its share of the increase. Water, in some form, had always been the biggest budget drain. However, the costs of supplying every household with good drinking water were a pittance compared to the costs of holding back the sea.

(c.1925) Lake Drive, with the Episcopal church of Saint Peter's-by-the-Sea on the left, was a narrow gravel lane, typical of the streets in the Point in earlier years. *Courtesy of William W. Dickhart, Jr.*

Dishonorable Discharge

First to go were the original privies. By the 1930s, these relics of sewage disposal were pretty much history. Few mourned their passing.

In 1938, a new sewage disposal plant at the corner of Yale and Coral Avenues was a significant improvement to the community's sanitary waste system. One problem remained: where the untreated waste was discharged. Although it had been that way for years, the adjacent Cape May meadowland was not a suitable place to dump the Point's sewage. That's what the State Department of Health was saying when they gave an ultimatum in October 1941 – find another solution by next June, or face heavy fines until you do.

It didn't happen that fast, but Cape May Point got the message. It was going to be costly. They negotiated with Cape May City to tap into their line on Sunset Boulevard for an annual use fee. The federal government had its Division of Public Works construct the necessary force main with Cape May Point responsible for half the cost. It was completed and approved in 1944.

Fifteen years later the same problem reappeared. Cape May's sewer line along Sunset Boulevard was dumping its effluent into the Delaware Bay near Sunset Beach. Beginning in 1951, the State Department of Health repeatedly warned that this was polluting the bay. Cape May kept stalling. Finally the state's Attorney General ordered the construction of a sewage disposal plant and gave them a deadline of January 1960 to complete it. Failure to finish on time would result in heavy fines every day until the plant was approved.

Cape May Point and West Cape May, both of whom used the line, agreed to share in the cost. The new plant was built across Sunset Boulevard just east of the Cape Avenue entrance. It missed the deadline by almost a year but avoided the fines when the Attorney General removed the judgment he had filed.

The last step in the modernizing of the Point's sanitary waste system came in 1980 with the establishment of the Cape May Point Water and Sewer Utility as a separate entity from the borough government. Plans were drawn and bonding secured through the US Department of Agriculture for a town-wide system that was completed in 1989.

(c.1958) Cape May City had its annual Baby Parade on the boardwalk, but in the 1950s, the Point preferred a more grown-up version in the person of "Miss Cape May Point." *Courtesy of the Borough of Cape May Point.*

117

Storm Water Matters

For a long, long time Cape May Point never needed storm sewers. The soil was more than sandy; it was *mostly* sand with several inches of topsoil. The unpaved streets and scarcity of houses ensured quick runoff even after heavy storms. When a northeaster broke across the bulkheads bringing in flood tides, it wouldn't be long before the seawater would be absorbed.

After the gravel streets were tarred, a few curbs and sidewalks installed, and more houses built, a heavier concentration of storm water had fewer places to go. If a big storm came along, with persistent heavy rains, large parts of the borough would become flooded. The great hurricane of 1944 was the messenger that told how things would be from then on.

The Cape May meadowland was so deep in seawater that Sunset Boulevard became impassable. The waters had rushed across Lighthouse Avenue and inundated the Point. Lake Lily, the community's natural drainage pond, spilled its banks and wiped out much of Lake Drive. It took days to clear the higher areas, longer for the many low spots.

Cape May Point was accustomed to some flooding after a heavy storm. The low-lying streets might take on a foot or so of water, but things usually cleared up in a matter of days. The 1991 Halloween storm changed that. The ocean had rushed through the South Meadows dunes and pushed the sand into the natural drainage swale there that had always carried off the Point's excess storm water.

A few months later, a January storm followed suit, flooding one third of the borough. Lake Lily, the Point's natural drainage basin, was filled almost to overflowing, the water table was at its highest level, and the storm water had no place to go. Its natural outlet to the ocean was blocked.

The borough engineers recommended piping water from Lake Lily to Lighthouse Pond just across Lighthouse Avenue in the State Park. That pond flows into the neighboring Shallow Pond, not far back from the damaged dune line. A second pipeline would run from there to the ocean and restore the historic drainage route of the Point.

Dubbed "Drainage East," it was the first half of a more ambitious plan for a permanent solution. Permits and approvals from government agencies were finally obtained, and the work completed in 1994.

Pete Bowers, a Cape May Point resident, suggested back in 1992 the alternate drainage system that came to be known as "Drainage West." Pete knew that there was an abandoned sewer pipe that ran along Sunset Boulevard and discharged into the bay at Sunset Beach. Installed in 1982 by the county Municipal Utilities Authority, it went out of service in 1990. Why not pump water from the north end of Lake Lily through a pipe connection to this old MUA line? In that way, he reasoned, the borough could have complete control over flooding.

Six years later, with all plans reviewed, all funding arranged, and all permits in place, his vision was to become a reality. Construction was completed in 1998. In the "Drainage East" plan the water level in Lake Lily, Lighthouse Pond, and Shallow Pond was to be kept no higher than three and a half feet above sea level. If, under severe weather conditions, Lake Lily rose more than a foot above that, the borough would pump the additional water out through the "Drainage West" line and keep the lake from overflowing. The final safety measure was now in place to ensure against flooding from the big storms.

(c.1992) Before the "Drainage East" and "Drainage West" storm water projects were completed in the 1990s, many heavy storms brought severe flooding to the east end of town. *Courtesy of the Borough of Cape May Point.*

Chapter 14
Contentious Issues

Them's Fightin' Words

Decorum usually reigns at the borough commission meetings. Attendance is low. Controversial issues are rare and there's a feeling of trust that the commissioners will do the right thing. Public confidence has not always been so high. During the 1930s and 1940s, when the big storms were wiping out beachfront properties, the borough officials seemed powerless to deal with the crisis. The taxpayers, feeling frustrated that nothing constructive was being done, took command and led the battle for beach protection. They wrote letters to their congressmen, they met with agency officials, they lobbied the legislature – they just took over!

Controversial issues, though infrequent, have been known to stimulate passionate debate. An ordinance, introduced in 1954 to prohibit boating, fishing, and hunting on Lake Lily, is a good example. Ducks had been introduced to the lake to control the grasses and weeds that were growing out of control. Was Lake Lily going to turn into a prairie? The ordinance was meant to ensure that the ducks could do their job in peace.

Some thought this was a stupid idea. Many lakeside residents considered the birds little more than a noisy nuisance.

"Turn Lake Lily over to the birds? How about the kids who for years and years have been boating or fishing from its shores? Was the muck they were eating good for the ducks? Should children be deprived of the use of the lake – for ducks?" The idea that children and ducks might be able to coexist never came up. The birds won. The ordinance passed unanimously.

Generally it has been such "you can't do this, you can't do that" ordinances that have caused outbursts of anger from the taxpayers. New regulations in the 1960s forbidding the burning of trash or fires on the beach brought bitter resentment from some old-timers. Burning papers and leaves in your backyard was the traditional way of disposal. Everyone had a fifty-five gallon oil drum or cinderblock enclosure for this purpose. It meant no trip to the town dump or less trouble for the trash collector. That's the way it had always been done. And now they want to fine us if we do this?

Prohibition of beach fires was greeted with similar indignation. Beach parties were another century-old tradition. What was a beach party without a fire? The outcry came from the younger set, the only ones who have beach parties. However, they don't attend borough meetings and, from then on, they didn't attend beach parties at the Point.

(c.1925) The intersection of Ocean and Beach Avenues is now part of the impressive dunes that line the beachfront, and Saint Peters-by-the-Sea is across from the entrance path to the beach. *Courtesy of William W. Dickhart, Jr.*

Licensed Landlords

From the early days of Sea Grove on, summer rentals have been a fact of life in Cape May Point. Almost one third of property owners in the Point rent out their houses for at least part of the year. When the mayor introduced, in 1993, an ordinance requiring these part-time landlords to pay $200 for an annual permit for each rental unit, the taxpayers' reaction was explosive.

"Why is this needed? We don't want "Big Brother" telling us whom we can or can't rent to! It's an unfair tax on those who need the rental income to pay down their mortgage and taxes. It's one more unnecessary intrusion by the borough. " Suspicion was strong that the reasons for the permit were a cover for something else. It had no support from the taxpayers. The opposition was so strong that it was tabled for further study.

A revised version lowered the fee to a more reasonable $35 per rental unit, supposedly an amount necessary to cover the borough's costs of administering, inspecting, and enforcing the new regulations. The mayor maintained that it could help deal with troublesome tenants and keep owners from creating illegal rental units in single-family dwellings. It passed, but not without resentment, for many still believed that its real purpose was simply to bring in more money to the borough.

(c.1890s) South Cape May's seawall could not hold back the storm tides that periodically flooded the railroad tracks that had been built too close to the beach. *Courtesy of H. Gerald MacDonald.*

Wide Open Spaces

Possibly the most divisive legislation ever enacted was the proposal in 1999 to sell three of the few remaining lots still owned by the borough. Real estate prices had skyrocketed in the 1990s – a combination of the national wealth factor and a crucial shortage of buildable lots. Talking about shortage, one new property owner recently complained that he had met the asking price on five houses, only to be outbid each time. Cape May Point seemed overbuilt to those who had lived there for many years. There was talk of ultimate build-out within a few years.

More building translated into less open space. Everyone sensed the change and many worried that in no time, the only remaining open space would be the lake, the beach, and Pavilion Park. The three lots on Coral Avenue were contiguous and a number of people thought they should remain undeveloped. More open space translated into a better quality of life.

The borough's position was: it would soon need a great deal of money for its share of the cost of ambitious beachfront projects. The lot sales would take care of the lion's share of the required borough appropriation. It was either sell the lots or raise taxes. At the borough meeting everyone present preferred to bear an increase in the real estate tax rather than see the land developed. Discussions grew heated and tempers grew hot. Some dreamed of raising enough money through voluntary contributions from the taxpayers to match the money that could be gained through the lot sales.

The Taxpayers' Association swung into action. Out went a questionnaire to every household. Two thirds of them came back with fifty-two percent opposed to the sale, forty-six percent in favor. The Environmental Commission and the Planning Board voted unanimously to keep the lots as open space. The preference of the taxpayers was clear. However, the commissioners voted two to one in favor of the sale. A public auction did bring in more money than had been anticipated, but it brought little satisfaction to the taxpayers who felt the will of the people had been ignored.

(c.1935) Only four of the buildings seen in this 1930s scene along Harvard Avenue are still in place: the Braun cottage on the far left, the Tower cottage to the right of the Braun cottage, the Sea View cottage (now called Brigadune) in the center, and Saint Mary's-by-the-Sea in the background. On the far right are the Hazzard cottage and the Harrison cottage. *Courtesy of William W. Dickhart, Jr.*

Trash and Trailers

One man's garbage cans became another man's grief. The endless garbage controversy created as much grief as would a trash-man's strike. It wasn't the garbage per se; it was where it was kept. The proliferation of curbside trash corrals had had a stimulating effect on the general health in Cape May Point. It had raised the collective blood pressure to dangerous levels. The clash of opinions was deafening.

The issue was: should residents be allowed to place their trash and garbage in closed containers near the curbside instead of somewhere behind the front of their house.

Proponents advanced the following arguments: "the tasteful enclosures we have built screen the trash containers from public view. Other residents put out their ugly trashcans and bags for everyone to have to look at – sometimes for days on end. Many of us rent our houses during the season and cannot depend on our tenants to put the trash out on the collection day; curbside trash corrals solve this problem. Our trashcans and covers are replaced in the corrals after trash pickup, not allowed to blow around the street after the trashmen leave."

Opponents screamed back the following: "the stink from your garbage spoils my daily walk around the Point; it's like walking through a garbage dump! They are so ugly – you walk down the street and all you notice are these trash corrals. If you can't train your tenants to put out the trash on collection days, hire a handyman to do it. Our tenants do put out their trash on collection days or they forfeit a substantial security deposit. You are breaking the law; your corrals are being built within the street right-of-way, not on your own property!" In 2002, the controversy was still unresolved.

Boats in Cape May Point front yards? "This is a residential community, not a marina!" Such were the sentiments of most in the Point – excepting, of course, the few boat own'ers. "This is my property and I can store my boat here like I've always done." So went the mariners' response. "Eye-sore," howled the accusers. "No law against it," countered the boat owners.

For months the debate raged. At issue were the rights of the individual versus the resentment of the community; the way things were versus the way things should be. Compromises were sought. Hardliners said: "Boats belong on the beach, in the water, or at a marina, not in my neighbor's front yard." Moderates favored leniency – let the boats stay, but keep them far back from the street and out of sight. Based on this compromise, an ordinance finally passed permitting boats to remain on residential lots, but restricting where they could be placed.

(c.1890s) The Idlewild cottage, pictured in a promotional brochure for the Shoreham Hotel, is now at the southwest corner of Lake and Yale Avenues. *Courtesy of the Cape May County Historical Society.*

Chapter 15

Saving the Strand

Hurricanes Make *News* – Northeasters Make *Waves*

Cape May Point gets both, but the storms that sometimes come in the fall, winter, or spring, with their fierce northeast winds, are far more frequent and bring much more grief. It's the wind-driven ocean storm surges of the northeasters, not the hurricanes, that have been responsible for gobbling up twenty percent of the Point's land over the past 125 years.

The news media love to hype the path of hurricanes and to paint shocking word pictures of the devastation about to visit every shore community along the Atlantic coast. Cape May Point has always been spared. The hurricane of September 1944 is a case in point.

Much of the Atlantic coast felt its fury, and by the time it hit the Jersey shore it had lost little of its venom. Cape May City got hit hard. A gigantic wave, pressed on by the hurricane winds, crashed through the boardwalk and ripped across town. The city lost its fishing pier, half of its convention hall, and its entire two-mile boardwalk. Few beachfront cottages escaped serious damage.

The wave that had pounded Cape May City spared both its neighbors, Cape May Point, and Wildwood. The Point experienced the usual consequences of every coastal storm – beach erosion and flooding. Sea front cottages were weakened but few suffered significant damage. This was a hurricane to be reckoned with – the worst storm in Cape May City's history

Everybody remembers the nor'easter of 1962. Meteorologists saw it coming, but they couldn't foresee how bad it would be. Nothing like it had ever happened in New Jersey's recorded history. It was *the really big one!*

March can bring tough coastal weather. Spring tides commonly run a foot or two higher than normal at new and full moons. That's to be expected.

For several days in early March, the weathermen had been tracking a heavy storm roaring southeast across the continent heading toward the coast. Simultaneously, high winds swirling over the Atlantic Ocean were pushing in a northwesterly path. The two weather patterns met well out to sea, increasing in ferocity as a high-pressure ridge over New England deflected them toward the east coast.

The impact was staggering. By Sunday night the wind, now blowing from the northeast, had reached gale force. The full moon brought in flood tides five or more feet above normal on Monday morning. The waves were terrifying. Reaching fifteen to twenty feet above the swollen surface, they ripped through dunes and bulkheads on a path of destruction.

Cape May Point had little protection to offer. There were no dunes – they had been absent since 1875. Its few pilings, jetties and bulkheads were pitifully inadequate barriers. Seawater soon inundated the borough, flowing into Lake Lily and making Lake Drive impassable. Cape and Lighthouse Avenues also flooded, isolating the 150 residents who were braving the storm. Several had to be evacuated by helicopter.

The Point escaped the terrible fires that raged in Cape May and Wildwood. There, firemen, attempting to control flames caused by electrical short circuits created by the storm, were captives of the flooded streets. They couldn't get to the fires, and house after house burned out of control.

(c.1940) A beachfront cottage in the 1930s and 1940s was constantly in danger from coastal storms and beach erosion. Many were moved back to safer ground but the Rockwell cottage was simply abandoned by its owners. *Courtesy of the Cape May County Historical Society.*

Beachfront cottages on the ocean side had no chance of avoiding damage or destruction. Harvard Avenue was like a war zone. The old Lankenau Villa, most recently reincarnated as the Chelsea Hotel, surrendered after more than a fifty-year standoff. Just down the street, at the foot of Ocean Avenue, the Morris cottage was swept away. Further along, the surf carried the Speer cottage off its foundations and spun it around in its wake.

The West and Mitchell properties received an unwelcome visitor as a neighboring house came crashing into them. A bungalow on Yale Avenue found a new home on Coral Avenue. The stately Harrison cottage, Wanamaker's gift to the president's wife in 1890, managed to survive, only to be abandoned, boarded up and soon condemned as a public nuisance.

The siege lasted for three fear-filled days. Seven successive storm tides had erased the line between beach and borough. Harvard Avenue was one big sand-pile streaked with debris. Cape May Point was not alone. From one end of the state to the other the storm had battered the seaside communities. On Tuesday, New Jersey's governor declared the coastal zone a disaster area and asked for immediate federal aid.

There was a silver lining. Substantial federal assistance, for which Cape May Point had been begging for half a century, finally came to pass. With Public Law 875, the 81st Congress responded.

(c.1962) Everybody remembers the nor'easter of 1962. Meteorologists saw it coming, but they couldn't foresee how bad it would be. Nothing like it had ever happened in New Jersey's recorded history. It was the really BIG one! *Courtesy of the Borough of Cape May Point.*

The Dunes Reappear

The 1962 northeaster had ravaged the coast of half a dozen states. In response to desperate appeals from the state governors, the President had declared the entire coast, from New York to North Carolina, a disaster area, and congress supported him. The US Army Corps of Engineers was charged with the colossal task of repairing all of the damaged beaches and dunes.

Cape May Point was at last to get its share of federal aid. The army engineers had the manpower and resources to act quickly, and they did. There was great concern that if emergency protection was not completed before mid-August, the coastal communities would be at the mercy of further northeast storms and hurricanes that might develop in the fall. By late April, Cape May Point's survey had been delivered to the Philadelphia office, and by May 28, 1962, the Army Corps' master plan had been developed and approved.

The plan's goal was to install emergency shore rehabilitation and protection against a ten-year storm. It was not intended to be long-range protection, because there were significant limits on the amount of earthmoving equipment and barges that could be mustered over such a large area in a period of a few weeks.

Buckley & Company, a large excavation company from Philadelphia, had started beach repair operations on their $345,000 contract by July13th, and, by working twelve-hour days, and six-day weeks, they were able to complete the job by the 17th of August. The deadline had been met.

The sand for beach restoration and dune construction had not been pumped in from an offshore barge. This commonly used method proved ill-suited for Cape May Point's steep sloping beaches. The Army engineers had to devise a special section that differed from their typical design for the dune construction, because the existing beach was so narrow.

(c.2002) The artificial dunes that were created after the devastating 1962 storm have provided the only effective protection since 1875 against the persistent erosion that has transformed the Point's shoreline. *Courtesy of the Author.*

Sand was taken from the south side of the Cape May Canal, from the place where the excavation spoils had been dumped when the canal was built in 1942. Loaded onto dump trucks, it was driven to the beach sites, where large bulldozers shaped the artificial dune line from the west end of the borough at Alexander Avenue, all the way along the South Cape May Meadows to Cape May's western end at Third Avenue.

The profile that resulted was a sand bank, a full thirty feet wide along its crest, which was ten feet above mean sea level, with a fifteen percent slope on the sea-ward bank, and a twenty percent slope on the land-ward side. No vegetation was planted, but a zigzag snow fence ran the full length of the dune line. Cape May Point was finally ready to face the fall and winter storm season

This massive federal dune project was a short term solution and there was a keen awareness that the Point still needed a coordinated long term project. By 1965, the Cape May Point Taxpayers' Association was at odds with the Borough commissioners.

The taxpayers sought as much publicity in the press as they could get, hoping to keep state and federal agencies aware of the serious erosion, and influence their position on funding beach projects. The commissioners feared that the extensive publicity would turn away vacationers and homebuyers. The borough did inform the state and federal agencies of their willingness to provide $75,000 as the community contribution toward beach improvement work.

A plan was developed to seek $1,350,000 from the state and federal government to rebuild the unstable emergency dunes and to install a network of stone groins from one end of the borough to the other. In November of 1966, the governor had approved a $300,000 appropriation for groins at Lehigh Central, and Stites, and these were completed the following year.

The New Jersey Department of Conservation and Economic Development was the state agency in charge and their master plan called for dune reconstruction, beach nourishment and a total of nine groins using creosoted timber and granite boulders. The federal government never appropriated funds and the state eventually spent over $3,000,000 for the work. There was delay after delay, caused by agonizing political stonewalling from each changing opposition party.

Total reconstruction of the dune from Lehigh Avenue to Ocean Avenue started the project in 1968, and the remainder of the dune system soon followed. That first section was reinforced with several dozen gigantic concrete submarine anchors that had been obtained from the federal government as war surplus material. They were buried in a core of I-95 gravel, and this formed a roadbed about six feet deep and twelve feet wide for the earthmoving equipment, which then shaped the final dune profile.

The section west of Ocean Avenue used huge nylon bags filled with ten cubic yards of sand on the landward side as the stabilizing units, instead of the concrete submarine anchors. All of this was placed on top of the emergency dunes the Army Corps of Engineers had built in 1962.

The whole beachfront work took four years, but by 1971 the Point had its nine stone groins stretching out 150 feet from the shore, a significant amount of beach fill, and a strong artificial dune.

For fifteen years the dunes were without any stabilizing vegetation except what little had seeded itself. Volunteers from the Crest Haven School for Special Services started the first organized planting of dune grass in the mid-eighties, and in 1988 the Taxpayers' Association formalized a Dune Day each spring and fall to plant grass, shrubs, and trees. This program has paid off handsomely and created a seafront that bears no resemblance to artificially created dunes. Today the dune's crest has grown as high as thirty feet in some places.

(c.2002) Cape May Point's dunes have grown so high with wind-blown sand and vegetation, that bathers along the beaches can seldom see that a town rests behind them. *Courtesy of the Author*.

(c.2002) The construction, in the 1960s, of nine stone groins from the beach at Lighthouse Avenue to the beach at Alexander Avenue has slowed erosion and provided anglers with an opportunity to fish in deeper water. *Courtesy of the Author*.

Artificial Reefs

The concept of an artificial reef to control beach erosion had a long and bizarre history in Cape May Point. It started back in 1936 when the borough commissioners asked the War Department for a permit to sink six abandoned ships offshore and partially fill them with sand.

Subsequent ideas ranged from sinking barges, decommissioned navy destroyers, left-over military materials, to junked cars. Nothing ever happened until the early 1990s, when the New Jersey Economic Development Authority was sponsoring and funding the installation of submerged concrete barriers that would act as artificial reefs at three voluntary locations along the Jersey shore. Unlike previous concepts, this plan carried impressive scientific credentials, and most of the cost would be borne by the state. Cape May Point joined with Avalon and Belmar-Spring Lake to become one of the three selected sites.

A firm from Flemington, New Jersey, Breakwaters International, had developed the engineering design for the reef, working with experts from the Stevens Institute of Technology and the University of Delaware. Wave tank testing in the laboratory was producing promising results, but field-testing was essential under actual ocean shore conditions.

Cape May Point was an ideal test site. In May 1994, the pre-cast concrete modules were lowered into place from an offshore barge and carefully placed by a crew of divers to form a straight line connecting to the ends of the existing stone groins at Lehigh, Whilldin, and Coral Avenues. Every interlocking unit was ten feet wide parallel to the shore, sixteen feet long perpendicular to the shore, and stood 6 feet high above the sand bottom. Each was triangular in cross section and weighed twenty-one tons. The precise location was chosen so that the top line of the reef would be about one foot below the water surface at low tide.

Breakwaters International explains the operation of the reef in their company literature:

The Beachsaver reef system works with sand nourishment and ocean forces to protect and extend the life of beaches. The reef reduces the volume of sand required for a nourishment project, retains replenished sand as it is pumped onto the beach, and keeps added sand on the beach longer by slowing the rate of erosion.

The reef works to enhance the long-term performance of beach fills in two ways. First the reef forms a partial barrier, preventing suspended sand from moving out to see in the return wave. This sand settles instead in the near zone or emergent beach. Second, the energy of incoming waves is reduced by twenty to thirty percent as they cross the reef and as they break further offshore, taking less of a toll on the beachfront.

Did it work? Did it stop erosion and build up the beach? Answers are provided in a 1997 final report prepared by the Stevens Institute of Technology that had been monitoring performance since the reefs were first installed. There was good news and bad news.

On the plus side they found a significant gain on the Lehigh beach where the distance to the water's edge was forty-four feet further than it had been prior to the reef installation. The gain on Coral beach was only fifteen feet, but that compared favorably with the fifteen-foot loss on St. Peter's beach, which had no reef. Wave heights were found to be reduced ten percent in fair weather and even more during storms.

While there was a clear buildup of beach sand, the presence of the reef did little to prevent erosion at the toe of the dunes during heavy storms. Settlement of several of the connected modules did occur, but the continuous chain of units remained unbroken. Results had been encouraging enough to spark a new round of experimental projects in Cape May Point. In 2002, a new line of artificial reefs was installed at Cape Beach. On the adjacent Emerald Beach, a different type of reef barrier, consisting of inverted concrete double-T structural beams, was placed. Over the next five years, annual surveys of shoreline changes are planned to determine the effectiveness of the several different installations.

(c.1994) The reef works to enhance the long-term performance of beach fills in two ways. First the reef forms a partial barrier, preventing suspended sand from moving out to sea in the return wave. This sand settles instead in the near zone or emergent beach. Second, the energy of incoming waves is reduced by twenty to thirty percent as they cross the reef and as they break further offshore, taking less of a toll on the beachfront. *Courtesy of Breakwaters International Inc.*

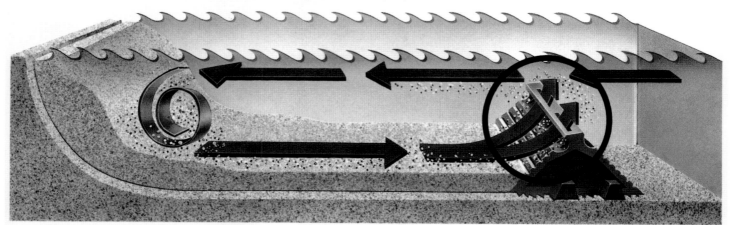

Offshore current channels through the Backwash Flume (right). This creates a curtain of water which suspends sand over the reef. Incoming waves then carry suspended sand back onshore.

(c.1994) In May 1994, the pre-cast concrete modules of the artificial reef were lowered into place from an offshore barge and carefully placed by a crew of divers to form a straight line connecting to the ends of the existing stone groins at Lehigh, Whilldin, and Coral Avenues. *Courtesy of Breakwaters International Inc.*

Reclaiming the Lake

c.1940 – Boating on the Lake "I used to hang around Sunset Beach where Kidder Hughes had his boat rentals when I was about fourteen. I loved boats and I'd help out Mr. Hughes in any way I could. The daily excursion trains, the "Fishermen's Specials" brought in a lot of customers and he was expanding his fleet to keep up with the traffic.

One day he offered me an old flat-bottomed rowboat that needed a lot of work before it would even float. I knew I could fix it up, so my pal Drew and I loaded this little fourteen-foot craft on my express wagon and pulled it down Sunset Boulevard to the lake. It took a lot of work to make it watertight, but we caulked her real good and gave her a coat of paint.

There were a few other boats on the lake; the Alvarez brothers had a couple at their dock about where Seagrove Avenue comes into Lake drive, and they would rent them out. They were all rowboats – motors were forbidden. But one night after dark we hitched up a little outboard and went chugging around the lake. The motor was small but it sure wasn't quiet!

Pretty soon we saw the headlights of Kidder (the mayor) Hughes' white pickup come running toward Lake Drive. Somebody must have called him about the noise, so we hightailed it down to the far end near Sunset Boulevard hoping we could hide there and wouldn't get caught.

We found Mayor Hughes standing on the shore right there waiting for us. "Boys" he thundered "you just got me out of a sound sleep and I have to be up before five tomorrow morning. I don't want you ever to have me do that again" We never did, and I'll bet that was the only time there was an outboard motor boat on Lake Lily."

—Dick Hall

Lake Lily has always been one of Cape May Point's star attractions. The Sea Grove Association had transformed it from an obscure hidden pond to a lovely park for public recreation. They dredged it for boating, stocked it for fishing, and cleared the underbrush for easy access to its shores. Leisurely boating, competitive sailing and fashionable parties marked its early days. For seventy-five years it saw little physical change, although its social role diminished considerably after the turn of the century.

The November nor'easter of 1950 may have been the first culprit to seriously upset the lake's equilibrium. It brought thunderous ocean waves ripping across the South Cape May Meadows and flooding the Point. So deep was the flood that the local milkman had to struggle through chest-high water to make his deliveries. When the storm ended, the receding floodwaters poured into Lake Lily carrying more than the usual amount of poisonous oils, fertilizers, and pesticides.

Excessive weed growth began to show up in the lake – a clear indication that something strange was occurring. The New Jersey Division of Fish and Game was called to the rescue but they had no sure remedy to offer. They tried adding several chemicals, using different concentrations at various locations, but the results showed little promise.

The weeds grew vigorously, and a dry spell in the summer of 1953 had so lowered the water level that the basin seemed more grassland than lake. The weed grass was dying as well as growing. The stench was offensive. In desperation the borough spread tons of lime over the surface, a temporary solution at best. Resolution of this problem would take another half century!

Not everyone was unhappy. Waterfowl that occasionally spent the warm months on the lake were delighted with the new menu. Some stayed for the winter, enjoying all that free food. The cottagers along the lakeshore were not so happy with the noise of the ducks and geese, or with the Canadian geese that were leaving mementoes on their lawns and walks. The borough commissioners on the other hand thought that the birds were the answer

As the grass plantation shrunk, the waterfowl population surged. The Cape May Point Civic Club settled a pair of mute swans there and made sure all the birds were adequately fed during the cold months. During the warm months tourists fed corn from the General Store to the quacking and honking hordes. The birds loved it, and each season seemed to bring in new avian settlers.

There was a price to be paid. The birds ate the waterweeds and then deposited tons of excrement on the bottom of the lake. The water didn't like that – it was becoming more of a sewer than a lake. It had already lost its fabulous water lilies, victims of the ocean water that had flowed in with the devastating northeaster of 1962.

Serious study of Lake Lily's condition started in the late 1970s with an eight-month survey by the New Jersey Department of Environmental Protection. Their final report on the physical, chemical and biological conditions was published in 1983. The following year two more surveys provided further evidence of the severity of the problem.

A group from the US Soil Conservation Service concentrated on the lakeshore habitat and aquatic plants, while volunteers from the Delaware County Aquarium Society did a fish count and studied the water quality. It was agreed that the waterfowl excrement was hurting the water quality and that the bird population had to be stabilized or reduced.

A decade later a Lake Committee was formed with Roy Keiser as chairman. He summarized the findings of the three previous studies in the fall 1994 edition of the Taxpayers' Association Newsletter:

> The lake seems to be deficient in in-flow of sweet clean water and has very slow circulation and exchange of water.
>
> Sediments and organic matter are building up too rapidly, producing a lake rich in nutrients.
>
> The shallow, enriched water promotes rapid plant growth (algae blooms) reducing the dissolved oxygen content and accelerating aging.

> The abundant plant growth dies, sinks and decays, adding to the muck on the bottom and to the nutrients in the water.
>
> The excrement of resident waterfowl increases nutrient load, (one duck deposits 80 pounds of manure annually and geese and swans contribute much more) lowers water quality and adds to the muck on the bottom.
>
> The shallower water becomes hotter in the summer, increasing the rate of these processes.
>
> The oxygen-deficient waters are unsuitable for other aquatic animal life and cause the bottom sediments to give off bad odors.
>
> The larger fish are gone and cannot return. The lake is populated only with small water animals and fish.
>
> Nutrients, minerals and pollutants are also entering the lake in storm runoff and possibly with any underground water that exists.
>
> The water is hard, alkaline and unfriendly to large fish.

The conclusions were discouraging. The Delaware County Aquarium Society returned in 1995 and found little changed from their previous survey. Restoration activities were clearly needed and they would be costly. The borough looked to the state for help, and legislation slowly worked its way through the political barriers.

A first attempt in 1998 didn't succeed in reaching the committee stage, but two years later the $625,000 appropriation bill got committee approvals from the Assembly. It was a good first step, but the final bill took two more years for passage, with the governor signing off on three quarters of the amount originally requested, leaving the Point to come up with the rest.

An environmental consultant, F. X. Browne, had been retained two years earlier to design the cleanup operations. He recommended pumping the bottom sludge and water to a dewatering site and depositing the final waste on a site off Sunset Boulevard owned by the New Jersey Fish and Wildlife Management Division. Here it would become part of a re-vegetation plan on the former Magnesite Plant site. The dredging operation was finally scheduled to start in the winter of 2003.

(c.1900s) Leisurely boating, competitive sailing, and fashionable parties marked the early days of Lake Lily around the turn of the century, when it was a healthy fresh water lake, filled with lily pads. *Courtesy of John Mather.*

Looking Back

The establishment of seashore resort towns, based on religious principles and preferences, is unlikely to occur again in America. We will see no more Oak Bluffs, no more Ocean Groves, no more Rehoboth's, and no more Sea Groves.

Sea Grove lasted only three years, the Sea Grove Association lasted but six. But its roots were strong, and its harvest is still with us. Significant reminders of nineteenth century Sea Grove (alias Cape May Point) can still be found today. The most obvious remnant is Sidney's radial street plan, with Pavilion Circle at its center. All the streets are the same – even their names. What's not the same is the disappearance of many, but they were all present and accounted for as late as 1900.

Throughout the town most of the pre-1900 cottages have survived. A number have been moved, and most are substantially altered. For about three dozen of them, the changes have been superficial. Although dispersed among the twentieth century houses, they are easily recognized, and help to give the Point its special character. The little cabins along Knox Avenue are a case in point. Half have been severely transformed through additions, but all remind us of the old camp meeting grounds that bore them.

Three of the five churches built in the 1880s still exist, with only St. Agnes at its original location. The Beadle Memorial on Cape Avenue has been moved twice. St. Peter's on Ocean Avenue is at its fourth address. The African Methodist Episcopal Church on Alexander Avenue was lost to fire, probably arson, in the 1920s. At the corner of Cape and Pavilion Avenues stands the Union Chapel, rebuilt in 1968 after an electrical fire took down the original building.

The hotels were less fortunate than the churches. Today the old Shoreham (now St. Mary's-by-the-Sea) is all that's left of the Point's four nineteenth century hotels. If it were not for the Catholic Sisters of St. Joseph, who acquired it as a summer retreat house in 1909, they would all be gone. Another holdout was the Carlton Hotel, also occupied as a retreat house (Villa Maria-by-the-Sea) by Catholic Nuns, but it succumbed to the sea in 1936. The first to disappear was the Centennial Hotel in a disastrous fire in 1888. By 1910, only the two Catholic retreat houses remained.

Long gone are the dozens of stores that were scattered around the Point. Only one remains – the Cape May Point General Store at Cape and Pavilion Avenues. The signal station on Beach Avenue, designed by J. C. Sidney, which for twenty years had monitored many a storm, came down soon after 1900. The old Life Saving Station, which, like the lighthouse, always seemed to be a part of the Point, was one of the last landmarks to go.

We still have the old schoolhouse on Cambridge Avenue, now a well-restored residence. The natural landscape has changed dramatically. Dense woods of oak and holly that stretched from the circle to the turnpike are scarcely discernable today; they became victims of twentieth century housing development. On the other hand, block after block east of Ocean Avenue, which had been barren of vegetation in the nineteenth century, is today dense with trees and shrubs, giving the town a visual homogeneity that the Point had lacked from its birth.

The last decade of the twentieth century witnessed such rapid growth on the Jersey shore that it could be characterized as a building frenzy. The residents of the Point started talking about buildout – the number of vacant lots remaining that could be built upon. They realized that at the rate new houses were going up there would be no vacant land left. Land prices rose rapidly in response to this scarcity.

Looking Ahead

How will Cape May Point change? Perhaps the right question is: how will it not change? It seems sure to remain a quiet residential community of single-family houses, with no commercial intrusions. The reconstruction of the dunes and installation of the groins, which the state of New Jersey brought about in 1968, appears to have tamed the erosion that has threatened the beachfront since 1875. A long-term program of beach repair and replenishment has been planned by the Army Corps of Engineers, and is awaiting stable funding. The experimental placement of artificial reefs on half of the point's beaches shows promising results for beach buildup.

Lake Lily is scheduled for a thorough cleanup. Dredging operations are planned this year. When the sediments and organic matter are removed, it is likely that the lake will be able once again to sustain water lilies and fresh water fish. There is nothing to prevent the return of boating, even a small dock or boathouse, if the residents favor such an addition to the available recreational opportunities.

Two significant changes are well underway – one is social; the other is visual. When Sea Grove was founded, the cost of house construction was about four times the cost of the lot. Today a new house can be built for as little as half the cost of the land. Tax assessments on the modest bungalow lots have risen, and some families are deciding to sell and move out. The pressures of economic hardship, or for economic profit, are formidable.

Some who bought their property decades ago cannot resist selling at twenty times what they paid. People of modest means will be leaving, and a more affluent group moving in. It will be the reverse of the social change of the early 1900s, when the wealthy moved away and the middle class moved in. Real estate values in 2002 skyrocketed – last year the average sale price was $600,000 and there was nothing to be had under $400,000.

As the demand for property continues, the little bungalows that were built up until World War II, will be bought and demolished. So will the smaller cottages of the 1950s and 1960s. They will be replaced by new homes as large as the zoning laws permit. Many of the nineteenth century cottages will share the same fate. New buyers will often not look kindly on summer homes without insulation, without air conditioning, and without modern baths and kitchens. Cape May Point will lose some of its historic houses, and the visual character that attracted so many current residents will gradually change.

On the brighter side, Cape May Point's good fortune is its landlocked position that guarantees no peripheral development. It is now surrounded by protected lands on the east and west, and by the ocean and bay on the south. Its exposed northern border is just one block long. While adjacent development could have occurred in the past, it didn't, and so the Point remains as it always had been – an island. If the dreaded 100-year storm finally comes along, it may become a real island, and a very changed community.

Part 4

Cape May Point's

Neighbors

Chapter 16
Higbees Beach

The Hermitage Hotel

In 1823, Joseph S. Higbee purchased a bayside plantation of about 200 acres stretching from Pond Creek on the South to New England Creek on the North. The land included an old inn, known as the Hermitage Hotel, that had been offering food, drink and lodging to travelers for many years. It was reported to have forty-four rooms, making it a good bit larger than the Delaware Bay House that accommodated travelers at Sunset Beach in 1878.

Both creeks that formed the property boundaries are gone now. Pond Creek had flowed into the bay scarcely a hundred yards north of Sunset Boulevard. It must have been a sizable waterway in 1875, since the Hughes brothers were able to widen its mouth and bring in light draft vessels to deliver some of the timber that built Sea Grove. The mouth of the Cape May Canal, some two and a half miles up from Cape May Point, marks the spot where the New England Creek used to flow into the Delaware Bay.

When Higbee died in 1872, he left the property to his brother, Tom Higbee. It left the Higbee family seven years later, upon Tom's death, but the name "Higbees Beach," or "Higbee Beach," or "Higbee's Beach" persists to this day. The remains of the old inn, with its four story high east wing, had been a well-known local landmark until its demise around 1940.

Such an old structure often breeds myths and the Hermitage Hotel was no exception. Local legend has pirates bringing captives to the attic where they were bound and held for ransom. Of much more substance, considering the presence of the inn, are reports that the place had been the early landing location for vacationers, brought down by schooner, and transported by stagecoach to Cape Island.

(c.1840s) The boat landing at Higbees Beach served early vacationers, who were brought down by sailing schooners from Philadelphia and Wilmington, and transported by stagecoach to Cape Island. *Courtesy of the Borough of Cape May Point.*

The Proving Grounds

c.1920s – The Big Bang "Sometime after the First World War my father found a five and a half inch artillery shell at the site of the old Bethlehem Steel Proving Grounds at Higbees Beach. Lots of boys went there looking for stuff, but my father must have been especially lucky to find such a treasure. As long as I can remember he kept that long brass shell in back of the woodstove in our kitchen. After his death I moved it into my basement where it would be safer. Then, many years later, I thought it might be a good idea to get rid of it, so I called the cops. The police department wanted nothing to do with it and suggested I contact the local Coast Guard Base. They were just as skittish and referred me to the Naval Weapons Station at Earle, New Jersey.

I wouldn't say the guys at Earle panicked when I described it, but they were really interested when I told them what it looked like. It was a big holiday time when I called, the Friday before the Labor Day weekend. Nevertheless, within a few hours several sailors rushed up in a jeep ready to pick up the shell, stow it carefully in a nest of three sand bags and carry it right back to the Navy Weapons Depot in north Jersey.

I learned later they had exploded it. It had blown a crater in the ground big enough to swallow a bus. I guess I finally did the right thing."

—*David Rutherford*

Old-timers remember the concrete remnants and other strange artifacts that were to be found along the shore and among the dunes at Higbees Beach. Locals often referred to this area as the Proving Grounds, because it had been leased by the Bethlehem Steel Company for artillery testing during the First World War. Little remains visible today because sufficient erosion has buried much of the material under the bay waters.

When the United States declared war in 1917, it lacked the necessary facilities for testing munitions. The Proving Ground at New Jersey's Fort Hancock, the nation's oldest facility, was thought to be too close to New York's active harbor and population centers. Desperate for an alternative site, the government chose a 70,000-acre parcel of farmland along the Chesapeake Bay near the town of Aberdeen in Maryland.

Within six months they had relocated 3,000 people and 12,000 animals under the right of eminent domain, and started construction. The primary mission was for proof-testing field artillery weapons and ammunition. It is probable that the Higbees Beach site was used for similar activities. The Bethlehem Steel Company was a key player in the war effort, and it seems likely that they were able to more quickly set up operations here than the Army had been at Aberdeen. The president of the steel company, Eugene G. Grace, had grown up in nearby Goshen, and it may have been his knowledge of the Higbee area that led the company to choose this site.

The Aberdeen Proving Ground has gone on to engage a workforce of over 14,000 and is referred to proudly as "The Home of Army Ordinance." The Higbees Beach Proving Ground shut down shortly after the war ended, leaving telltale reminders of its wartime past.

DANGER
TARGET RANGE - KEEP OFF BEACH
WARNING: FIRING WILL BE CONDUCTED DURING CLEAR WEATHER 1½ HOURS BEFORE AND AFTER HIGH TIDE. RED FLAGS HOISTED INDICATES FIRING. A SALUTING GUN WILL BE FIRED 15 MINUTES BEFORE FIRING STARTS.
BETHLEHEM STEEL COMPANY.

(c.1918) Old-timers remember the concrete remnants and other strange artifacts that were to be found along the shore and among the dunes at Higbees Beach. Locals often referred to this area as the Proving Grounds, because it had been leased by the Bethlehem Steel Company for artillery testing during the First World War. *Courtesy of the Cape May County Historical Society.*

Davy's Lake

c.1920s – Davy's Lake "From time to time a lot of the kids my age went out to Davy's Lake for a swim. The grown-ups never heard of it, or if they did, they had no idea where it was. And we didn't tell them – it was our secret. It was our big adventure. To get there you had to walk about a mile up the beach from the end of Sunset Boulevard and you had to know just when to cross over the dunes and into the woods or you'd never find it. Sometimes we would approach it from Sunset Boulevard instead, but this way was even more confusing and mysterious. There was a kind of trail and certain markers to look out for but you really had to pay attention or you'd never find the lake. This route brought you right to the swimming place, so you didn't have to wander around the long shoreline as you would if you came in from the beach.

We would cautiously strip out of our clothes, making sure that no one could see us. Long ago, somebody had rigged up a diving board, so we would run down the steep sandy dune and plunge into the clear water. You dove in only a few yards off shore but it quickly got so deep that you actually had to swim down before you could touch bottom. We mostly stayed pretty close to shore where the water was warm and we felt safe – a little further out it was cold as ice because the sun would only warm the surface. The best part of skinny-dipping was the feeling that you were doing something forbidden. We kept a sharp lookout for strangers who we thought might suddenly appear and catch us in the nude. From time to time we sent out a scout to ensure that we were alone. Occasionally an adult might stumble upon the hidden lake and then we would breathlessly scramble into our shorts – our hearts pounding in the fear that they may have seen us before we saw them.

It was a long time before we learned that some young girls had discovered our swimming hole and one day had been watching us from the bushes along the top of the dune. We were about nine to eleven years old and I don't know whether the thought of having been secretly seen by some young girls was humiliating – or titillating."

—Bob Grubb

In the thirties and forties Cape May Point had a small but fairly stable population of summer renters and regular residents. The vacation families would come down for the whole summer, year after year, and all the kids pretty much knew each other. They also knew Davy's Lake, because, unlike the too shallow Lake Lily, you could swim there.

It seemed kind of mysterious, this fresh water pond so close to the Delaware Bay, buried deep in the dunes and scrub woods that made up the bay's undisturbed shoreline. Nobody knew how it got its name, and the kids never gave it a second thought. In 1952, Robert C. Alexander wrote this about the lake in the annual bulletin of the Cape May Geographic Society:

> North of Pond Creek and half a mile above Sunset Boulevard, a man-made fresh-water lake fed by springs, called Davis Lake or Davy's Lake, lies among the dunes about 125 yards from the bay. The lake was named for two employees of the Cape May Sand Company, S. Walter Davis and David Wilkshire, who operated cranes and helped to dredge it when sand was dug there commercially about 1910.
>
> It is over 300 yards long, nearly ninety yards wide, and parts of it are twelve feet deep. After dredging operations were abandoned, the lake became a favorite swimming hole. The state has stocked it with bass in recent years for fresh-water fishing.
>
> Sections of the old railroad used to haul sand, with some of the ties still in place, a mound of cinders, coils of rusted steel cable, and a rectangular wooden bulkhead used to support dredging apparatus, almost submerged in the water, can still be seen there. Signal Hill, the highest dune on this part of the bay shore, stands a short distance north of the lake. Formerly a vantage point used to signal ships in the bay, it has become an observation spot for bird watchers.

(c.1935) Davy's Lake was named for two employees of the Cape May Sand Company (whose railroad tracks ran along Higbees Beach), S. Walter Davis and David Wilkshire, who operated cranes and helped to dredge it when sand was mined there commercially around 1910. *Courtesy of the Cape May County Historical Society.*

Nudes and Prudes

For perhaps the past forty years, Higbees Beach has been well known, not as the earliest boat-landing site, not for its First World War proving grounds, not as the home of Davy's Lake, but for the scores of naked men, women and children who claimed this secluded stretch of bathing beach as a nudist paradise. The location is well concealed – a two-mile stretch of virgin strand, bordered by a wilderness of dunes and rough brush, and accessible only from Sunset Boulevard and from New England Road.

No one seems to know when naturists first used Higbees Beach, but it is likely that the practice developed sometime after the First World War. In the sixties and seventies, Higbees' popularity grew, and scores of bathers unofficially declared it a clothes-optional beach. Nudist families, couples, singles, and gays mixed without incident on the half mile section they had claimed, while clothed sightseers and voyeurs occasionally strolled by hoping to get a good look at some naked bodies.

The public's interest in nudists may be curiosity, lust, or indignation. Besides the occasional passersby, the bathers were to be found in the binoculars of countless seafarers and fishermen whose powerboats assembled close to the shore for a really good look. Even the giant ferryboats listed to starboard or port as their passengers gathered at the rail to see what they could see on Higbees Beach as they were entering or leaving the nearby ferry terminal.

Higbees Beach wasn't always South Jersey's most famous destination for naturists. That distinction belonged to Sunshine Park on the Great Egg Harbor River near the town of Mays Landing in nearby Atlantic County. Established in 1935 by an unlikely visionary, Ilsley Boone, a Baptist minister, it grew into a successful campsite that hosted thousands of visitors each year. Boone had hoped to create a utopian community where social nudism would eliminate class distinctions based on wealth or position. That goal was never reached, but the park became one of the early and best-known naturist resorts in the country.

The camp's bathing beach and diving pier were in a private cove on the river, partially hidden from the constant parade of boats motoring to or from the Great Egg Harbor bay. Most of the passing boats would slow almost to a halt as they passed the camp site, and an astonishing number seemed to develop engine trouble in order to get a good look at the nudists, often with the aid of binoculars. The bathers ignored them.

The camp had established strict rules to guard against promiscuous behavior – excluding single male adults, forbidding drinking, dancing or any questionable physical contact in public. By the 1970s the park's heavy attendance and its crude sewer systems were polluting the river waters, and the state forced it to close down.

The shut down of Sunshine Park probably brought more nudists to Higbees Beach, but it was the new fame generated with the advent of the Internet that accounted for the largest increase in attendance. Suddenly people were coming from far and wide and virtuous residents of Lower Township decided it was time to rid their area of this abominable nuisance.

Under pressure from a few residents who claimed that there were incidents of lewd behavior going on there, the Lower Township commissioners passed an ordinance in 1986 that banned nude sunbathing. A group of naturists successfully challenged the legislation the following year, claiming that the township lacked jurisdiction since Higbees Beach had been a state park since 1978 and the park's regulations had no prohibition against nude bathing or sunbathing.

The court agreed and issued an injunction prohibiting township police from disturbing the naturists, and the sunbathers returned. The township never gave up and the arbiters of public morals were finally able to induce Senator Cafiero to push through state legislation in 1999 allowing municipalities to enforce anti-nudity laws on state-owned property.

That same year a woman naturist publicly flaunted the new law by going topless on the beach in order to bring a test case before the Appeals Court. The court decided against her, but it is likely that the naturist organizations will carry the battle all the way to the U.S. Supreme Court.

At this point in time Higbees Beach is fully clothed – the nudes have lost this battle, and the prudes have won. However, this war may not yet be over.

Even the giant ferryboats listed to starboard or port as their passengers gathered at the rail to see what they could see on Higbees Beach.

Chapter 17
Sunset Beach

The Steamship Landing

A century has passed since a trip to what we now call Sunset Beach meant a trip to the site of the Steamboat Landing, known much earlier as Cape May Landing. Steamship travel to Cape May had been common throughout the nineteenth century. A member of Alexander Whilldin's clan, a Captain Wilmon Whilldin, has been credited as the pioneer in steamboat travel from Philadelphia.

An article in a 1954 issue of *The Cape May Star and Wave* had this to say:

> It was as early as 1822 that Captain Whilldin, one of the most enterprising men of his time, started the first steam packet line to Cape Island…. The landing of passengers and freight at first was done by boats through the surf on the bayshore…. It was not until 1830 that a wharf facilitated the traffic, and for this accommodation a charge of ten cents was made upon each passenger, that the cost of building might be gotten back.

The early steamboat landing was an ever-changing and untrustworthy wooden pier according to a visitor's letter in 1846, quoted in Robert Alexander's *Ho! For Cape Island.*

> After a most pleasant ride down the river on the steamboat Ohio … we arrived at Cape May Landing …The approach to the landing is beautiful…while the landing itself, delicate and fairy-like as it looks from the boat when you first make it out, resolves itself into a long wharf supported by tall, slender poles of so fragile an ar-

rangement as to make communication with land by it a thing by no means as safe as one's dislike of lofty tumbling would desire.

A number of steamboats, all iron side-wheelers, saw service to the Cape, from Whilldin's *Delaware* to the *Richard Stockton*, the *Ohio* and finally the celebrated *Palace Steamer Republic*, which had a quarter-century run from 1878 to 1903.

Cape May Landing—1859

(c.1859) The early steamboat landing at Higbees Beach was an ever-changing and untrustworthy wooden pier supported by tall slender poles according to a visitor's letter written in 1846. *Courtesy of the Borough of Cape May Point.*

(c.1902) A number of steamboats, all iron side-wheelers, saw service to the Cape from Whilldin's *Delaware* to the *Richard Stockton*, the *Ohio* and finally the celebrated *Palace Steamer Republic*, which had a quarter-century run from 1878 to 1903. *Courtesy of the Cape May County Historical Society.*

The Delaware Bay House

Nothing much had been built at the beach except the steamboat pier until 1878 when the owners of the *Republic* built the Delaware Bay House as an excursion house to accommodate the thousands of passengers who were arriving at the landing. They bought up 700 feet of shorefront stretching southward from the pier toward Sea Grove.

The two-story hotel building had a modest footprint of only forty by sixty feet, but its gigantic two-story veranda was an impressive sight, running 200 feet along the beachfront and connecting with a second building that housed three bowling alleys on the ground floor and billiards tables on the floor above.

Scarcely fifty feet away was the station platform for the *Delaware Bay and Cape May Railroad*. Whether visitors arrived by steamboat or steam-train, the Delaware Bay House (sometimes referred to as the Steamboat Excursion House) stood ready to cater to their whims.

As the hotel prospered, bathhouses and amusements were added to occupy the time of those waiting for ship or shore transportation. A nearby toboggan slide had been a popular thrill ride until a fateful day in the summer of 1893, when two of the cars, loaded with laughing vacationers from a group of Christian Endeavor Societies, suddenly collided in a crash that sent one home unconscious and injured half a dozen others. The group had just arrived on the *Republic* and fortunately several doctors on board were able to render first aid to the accident victims.

The hotel complex probably closed after the steamship *Republic* made its final run in 1903. For years it had been the place to go for seafood, especially the clams and oysters harvested from the Delaware Bay. In 1895 the *Star of the Cape* reported on a clambake where 10,000 clams were to be roasted – that's a lot of clams! The last reported activity was a dance organized for a hundred guests from Cape May Point.

Around 1900, Franklin Rutherford had been in charge of assembling and dismantling the steamboat wharf each spring and fall and it is likely that he was also responsible for the demolition of the Delaware Bay House, because he used some of its timber to build a barn on his farm. When the barn burnt down around 1902, it was rebuilt with additional material he had removed from the old excursion hotel. This second barn now stands off Seagrove Avenue next to the house of his grandson, David Rutherford.

(c.1900) Whether visitors arrived by steamboat or steam-train, the Delaware Bay House (sometimes referred to the Steamboat Excursion House) stood ready to cater to their whims. Scarcely fifty feet away was the station platform for the *Delaware Bay and Cape May Railroad. Courtesy of H. Gerald MacDonald.*

COMFORT COTTAGE,
STEAMBOAT LANDING,
CAPE MAY, N. J.,
C. HAGGERTY, Proprietor.

(c.1890) The Delaware Bay House was not the only place for lodging when visitors arrived at the steamboat landing. Nearby was the much smaller Comfort Cottage, run by a Mr. Haggerty. *Courtesy of the Cape May County Historical Society.*

The Cape May Sand Company

The mining of beach sand is seldom if ever seen along the Jersey coast, but for many years there was such an odd industry at Sunset Beach. The Cape May Sand Company built a plant there in 1905 to take advantage of the plentiful sand, cheap land and nearby tracks of the *Delaware Bay, Cape May, and Sewell's Point Railroad.*

Beach and dune sand have extensive industrial uses, and such mining operations have now shifted from the sea coast to the shores of some of the Great Lakes and to the desert lands of the far west. Sand deposits rich in quartz are preferred for glass manufacture, and many sands are needed by foundries to make molds and cores.

Set back a few hundred yards from Sunset Boulevard, the curious contours of the six-story washhouse made a strange sight indeed. By the nineteen thirties the wind driven salt air had so blackened and warped and twisted its clapboard cladding that one wondered what was holding the giant pile together. Nearby, puffs and plumes of white smoke rose up from the engines of the several steam shovels as they plundered sand from beach and dunes.

The total impression was of an otherworldly activity – something too strange to be found on the pristine shores of the bay and so close to Cape May Point. It had the primitive look of a nineteenth century industry and indeed the operations were simple enough.

The steam shovels would scoop up sizable bucket-loads of sand from just past the waters edge and drop them, dripping wet, into small dump cars lined up along the tracks. From there the sand went to a sorting machine where it was screened into its various sizes and finally to the mill building to be washed clean before being reloaded onto rail cars for shipment to Cape May, Philadelphia, and other final destinations.

Some of the sand was mined from the dunes and other sand deposits far back from the beach. Davy's Lake (far north of the Sand Plant and well back from the beach) is one of these abandoned sand washes that the plant excavated over the years.

The rail line along the beachfront from Cape May Point through South Cape May (now called South Cape May Meadows) to Cape May City was a perfect transport route for the sand – but there was one big problem. Every violent fall and winter storm brought wave after wave crashing across the tracks, often undermining their foundations and halting travel until repairs could be made.

Desperately seeking an alternative route, the Sand Company approached the *Atlantic City Railroad* to build a two-and-a-half-mile track inland though Lower Township to Cape May, suggesting that the proposed ferry connection between Sunset Beach and Lewes, Delaware would justify the investment. The ferry never happened but the railroad was stuck with this losing investment until 1942, when the sand plant had closed and a new magnesite plant was about to open.

(c.1920) At the Cape May Sand Plant, puffs and plumes of white smoke rose up from the engines of the several steam shovels as they plundered sand from beach and dunes. *Courtesy of H. Gerald MacDonald.*

(c.1920) The sand went to a sorting machine where it was screened into its various sizes and finally to the mill building to be washed clean before being reloaded onto rail cars for shipment to Cape May, Philadelphia, and other final destinations. *Courtesy of H. Gerald MacDonald.*

(c.1920) Set back a few hundred yards from Sunset Boulevard, the curious contours of the six-story washhouse made a strange sight indeed. By the nineteen thirties the wind driven salt air had so blackened and warped and twisted its clapboard cladding that one wondered what was holding the giant pile together. *Courtesy of H. Gerald MacDonald.*

The Northwest Magnesite Company

Any resident or visitor to Cape May Point prior to the 1980s remembers (and not fondly) the magnesite plant at Sunset Beach. For forty years it was an important employer in lower Cape May County and a hated intrusion into the idyllic life of Cape May Point.

Its smoke stacks spewed out billowing clouds of white soot, and much too often southerly winds carried the heavy dust across the Point. It covered porches, cars, and gardens with a gray film so thick it had to be swept off. Some say it decimated the native oaks of Cape May Point, although a plant disease may have caused that terrible misfortune.

Before the war, magnesite for firebrick had been imported from Austria, the USSR, Turkey and Greece. With the wartime naval blockades these shipments stopped. Since the domestic U.S. output was insufficient to satisfy the steel industries' needs, the Office of War Production Management in August 1941 urged the Northwest Magnesite Company, subsidiary of the Harbison-Walker Refractories Company of Pittsburgh, "in the interest of national defense, establish facilities for the manufacture of 60,000 to 70,000 tons of dead-burned magnesite for brick making purposes at a plant to be situated on the New Jersey Coast. This production could, we understand, best be obtained from a combination of sea water and dolomite, and the output will be needed by April 1942."

World War II brought this unwelcome industry to the Point. The war created an extraordinary demand for the production of steel for the military. As the industry geared up for maximum output, a corresponding increase in the production of firebrick for steel production was essential.

With the government's assistance, a 350-acre site in Lower Township immediately adjacent to Cape May Point was quickly selected. The land straddled Sunset Boulevard and bordered the bay at Sunset Beach. Construction of the plant facilities was fast tracked and before the end of 1942 they were producing the synthetic magnesite.

This location provided sufficient ground area for plant construction, an unlimited supply of seawater, and access by rail and highway for the shipment of raw materials and finished product. It also offered reasonable proximity to the Catanach Quarry in Paoli, Pennsylvania, where the raw material, a dolomitic limestone, was mined, sized and shipped to Cape May Point.

The manufacturing process was not complex. The Pennsylvania limestone was crushed and reduced at the quarry to stone aggregate small enough to pass through 1-1/4 inch and 3/8 inch screens. Transported largely by rail to Cape May Point, it was then calcinated by lightly burning in kilns at 1850 degrees F. Meanwhile, enormous quantities of sea water (thirty-two million gallons per day) were pumped into large concrete storage tanks from a pipeline extending 1,500 feet into Delaware Bay.

After thorough cleaning and softening, the salt water was adequately purified to mix with the limestone. The seawater and calcinated limestone were then mixed in reactors to precipitate out the magnesia. While in slurry form, it was transferred to the filtration units inside the main plant, and fed into a rotary kiln for dead-burning at 3,250 degrees. This produced a high-density dolomite granule almost identical in chemical composition and structure to magnesite. This material was shipped to various fabricating plants where the final firebrick production took place.

The plant was in continuous operation twenty-four hours a day and seven days a week. Its production reached a maximum capacity of 108,000 tons. Following the war, the demand tapered off and in later years production dropped to 48,000 tons. The plant was operating in long shifts, producing for five months and then shutting down for another five months to avoid over production. More than forty years later, on July 31, 1983 the plant was finally closed down for good. No one wept in Cape May Point.

(c.1945) Any resident or visitor to Cape May Point prior to the 1980s remembers (and not fondly) the magnesite plant at Sunset Beach. Its smoke stacks spewed out billowing clouds of white soot, and much too often southerly winds carried the heavy dust across the Point. It covered porches, cars, and gardens with a gray film so thick it had to be swept off. *Courtesy of H. Gerald MacDonald.*

The Concrete Ship

Curiosities always draw crowds. Since 1926, crowds of Cape May County vacationers have come to Sunset Beach to stare at the broken hulk of the *Atlantus*, lying just a few hundred yards off shore. It was an odd thing indeed, this crippled concrete behemoth that looked like no other ship anyone had ever seen. How could a boat made of concrete ever float? How did it end up here of all places, and why?

For years after its arrival tourists went away baffled but satisfied that they had actually seen this strange derelict. The mystery of its origins has faded as countless articles and a few books have told its fascinating story.

After two years spent shipping a cargo of coal, the *Atlantus* found herself in the James River near Norfolk, Virginia, available for salvage. In 1926, a rescuer came in the form of Jesse Rosenfeld, who intended to use her hull as part of his planned ferry service from Cape May Point to Lewes, Delaware.

In her fact-filled recent book, *"Atlantus" and the History of Concrete Ships*, Connie Considene Kelly writes:

> After some repairs were completed, a tugboat took the *Atlantus* to Cape May Point. The plan was to have a channel dug into the shoreline. The *Atlantus* would be eased into the hallow, filled with sand, and put on an even keel.
>
> "Fifty feet of stern, facing seaward would be cut off and a hinged-type door would be mounted aft to form a ramp to join the moorings to the ferries. The ship's superstructure would be raised level with the main deck, while a hundred feet of causeway would run from the *Atlantus* to the parking lot.

It didn't work out that way. In his excellent history, *Cape May County, New Jersey*, Jeffrey M. Dorwart tells us:

Jesse Rosenfeld's project ran into trouble. The *Atlantus* slipped its mooring in a high wind and plowed bow first into the sand. Floated free, the hulk dragged its anchor and became fouled in the discharge pipe of the Cape May City sewer. The huge concrete mass could not be stirred further from its resting place...Rosenfeld failed to obtain support from either the New Jersey or Delaware legislatures, and his company fell apart.

A few of the myths about the *Atlantus* can be dismissed. It wasn't built as a troop ship during the First World War, although she did make several trips to France to return American troops after the war. In addition to the four concrete cargo vessels like the *Atlantus*, that are usually reported to have been commissioned at that time, another eight were launched as oil tankers.

The goal of the United States Shipping Board was to increase our merchant fleet by building concrete-hull ships instead of the conventional metal-hull because of the steel shortage created by the war. Between 1918 and 1921, all twelve had been turned out at various shipyards around the country.

Their sea-worthiness seems questionable. Like the *Atlantus*, several ran aground, four were damaged in collisions with another ship or with some fixed barrier, two suffered crippling damage in heavy storms, and one never even sailed. A few years after the first was launched, more steel became available for conventional ship design. Their useful life was amazingly short. Only three sailed longer than one year. Concrete ships could no longer compete.

Their final disposition was pitiful. Like the *Atlantus*, three ended stranded in shallow water, two sank in deep water, two were floated offshore as oil storage tanks, and another two became breakwaters.

Over the years, the light steel superstructure of the *Atlantus's* deck, railings and funnels has rusted away and the shifting sands have severed, then gradually swallowed up all but a morsel of the concrete hull. Today, it resembles a large rock outcrop and its total disappearance is well underway.

(c.1926) For years crowds of Cape May County vacationers have come to Sunset Beach to stare at the *Atlantus*, lying just a few hundred yards off shore. In 1926, when it was first towed here to serve as a landing for a proposed ferry to Delaware, this concrete behemoth looked like no other ship anyone had ever seen. *Courtesy of the Borough of Cape May Point.*

(c.1958) Over the years, the light steel superstructure of the *Atlantus's* deck, railings and funnels has rusted away and the shifting sands have severed, then gradually swallowed up much of the concrete hull. The sign painted on the bow advertises an agency selling boat insurance The Delaware bay ice flows can be seen as far as the horizon. *Courtesy of the Cape May County Historical Society.*

(c.1990s) Several decades after Jesse Rosenfeld's ferry project failed in 1926, The Delaware River and Bay Authority succeeded in establishing the much needed ferry connection between New Jersey and Delaware, with a modern terminal in Lower Township, across the canal from Higbees Beach. *Courtesy of the Cape May Star and Wave.*

Cape May Diamonds

Since the early 1800s, visitors to the New Jersey cape have been searching for Cape May Diamonds. These whitish quartz pebbles are seldom large, with few bigger than a lima bean or a cherry. Occasionally, however, a monster size shows up, and not necessarily at Sunset Beach, although that is a famous place for this collecting pastime.

John Pontiere, an amateur gemologist and outstanding collector of Cape May Diamonds, found one such in a gravel pit near Marmora, New Jersey. After the piece was cut in the conventional diamond style, it weighed in at 1,800 carats – almost the size of a baseball. He had in his extensive collection an even larger one, found just outside Ocean City, near Somers Point, which in its uncut state weighed over 2,400 carats! Because Sunset Beach had been the site of the steamboat landing and later the rail terminal, thousands of their riders, while waiting for the next departure, eagerly combed the beach in search of these wondrous stones.

Sunset Beach soon earned a reputation as the best spot (many think the *only* spot) in New Jersey to find these strange crystals. When, in 1925, the old gravel Cape Island Turnpike was paved in concrete in anticipation of the planned ferry line to Delaware, access by automobile brought more and more tourists to this Delaware Bay beach. The other residue of the proposed ferry service, the ill-fated concrete ship, not only attracted numerous additional sightseers, it probably deflected more of the stones onto Sunset Beach.

Cape May Diamonds probably started their trip to the Jersey shore torn from veins of quartz in the bedrock along the upper Delaware River, countless centuries ago. Known in the jewelry trade as white sapphires, these stones are almost indistinguishable from real diamonds, and are famous worldwide for their brilliance and beauty. For many years local stores have had the stones cut and polished and mounted into costume jewelry.

(c.1950s) Since the early 1800s visitors to the New Jersey cape have been searching for Cape May Diamonds. Sunset Beach has become a famous place for this collecting pastime.
Courtesy of Robert W. Elwell, Sr.

(c.1926) Cape Avenue became a dependable concrete highway in 1926, when it was intended to connect the planned ferry terminal at Sunset Beach with Cape May City. A colorful parade marked the opening ceremonies.
Courtesy of the Borough of Cape May Point.

God Bless America

Every evening at dusk, Kate Smith's stirring rendition of "God Bless America" resonates across the strand at Sunset Beach, signaling the start of the flag lowering ceremony that has been a popular tradition there for nearly half a century.

Hundreds stand in respectful attention as the National Anthem follows, then all heads bow as a bugle sounds Taps, and Marvin Hume, proprietor of the Sunset Beach Shops, slowly lowers the flag. Often assisted by a visiting young child, whom he introduces by name and home address to the crowd, he then patiently instructs his helper in the proper way to fold the flag for the night. Youthful volunteers for this honor are plentiful, so they must sign up weeks in advance.

Preston Shadbolt, the previous owner of Sunset Beach, started the flag ceremony after he acquired the property from the estate of Frank Hughes in 1955. Hume added the Anthem and Taps. He also introduced the large casket flags that have been donated by veterans' families.

The crowds come here all year, to check out the concrete ship, to collect Cape May Diamonds, to watch the spectacular sunsets over the Delaware Bay, and always to shop endlessly for souvenirs and gifts. On summer evenings the parking lots are packed full and latecomers are forced to line both sides of Sunset Boulevard almost to Cape May Point's entrance.

These family businesses started late in the nineteen twenties when a young and enterprising Frank Hughes set up a boat livery business along the beach in front of the derelict Cape May Sand Plant. Dozens of clinker-built rowboats lined the shore, available for rent by the hour or by the day. The boats came with oars but you had to supply your own outboard motor. Business was good and so was the fishing.

By noon the bay was alive with fishermen in Hughes's boats, often clustered around the sunken ship like chicks to a hen. At the end of the day, with suppertime approaching, Hughes and a few helpers pulled each beached craft from the water's edge to high ground using a cable rigged through a series of pulleys and powered by an old Ford engine bolted to a concrete foundation. The boats slithered up the sand one by one as onlookers marveled at the speed and efficiency of the operation.

Frank's wife Leah ran the little restaurant that offered family fare at modest prices. Not long after Hughes died in 1954, his widow tired of running the restaurant and the new owner, Preston Shadbolt, turned it into a small gift shop selling shells, Cape May Diamonds and other exotic minerals.

The present owner, Marvin Hume, acquired clear title to the Sunset Beach property from the State of New Jersey, when the state's Green Acres program bought up the holdings of the Northwest Magnesite Company in the mid-1990s, with the stipulation that he would continue to operate his shops and grille as a small family business.

Sunset Beach has had many lives and catered to many interests. Starting in the nineteenth century, it served an important role as the Steamboat Landing until 1903. From 1875 until 1916, it was a terminal for the railroad and electric trolley lines. After 1878, it provided hotel accommodations and amusements at the Delaware Bay House adjoining the terminal.

The twentieth century brought in five industrial or commercial enterprises. At the beginning of the twentieth century, the Cape May Sand Plant moved in, and lasted until the Northwest Magnesite Company was built on its site at the start of World War II. In the 1930s, Frank Hughes started his boat livery business and his wife operated a small family-style restaurant nearby. The ferry would have dwarfed the other commercial businesses had it not been stillborn in 1926, leaving behind the famous concrete ship as a reminder of its grandiose plan. The Hughes restaurant, taken over by Preston Shadbolt in 1955, was not the last commercial venture – that distinction belongs to his successor, Marvin Hume, who turned a sleepy dead end into a thriving set of stores and an outdoor grille that promises to be around for a very long time.

(c.1940s) Leah Hughes ran the little restaurant at Sunset Beach that offered family fare at modest prices. Not long after her husband Frank died in 1954, she tired of running the restaurant and the new owner, Preston Shadbolt, turned it into a small gift shop selling shells, Cape May Diamonds, and other exotic minerals. *Courtesy of the Cape May County Historical Society.*

Chapter 18
South Cape May

Mark Devine

More than a century before the development frenzy that gripped so many coastal regions worldwide, Mark Devine made his first investment in beachfront property. The year was 1840 and he picked up eighty-nine acres at a sheriff sale. The land was east of Stites Beach (later Sea Grove) going toward Cape Island (later Cape May City). It would be another thirty-five years before the adjoining Stites Beach became Sea Grove.

Over the next forty years, Devine assembled, piece by piece, a tract of 225 acres stretching a mile and a quarter along the beachfront from Patterson Avenue in Cape May almost to Cape May Point. The land seemed marginal, half meadow and half tidal marsh with shallow ponds and little tributaries of Cape Island Creek meandering through the grassland. It was, however, a financially successful venture – a five hundred percent gain on investment when Devine sold his entire holdings to a development group, The Cape May City Land Company, in 1882. It made possible the Borough of South Cape May.

(c.1910) The trolley line that ran along the beachfront between Cape May Point and Cape May City provided the residents of South Cape May convenient transportation, but constant storms assaulted the rail line. *Courtesy of H. Gerald MacDonald.*

Mr. Reger's Jumbo

Land development is a high-risk business often dominated by entrepreneurs with a grand vision – and occasionally with far-out ideas. Theodore M. Reger seems to fit that image. His vision was the creation of the Mount Vernon tract that became South Cape May. His big idea was *Jumbo*, the larger than life size tin elephant, originally named *Light of Asia*.

Between 1882 and 1887 he formed three corporations to develop the Devine property, The Cape May City Land Company, The Neptune Land Company, and the Mount Vernon Land Company of Cape May. Reger was a key investor in all three companies. His Neptune Land Company built the elephant 300 feet back from Beach Avenue and the tracks of the *Delaware Bay, Cape May, and Sewells Point Railroad* on empty meadowland midway between Cape May Point and Cape May City. They started construction in the spring of 1884, and the giant beast was open for business the following season.

Was the construction of a forty-foot high elephant in the middle of nowhere a far-out idea? Perhaps, but not an original one. The inventor of tin elephants was a twenty-five-year old engineer named James B. Lafferty. He built *Lucy*, the first of these monstrous oddities in 1882 as a publicity device to grab the attention of press and public for his proposed land development south of Atlantic City.

With the aid of a lawyer and the U.S. Patent Office, Lafferty ensured that any copycats would be paying him a license fee. So two years later, Reger was starting to create South Cape May in the same fashion that Lafferty was creating what has become present day Margate – with an oversize pachyderm as the star attraction. He engaged Philadelphia architect N. H. Culver to design the fantastic creature. It would be a multi-purpose structure, part real estate landmark, part tourist bazaar, and part observation tower.

The name he gave it, *Light of Asia*, belonged to a real circus elephant supposedly imported from Siam in 1884. That moniker never caught on. The public preferred to call him *Jumbo*, after the popular circus elephant P.T. Barnum had brought in from Africa several years earlier. The word *Jumbo* had come to mean big, so it was an apt name for this strange new edifice.

Framed pretty much like a house with wood studs and joists, covered with wood lath and plaster, its belly housed a lofty room about eighteen feet wide and thirty feet long. According to an early advertisement, this was to be leased to vendors selling "soda water, fancy articles, advertising…ice cream, candies and dairy."

Like *Lucy*, the entrance was through the hind legs, then up several winding stairs to the sales hall. After having paid ten cents for admission, few would pass up the privilege of climbing another flight to the observation deck of the howdah atop the elephant's back. The view could hardly rival the one from the nearby lighthouse, but the environment was more exotic. For those less athletically inclined, there were refreshments available from stands in the two front legs and there was seating on the spacious wooden deck upon which *Jumbo* stood.

It takes a lot of visitors at ten cents each and the sale of lots of merchandise to cover a construction cost of $18,000. Since the only viable access was from a few rail cars passing by three times an hour during the summer season, it's understandable that *Jumbo* was a losing venture. Nevertheless, It did bring attention to the proposed land development, when in 1887 the words "New Mount Vernon" were painted across its side. *Jumbo's* lifespan was a mere sixteen years, much of it in neglect. In time vagrants replaced curious tourists, and by 1900 it faced a demolition crew.

(c.1895) Land development is a high-risk business often dominated by entrepreneurs with a grand vision – and occasionally with far-out ideas. Theodore M. Reger's big idea was *Jumbo*, the larger than life size tin elephant, originally named "Light of Asia" that stood in the meadows marking the place where South Cape May was starting to develop. *Courtesy of Marie G. Richards.*

(c.1852) A new hotel was under construction in 1852 that was meant to ensure Cape May's reputation as New Jersey's premier seaside city. The Mount Vernon Hotel was to be the largest resort hotel in the world; it's four stories to accommodate 2300 guests; its dining salon to seat 3000! *Courtesy of the Author.*

New Mount Vernon

In 1852, a new hotel was under construction that was meant to ensure Cape May's reputation as New Jersey's premier seaside city. The Mount Vernon Hotel was to be the largest resort hotel in the world; it's four stories to accommodate 2,300 guests; its dining salon to seat 3,000!

It was nearing completion on its sixteen-acre beachfront site at the edge of town, just west of Broadway, when, in early September 1856, a vicious fire consumed it within a few hours. It had attracted enormous attention in its short life, and the name Mount Vernon was not soon forgotten.

Hence the name, New Mount Vernon, which Theodore Reger and his partners adopted for the extensive development they were about to start in 1887. N.C. Price, their civil engineer, had laid out fourteen blocks along the beachfront with a total of sixty-nine blocks stretching back to what is now Sunset Boulevard in a relentless gridiron pattern. Almost 2500 lots were planned, most with a narrow thirty-foot frontage and a depth of one hundred feet. *Jumbo* was given a place of honor in the center of the beach block between 15th and 16th Avenues.

By the end of the summer of 1888 the new resort town was showing some progress. At the eastern end, 8th Avenue had been graded from Beach Avenue to the turnpike, and Beach Avenue itself graded all the way to Cape May Point. Eight cottages, all beachfront, were under construction or completed. A seawall and boardwalk were being built along Beach Avenue.

A new and decidedly more modest Mount Vernon Hotel went up on Beach Avenue right in front of *Jumbo* and the next block east offered a two-story pavilion and public bathhouses. The cottages were lined up like soldiers, one in the middle of each beachfront block, with several more built in the next block back. That was the extent of the development at the turn of the century. Even so, the tiny community, which had been part of Lower Township, incorporated as the borough of South Cape May in 1894.

By 1910, Beach Avenue had become *beach* and most of the houses and the hotel had been moved back a block so that they were still oceanfront, but now faced the railroad tracks along Mount Vernon Avenue. A three-story boarding house had opened for business. Further construction was slow in happening and the greater part of the land remained open meadow until 1925.

At that time, the splendid new Sunset Boulevard replaced the old gravel Cape Island Turnpike, under the expectation that the long awaited ferry to Delaware would soon have its terminal at Sunset Beach. Other developers bought up the unimproved land on the south side of the new boulevard, filled and graded it, and connected several of the previously planned avenues to Sunset Boulevard. A small village of pseudo-Spanish Villas sprung up, with clay tile roofs and exterior walls of lath and plaster – not the kind of construction to stand up against the hurricane winds and flood tides that were soon to come along.

(c.1900) The beachfront residence of John E. Lonabaugh, president of the Mount Vernon Land Company of Cape May, which developed South Cape May. *Courtesy of the Cape May County Historical Society.*

(c.1900) Peter Day's residence in the New Mount Vernon development, which ran fourteen blocks along the beachfront with a total of sixty-nine blocks stretching back to what is now Sunset Boulevard in a relentless gridiron pattern. *Courtesy of the Cape May County Historical Society.*

(c.1890s) The sea wall and beach pavilion were the first things to go up in the new development which became South Cape May. *Courtesy of the Cape May County Historical Society.*

(c.1895) By the end of the summer of 1888 the new resort town was showing some progress. Eight cottages, all beachfront, were under construction or completed. A seawall and boardwalk were being built along Beach Avenue. *Courtesy of the Cape May County Historical Society.*

The End of a Dream

There are reported to have been as many as fifty cottages in South Cape May at one time. Most had occupied two thirty-foot lots, so less than five percent of the parcels had been built on at any one time. This is not a prescription for a successful real estate development.

Beach erosion and storm damage had plagued the community from its earliest days. When the 1936 nor'easter brought in gale force winds of eighty mph, South Cape May was helpless. The beachfront homes of the mayor and his neighbor toppled into the sea shortly after the Coast Guard had rescued the occupants. Boats picked up several dozen residents from the flooded town.

The great Atlantic hurricane of 1944 brought floodwaters surging through the weakened community. At the height of the storm even Sunset Boulevard was impassable, and the water had inundated properties for four blocks on the other side of the boulevard. Houses not destroyed were so badly damaged that many were abandoned. By 1945, so few taxable properties were left that the borough could not collect enough revenue to meet its obligations, and, faced with bankruptcy, South Cape May decided to relinquish its status as an independent borough and become once again part of Lower Township.

The final blow came six years later on a Saturday morning in November. A fierce east wind drove abnormal tides caused by Friday's full moon into a tidal wave of such force that the floodwaters reached all the way to 6th Avenue in West Cape May! Almost everything still standing in the South Cape May meadows was swept away by the storm tide and hurricane force winds that had reached a peak of eighty-eight mph. The town was gone at last, and Sunset Boulevard was filled waist-deep with its wreckage.

(c.1948) By 1945 so few taxable properties were left that the borough could not collect enough revenue to meet its obligations, and, faced with bankruptcy, South Cape May decided to relinquish its status as an independent borough and become once again part of Lower Township. *Courtesy of the Cape May County Historical Society.*

(c.1944) The great Atlantic hurricane of 1944 brought floodwaters surging through the weakened community. At the height of the storm even Sunset Boulevard was impassable, and the water had inundated properties for four blocks on the other side of the boulevard. *Courtesy of the Cape May County Historical Society.*

(c.1936) Beach erosion and storm damage had plagued the community from its earliest days. When the 1936 nor'easter brought in gale force winds of 80 mph, South Cape May was helpless. *Courtesy of the Cape May County Historical Society.*

149

(c.1945) There are reported to have been as many as fifty cottages in South Cape May at one time. By 1945, few were still livable. Houses not destroyed were so badly damaged that many were abandoned. *Courtesy of the Cape May County Historical Society.*

Enter Mr. Weatherby and Dr. Mossell

An interesting new entrepreneur, J.H. Weatherby, got into the act in 1913, buying the remainder of the Mark Devine estate that had not been laid out for development by the Mount Vernon Land Company of Cape May. It was an even more ambitious undertaking than that of Theadore Reger.

He had his engineer, Ralph L. Goff, lay out sixty-eight city blocks between Cape May Point's Lighthouse Avenue and Reger's 21st Avenue in South Cape May. Most of the plot ran from the Beach north to Sea Grove Avenue, but a small portion to the west extended out to Sunset Boulevard. The street layout here was once again a boring gridiron pattern with 25 by 100-foot lots.

His first purchase from the Cape May City Land Company in 1912, in the name of his wife, Annabelle, was a two hundred-foot deep parcel with a frontage of 300-feet on the north side of Sea Grove Avenue, which included the old Stites family house. The following year he bought the remainder of the tract.

At some point in time he teamed up with a gentleman who would seem to be a most unlikely partner, Dr. Nathan F. Mossell, a brilliant Canadian, and the first negro graduate of the University of Pennsylvania's School of Medicine. Mossell had done graduate work in Ireland at Guy Queen's College, and in England at London's Saint Thomas Hospital. Passing up a position at the prestigious Pennsylvania Hospital, Dr. Mosell, in 1895, established the Frederick Douglass Memorial Hospital and Training School in downtown Philadelphia on the 1500 block of Lombard Street.

By 1912, when Weatherby was prepared to offer his first building lots for sale, Dr. Mossell had become a highly in-fluential member of Philadelphia's black society. His post as Medical Director and Supervisor of the Douglass Hospital, the first medical institution in the North to be staffed entirely by black doctors and nurses, placed him in contact with the local black political and social leadership.

In his promotional materials, Weatherby promised to enlarge and donate his "spacious old Colonial homestead" to the Frederick Douglass Hospital as a Sanitarium on the condition that the nearby lots be purchased by what he called "friends of the institution." The large headlines declared "Every Colored Man and Woman Should Take Advantage of this Offer" and suggested that this development would be "your only opportunity to own a real seashore home at a high-class resort." The text that followed was just as explicit:

The Sanitarium and the lots surrounding it are beautifully located, overlooking the sea, and close enough to the ocean to put on your bathing suit at the house and walk to the beach. This offer of Mr. Weatherby's gives an opportunity for the better class of colored people to obtain a real seashore home at a mere nominal cost.

The special price of $125 per lot, including cement sidewalks and curbs, which Mr. Weatherby has made to our friends is so exceptional that anyone who can at all afford to do so should subscribe without hesitation. So far as we know the lots cannot be duplicated anywhere else on the New Jersey coast at the price.

The colored people have never before had a real location at a summer resort offered to them. There are only about eight hundred lots set aside for these subscriptions and they are being rapidly taken up. Such an opportunity will not come again soon. If you are so situated that you cannot use the lots for a summer home, surely at the price, they are a good investment.

The names and addresses of Dr. Nathan F. Mossell and of J. Howard Weatherby are prominently listed for those desiring further information. The marketing message of the promotion piece seems more like the work of an entrepreneurial pitchman than that of a distinguished physician. In any event the project never went far. One lot was improved as a sample and some lots were sold, but neither roads, nor sidewalks, nor cottages ever appeared on the site. Today, it is once again open meadow, owned partly by the state of New Jersey and partly by the Nature Conservancy.

(c.1926) Margaret Aylsworth, one of the first residents of this final South Cape May development stands in the doorway of her Spanish Villa looking out to the nearby ocean. *Courtesy of the West Cape Café.*

(c.1926) A small village of pseudo-Spanish Villas sprang up, with clay tile roofs and exterior walls of lath and plaster – not the kind of construction to stand up against the hurricane winds and flood tides that were soon to come along. *Courtesy of the West Cape Café.*

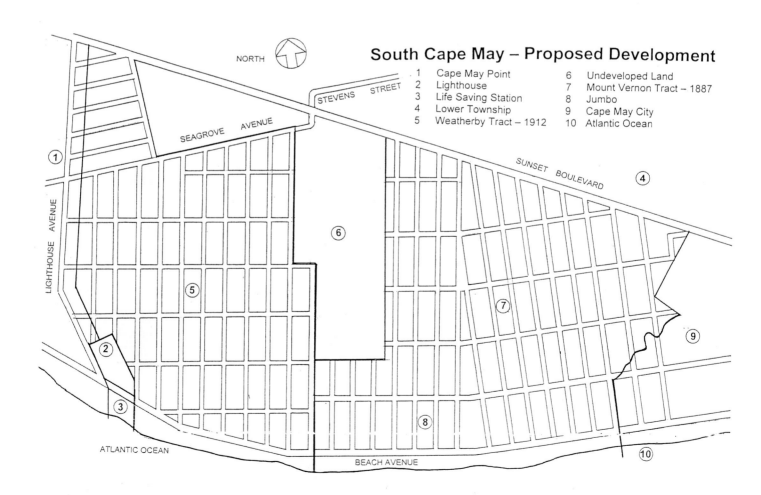

South Cape May – Proposed Development

NORTH

1 Cape May Point	6 Undeveloped Land
2 Lighthouse	7 Mount Vernon Tract – 1887
3 Life Saving Station	8 Jumbo
4 Lower Township	9 Cape May City
5 Weatherby Tract – 1912	10 Atlantic Ocean

STEVENS STREET

SEAGROVE AVENUE

SUNSET BOULEVARD

LIGHTHOUSE AVENUE

ATLANTIC OCEAN

BEACH AVENUE

Chapter 19
The Lighthouse

Early Lights

Few visitors to southern Cape May County pass up the chance to climb the famous spiral "hundred and ninety-nine" steps to the top of Cape May Point's lighthouse. Families who vacation here every season make sure that they make at least one trip back up to check out the astounding views. In 1868, just nine years after the lighthouse was built and seven years before Sea Grove even existed, one visitor had this to say in the *Cape May Ocean Wave*:

> The panorama spread before us repaid, a hundred times, the fatigue of the ascent. The view on all sides was grandly picturesque. To the right, Cape Island (Cape May City) was spread like a table-cloth, and its hotels and cottages glistened in the sunlight like a service of China. The little creek that separates the Island from the mainland, runs through the marshes like a silver thread. Beyond was the great ocean. Its breakers broke below our feet like ripples, and its distant boundary was the horizon. The white Jersey coast lost itself in a sunny mist.
>
> To the left, the pine forests shadowed the level mainland, and great sounds, like monster fishes swam miles inland. Bennett's station and the passing (railroad) cars looked like toys. The steamboat wharf lifted itself out of the water like a spine. Delaware bay could be traced to a threadlike river. Behind, the Henlopen light-house looked like a candle, and the golden Cape on which it stood, like a candle-stick.

Everybody loves lighthouses and the above account shows why. Countless millions of enthusiasts, in every coastal country in the western world, have gotten together to form lighthouse societies, organizations, associations and even foundations. Thousands of web sites and scores of books will tell you everything you could ever want to know about lighthouses. It's no wonder that almost a million curious visitors each year visit this famous shrine in Cape May Point, adjacent to the State Park. It is, after all, the second oldest continuously operating lighthouse in the nation, outclassed only by the light at Sandy Hook in northern New Jersey.

The present structure, erected in 1859, will probably be around a century from now (global warming and erosion permitting), but its predecessors had very short lives. The first tower went up in 1823 and was replaced only twenty-four years later, after the advancing surf started attacking its foundations.

The next one, built in 1847 by local contractors, operated only twelve years, a victim of poor construction, negligible maintenance, faulty equipment, and inexperienced operation. The Lighthouse Service had been under-funded for years and a mounting number of shipwrecks testified to the desperate need for management reorganization of the service and an infusion of capital to build proper lighthouses along the Atlantic Coast from New Jersey to South Carolina.

The first tower went up in 1823 and was replaced only twenty-four years later, after the advancing surf started attacking its foundations.

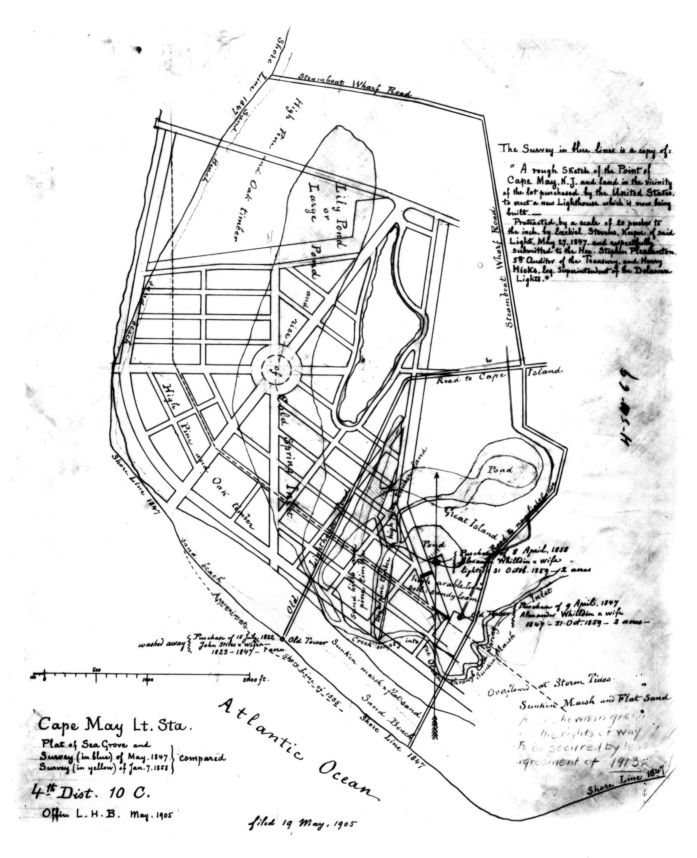

(c.1847 and 1905) This map was prepared by the Army Corps of Engineers in 1905. It shows the changed conditions of the coastline, of Cape May Point, and of the area where the first lighthouse was built in 1847, when Lake Lily, almost four times its present size, was connected by Cape Island Creek to Cold Spring Inlet, the present entrance to Cape May Harbor. *Courtesy of H. Gerald MacDonald.*

The Jersey Cape's New Beacon

With sufficient money, new technology, and improved design, the Army Corps of Engineers was able, in 1859, to manage the construction of the impressive tower that stands here today at twice the height of the one it replaced. The following year, twin dwellings were built for the lighthouse keepers and their families. The tower, the dwellings, a barn, vegetable gardens, and three little privies made up the several-acre complex. Sea Grove didn't open up for another fifteen years, so the only relief from relative isolation was the nearby Life Saving Station.

Its construction of brick, with a thick tapered outside cylinder enclosing a thinner inner cylinder, created a sturdy tower able to withstand any wind force nature might deliver. An elegant spiral stairway of cast iron, winding around a central steel column within the inner brick cylinder, carried the lighthouse keeper to the top. Here at the lantern level he kept the three lamps supplied with the sperm whale oil he carried up each day.

The miracle of this and other lighthouses was their ability to amplify the weak light of a simple oil lamp to such intensity that it could be seen from a distance of twenty-four miles. The secret ingredient that allowed this magic was the complex lens assembly that had been perfected by a French physicist, Augustin Fresnel, in 1822, when he was thirty-four years of age.

This giant lens, a cylinder six-feet around and almost eight-feet tall, enclosed the oil lamp at its center. Its combination of prisms and lenses could focus the lamplight into sixteen horizontal light beams. Driven by a clockwork mechanism, the Fresnel lens slowly turned, completing a revolution once every eight minutes (the current revolution is once every thirty seconds). Mariners, seeing each of the sixteen beams flash by every thirty seconds, could identify their position, knowing the source to be the Cape May Light. Had the beam flashed at intervals of ten seconds they would be seeing the Barnegat Light, at ninety seconds it would be the light at Cape Henlopen across the Delaware Bay.

(c.1909) Lighthouse keeper Captain James H. Eldridge in 1909. With a brass buttoned jacket, vest and trousers plus a shiny black-visored cap with splendid insignia, the keeper was able, starting in 1884, to hold his own in the company of other nautical dress uniforms. *Courtesy of the Cape May County Historical Society.*

(c.1910) The lighthouse tower, the lighthouse keepers' dwellings, a barn, vegetable gardens, and three little privies made up the several-acre complex. Sea Grove didn't open up for another fifteen years, so the only relief from relative isolation was the nearby Life Saving Station. *Courtesy of H. Gerald MacDonald.*

Now and Then

The Cape May Light is still operating, but its service to navigation has been largely supplanted by such advanced technology as GPS (global positioning systems). Since its erection in 1859, there have been significant changes in its technology, operations and ownership. A timeline best tells this story:

1865 – The lighthouse keepers finally get the safety of a metal railing as they climb the winding stair each day with their containers of oil.

1878 – Around this time the original whale oil lamps are replaced with five-wick kerosene lamps because the cost of whale oil has become too expensive.

1884 – Sartorial splendor arrives in the form of smart new uniforms for the keepers. With a brass buttoned jacket, vest, and trousers plus a shiny black-visored cap with splendid insignia, the keeper is now able to hold his own in the company of other nautical dress uniforms.

1896 – Lighthouse Keepers come under the Civil Service System as dedicated and well-trained career officers.

1932 – The commissioners of Cape May Point send a resolution to the Coast Guard registering their opposition to the rumored closing of the Cape May Point lighthouse.

1935 – The kerosene lamp is retired and replaced by an electric lamp. The keepers job is now much simpler, and within a few years, unnecessary.

1939 – The Coast Guard takes over the duties of the Lighthouse Service whose responsibility for all lighthouse matters dates back to 1851.

1941 – The US declares war and German subs prowl the Jersey coast. Lighthouses and coastal towns are under blackout restrictions for the duration.

1946 – The newest (and current) lamp uses a 1,000-watt incandescent bulb focused through an opposing pair of three-foot diameter Fresnel lenses that now make a complete rotation in 30 seconds instead of the previous time of eight minutes, thus changing the flash interval (the *characteristic*) to 15 seconds from the previous thirty seconds. The giant old Fresnel Lens is removed and is now on permanent display at the Cape May County Historical Society Museum, north of Cape May Court House.

1984 – The commissioners of Cape May Point send a resolution to the Coast Guard registering their opposition to the rumored leasing of the Cape May Point Lighthouse to the Mid-Atlantic Center for the Arts (MAC).

1986 – MAC leases the lighthouse from the state DEP Division of Parks and Forestry, who, in turn, lease it from the Coast Guard.

1988 – For the first time in years, people can again climb the lighthouse stairs after MAC completes minimum alterations to ensure visitor safety.

1998 – A series of grants from various agencies over a ten-year struggle provide the capital needed for MAC to complete the restoration work.

MAC has current plans to restore the lighthouse grounds with appropriate landscaping. The restoration has been a success, attested by the hundreds of thousands of visitors each year.

Chapter 20
The Life Saving Station

The Last Remnant

In 1959, after more than a century of heroic service, the last reminder of a vital maritime operation in Cape May Point disappeared in smoke. The old Coast Guard Station, that had been decommissioned and closed up for many years, became the prey of an arsonist.

It was privately owned at this time, having been purchased from the Coast Guard when they moved their operations to the Cape May Station at the harbor. Storms and tides had weakened it and its prognosis was not good.

At 6:45 P.M., the alarm had gone out. In no time, the volunteer firemen were on the scene. As soon as they arrived, Fire Chief Rutherford noted two distinct fires in the garage section – a sure sign of arson. Within a short time his team had managed to contain the blaze and it looked as if they might salvage the old fellow. But then came a setback as the wind picked up and shifted direction. In less than an hour the fire had won, and the last evidence of a colorful era in the Point's history had vanished.

(c.1950s) In 1959, after more than a century of heroic service, the last reminder of a vital maritime operation in Cape May Point disappeared in smoke. The old Coast Guard Station, that had been decommissioned and closed up for many years, became the prey of an arsonist. *Courtesy of Robert W. Elwell, Sr.*

In the Beginning

For a century before Alexander Whilldin set up Sea Grove, its coastline had been witness to (and often cause of) countless marine misfortunes. Its unpredictable array of shoals, and the fierce rip tides, where the Delaware Bay joined the Atlantic Ocean, took their toll on ships and sailors. Up and down the Atlantic coast shipwrecks were so common that they seldom got reported beyond their local district.

During most of this period, the federal government looked the other way and offered no assistance. There was no Coast Guard to respond to emergencies at sea, and the number of lives lost was tragic.

The first small step to provide some assistance occurred in 1848 when Congress tacked on an amendment to the lighthouse bill that provided some funds to construct and equip lifeboat stations on New Jersey's coast from Atlantic County north. The Point's opportunity came the following year when money was made available for six such stations from Little Egg Harbor south to the area that would become Cape May Point.

These stations were little more than small boathouses with only the most basic equipment needed for sea rescue. There was no one responsible for repair or maintenance. All too often the buildings suffered such neglect that after some years repairs were not possible and replacement or abandonment were the only options.

Neglect was not the only culprit – outright theft of lifeboats and gear was commonplace. The 1854 wreck of the *Powhatten* off Long Beach Island cost the lives of more than two hundred, a tragedy severe enough to move Congress to action. The Treasury Department was authorized to appoint station keepers and superintendents and, in effect, the United States Life Saving Service was born.

It wasn't until 1870 that permanent crews became the norm at the stations along the New Jersey coast. Even then, it only amounted to six surf men assigned to every other station, but it was an improvement on the prior arrangement that depended entirely on volunteers. In spite of these limitations, the stations had proven their value in rescuing lives and safeguarding property.

(c.1877) Cape May Point's unpredictable array of shoals, and its fierce rip tides, took their toll on ships and sailors. Up and down the Atlantic coast shipwrecks were so common that they seldom got reported beyond their local district. *Courtesy of Joan Viguers.*

The Cape May Point Station

(c.1870s) The new boathouse was an engaging example of high Victorian architecture, adorned with brackets, fretwork and gingerbread. Cedar shingles crowned the steep gabled roof and heavy timber buttresses pressed against the stick-style façade, ensuring that the sea-front structure could stand up to the fiercest hurricane winds. *Courtesy of the Cape May County Historical Society.*

The first Life Saving Station at the Point was built in 1849. Like many of these early stations, it was nothing more than a boathouse equipped with several surfboats of galvanized iron and metallic life-cars. Lanterns, rockets, shot lines, ropes, and shovels made up the meager supplies.

In 1871, the Treasury Department picked a young lawyer, Sumner Kimball, from its auditing department to head what was then called the Revenue Marine Bureau, that soon became the United States Life Saving Service. The choice was an excellent one. Kimball was not your usual bureaucrat – he was a fine manager and a man with a mission. He immediately instituted reforms and created an effective organization that he oversaw for the next forty-four years.

In 1876, he was able to report the loss of only sixteen lives along the coasts of New York and New Jersey in the five years since he had taken office, whereas in the prior twenty years the number of fatalities had probably exceeded fifteen hundred! Kimball required all stations to file an annual report detailing their rescue missions and the outcome of each. The reports filed by James W. Eldridge from the Cape May Point Station between 1885 and 1915 reveal the life of the crews to be one of boredom, hardship, and frustration; consider his report of an incident on February 10, 1902:

> About 6 P.M. we discovered what was supposed to be a burning vessel E.S.E. from this station. Hauled surfboat over the ice and after working about one hour we reached clear water. We then went off shore about six miles and there she did not seem any nearer than we left the beach. The sea breezed up and the sea become quite rough and we headed for the shore and landed at Cold Spring Station left our boat and walked to our station arriving at 11:30 P.M.

It is probable that the original boathouse was replaced in the early 1870s, when the Life Saving Service developed standardized plans for new station construction. This new boathouse was an engaging example of high Victorian architecture, adorned with brackets, fretwork and gingerbread. Cedar shingles crowned the steep gabled roof and heavy timber buttresses pressed against the stick-style façade, ensuring that the sea-front structure could stand up to the fiercest hurricane winds.

The two-story main building for the crew was also an attractive building, but its simpler lines and absence of gingerbread suggest that it was added around the turn of the century. Erosion was bringing the surf too close to the complex by 1934, and the Coast Guard, which had replaced the Life Saving Service in 1915, moved the main building back thirty feet from the beach and erected a sheet steel bulkhead to protect the property. The boathouse remained untouched.

Only three years later, in 1937, the Treasury Department announced plans to decommission the Point Station, along with others at Wildwood, Avalon, and Sea Isle City. So many closely spaced stations, that had been necessary in the nineteenth century when the surfmen rowed out on rescue missions, were no longer needed, since the introduction of high-speed powerboats could cover a much larger area. After World War II, it was completely shut down and finally sold in the 1950s to an Ernest Romeo, from Port Norris, New Jersey.

For Mr. Romeo, that probably turned out to be an unwise investment. Storm-tides tore away at its foundations, causing severe structural damage. The cost of repairs and bulkhead improvements would have been prohibitive. A fire of unknown origin burned it to the ground in 1959. Arson was suspected, but not proven.

Cedar shingles crowned the steep gabled roof and heavy timber buttresses pressed against the stick-style façade, ensuring that the sea-front structure could stand up to the fiercest hurricane winds.

Chapter 21
The State Park

First The Army

World War II brought forth two strange enterprises to the perimeters of tranquil Cape May Point – the sizable army post (now the lands of the State Park) next to the lighthouse, and the industrial complex of the Northwest Magnesite Company, stretched out along Sunset Boulevard as far as Sunset Beach.

It was late 1941, just after war had been declared, that the Army laid claim to over a hundred acres of meadowland adjacent to the small government owned plots where the lighthouse and Coast Guard Station stood. Back in 1934, its Delaware Coast Artillery Plan had called for gun batteries to be installed at Cape May Point and at Fort Miles across the bay in Delaware, to protect merchant shipping in the event of war.

Now it was time for action, and the Army moved quickly to place four concrete platforms along the beachfront following the designs that had been prepared in the early 1930s. Two stood a few yards east of Saint Mary's convent just behind its bulkhead and the other two flanked the nearby Coast Guard Station. They were the familiar Panama mounts, carrying 155 mm coast artillery guns, capable of anti-aircraft and anti-submarine fire. These would allow crossfire to the heavier armament at Fort Miles as part of the Harbor Defense Plan.

For many years, the most conspicuous remnant of these wartime installations (excluding the magnesite plant) has been the mysterious concrete bunker standing defiantly at the waters edge, a formidable giant resting precariously on spindly wooden pilings.

It didn't start out that way. When first built by the Army Corps of Engineers in 1942, it was underground in the meadows nine hundred feet from the shoreline. The hundreds of wood pilings driven deep into the sandy soil provided a firm foundation for the massive labyrinth of cells and passages that made up what the Army called battery #223. It was indeed a bunker whose six-foot thick reinforced concrete walls and roof could handle almost anything thrown at it.

Inside were rooms for artillery shells and powder, a plotting room, radio room, latrine, and storeroom. Power generators made it self-sufficient and special air-handling equipment could take care of a gas attack. Completely covered with sand and gravel, it would have appeared like one of the many neighboring sand dunes. Flanking each side were massive gun blocks to house the formidable six-inch guns the bunker was built to support.

While few of us have seen anything like this peculiar construction that now dominates a stretch of Cape May Point State Park beach, perhaps fifty similar installations were to be found during the war years, and the layout of Cape May Points bunker is not unique. It became fully operational in 1944, but several years later was decommissioned and the troops moved out.

Fear that a German submarine might send a landing party ashore prompted the army to run constant horseback patrols along New Jersey's beaches. In Cape May Point they took over the lighthouse keeper's barn as a stable. Troops were housed in the Convent of Saint Mary's-by-the-Sea during the war years; the Sisters had agreed to give up their summer retreat house as their part of the war effort.

One casualty of the army's presence was the loss of Mount Vernon Avenue, often affectionately called the 'back road' by Point residents who frequently used it (rather than Sunset Boulevard) to get to Cape May City. It ran right through the Coast Guard property, then along the beach and past what remained of the borough of South Cape May, connecting Lincoln Avenue in Cape May Point with Beach Avenue in Cape May. For security purposes the army had fenced it off limits. Even before the war was over, the formidable 1944 storm had torn up a great deal of the roadway beyond the Army compound. The government held onto the land it had acquired for military use, so the road never again connected the two towns.

For many years, the most conspicuous remnant of these wartime installations has been the mysterious concrete bunker standing defiantly at the water's edge.

(c.1990s) For many years, the most conspicuous remnant of the US Army's wartime installations has been the mysterious concrete bunker standing defiantly at the waters edge, a formidable giant resting precariously on spindly wooden pilings. When first built by the Army Corps of Engineers in 1942, it was underground in the meadows 900 feet from the shoreline. *Courtesy of the Cape May Star and Wave.*

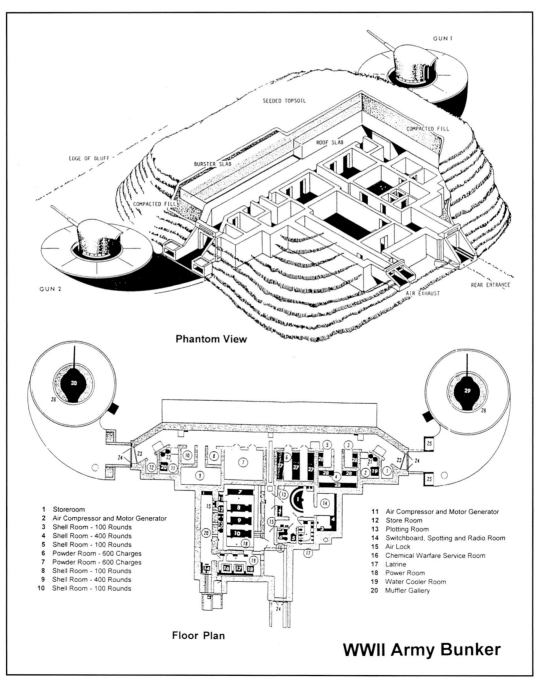

Phantom View

1 Storeroom
2 Air Compressor and Motor Generator
3 Shell Room - 100 Rounds
4 Shell Room - 400 Rounds
5 Shell Room - 100 Rounds
6 Powder Room - 600 Charges
7 Powder Room - 600 Charges
8 Shell Room - 100 Rounds
9 Shell Room - 400 Rounds
10 Shell Room - 100 Rounds

11 Air Compressor and Motor Generator
12 Store Room
13 Plotting Room
14 Switchboard, Spotting and Radio Room
15 Air Lock
16 Chemical Warfare Service Room
17 Latrine
18 Power Room
19 Water Cooler Room
20 Muffler Gallery

Floor Plan

WWII Army Bunker

Then the Navy

Sometime after World War II the Navy established a communications center on the old army site. When the Korean War broke out in 1950, it served as a transmitting station for the Atlantic fleet. Yet four months after an armistice had been signed to end that conflict, the Navy embarked on an expansion program at the site.

In October of 1953, a contingent of Seabees pulled into the receiving station in Cape May harbor on a landing craft loaded with bulldozers, trucks, and construction equipment and headed to the Cape May Point base. In no time they had put up barracks as living quarters, an operations center for radio transmission, and an oceanographic research facility.

These operations were short-lived. Ten years later, concerned about the danger posed to its facilities by continuing erosion, the Navy deactivated the radio transmission station and moved the operation to Lewes, Delaware. In 1964, they turned the 133-acre military site over to the General Services Administration (GSA) for disposal. The GSA in turn sold the property to the State of New Jersey, stipulating that it be used for recreational purposes, not for residential, commercial or industrial development. It was assigned to the Department of Environmental Protection's Division of Parks and Forestry – the seeds for the Cape May Point State Park had been sown.

Finally the Park

With the closeout of all military operations the public was finally able, after over forty years, to gain free access to this beachfront area on the west end of the South Cape May Meadows, at the eastern border of Cape May Point. Dedicated birders were quick to take advantage of the opportunity and the New Jersey Audubon Society began studies of the natural environment and pressed the Park Service to plan suitable improvements. Response from the state was sluggish – it took ten years before a full-time staff was assigned.

The New Jersey Marine Services Consortium, founded in 1969, established its first program there in 1970 after the state provided them with a special use permit. Its mission was to conduct research in the field of environmental and marine science and to offer educational programs to the public. Unfortunately the General Services Administration intervened, claiming its program was not recreational, and closed it down after one year. It moved its operations to Sandy Hook in north Jersey, where its program is now conducted with the support of twenty-nine colleges and universities.

The Cape May Point State Park, as we know it today, really got started in 1974 when an officer-in-charge was appointed together with a full time maintenance worker. Within a few years, they had converted one of the former military buildings to the park office with space for a museum and visitors' center

The old bunker had long been a prime attraction for visitors, and when the park service in 1977 provided ramp access from the beach and safety fencing around the roof, it became an immensely popular elevated platform for sightseeing and fishing. The next two decades brought the waters edge in so far that this diversion had to be abandoned.

Annual budgets had always been tight, so the park improvements developed slowly. Assisted by a group from the Youth Conservation Corps, the popular nature trails were laid out, and a bird blind was constructed to better enable visitors and researchers to study wildlife. Significant work got underway in 1980, and the result was a large parking lot, the first picnic shelter, and the original hawk platform. The following year an environmental education center was created in another old military building.

By 1986 the deteriorated boardwalks along the nature trails had been replaced. That same year the Cape May Point Natural Area Management Plan had been adopted as part of the New Jersey Natural Area System, ensuring the preservation of the park's natural character. Eighty percent of the park is designated a Natural Area with diverse species of animals and plants.

Today, almost forty years since the military base had been taken over, the Cape May Point State Park has grown to 190 acres. The first attendance records, dating from 1977, record over 80,000 visitors. Today, twenty-five years later, the count has increased tenfold to 800,000 each year.

Cape May Point State Park

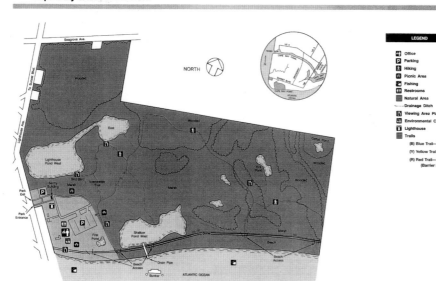

Map of the Cape May Point State Park. *Courtesy of the New Jersey Department of Enviromental Protection, Division of Parks and Forestry.*

Chapter 22

Birding at the Point

Birders' Paradise

Recreational birding has become, in recent years, the second most popular outdoor leisure activity in the country – after gardening. Over the past several decades, the Cape May Bird Observatory (CMBO) has been an outstanding force behind this phenomenal growth. Since its founding in 1976 by the New Jersey Audubon Society, CMBO programs and publications have had a marked influence on the world of birding. Its success can be attributed to two factors: the dynamic leadership of several inspired directors and its incomparable location at the tip of the New Jersey peninsula in Cape May Point.

The peninsular form, diverse natural habitat, and dominant winds from the west combine to make this area the most exciting hotspot for birding in North America. Its fame has spread worldwide. Sandy beaches, tidal pools, wetlands, freshwater ponds, meadows, and woodlands are environments that cater to over four hundred species of birds.

The season for bird watching and migration is yearlong. January introduces the northern spring migration; that continues until July, just as the first shorebirds start heading south. In late May, legions of shorebirds descend on the bay beaches, devouring the eggs of horseshoe crabs in a spectacular feeding frenzy that lasts for almost two weeks.

Songbirds, shorebirds, and birds of prey can be found in such numbers and such variety that Cape May Point is acknowledged as one of the world's pre-eminent birding centers. It's hard to beat the Point's tally of eight species of owls, seventeen of sparrows, thirty-six of warblers, forty of shorebirds, and twenty-four of hawks. Over four hundred species of birds have been recorded in Cape May County.

The Early Birds

It's not surprising that all three of America's celebrated ornithologists visited south Jersey for bird studies in the early 1800s. Alexander Wilson, the Philadelphia author of the nine-volume *American Ornithology*, published in 1808-1814, came half a dozen times to observe, record, and illustrate the magnificent birds of the region. On some of his trips, his intimate friend, George Ord, joined him. Ord was another Philadelphia student of natural history, who became Wilson's biographer and later republished several of Wilson's volumes,

The legendary American ornithologist, the French-born John James Audubon, came to depict the birds of New Jersey a bit later, perhaps in 1829. Coincidentally, his first home in America in 1806 was also in the Philadelphia area – just outside the city in Montgomery County. His stay there however, was a short three years. His return to Philadelphia in 1824, where he showed his splendid portfolio of paintings of birds to the members of the Academy of Natural Sciences, was a major disappointment.

His brash criticism of the bird paintings of his predecessor, Alexander Wilson, a deceased but revered former member of the Academy, offended the group. George Ord, Wilson's friend, biographer, and about to be publisher of Wilson's work, made sure that the members would not support Audubon, and he failed to get the engraver and publisher he had sought in Philadelphia.

His monumental *The Birds of America* was first published in 1827 in England, etched, engraved and aquatinted by the gifted George Havel. The masterful work was well received and his reputation grew. Philadelphia's prestigious Academy of Natural Sciences, which had rejected him only seven years prior, made him an honorary member in 1831.

The most important ornithologist in documenting the south Jersey birds was Witmer Stone, curator of birds at the Academy of Natural Sciences. After decades of study, in 1937 he published his definitive *Bird Studies of Old Cape May* in two volumes that have fortunately been republished just two years ago. Cape May Point was fortunate in having this distinguished scientist as a resident during the last twenty years of his life. A wildlife sanctuary in Lower Township, on the south side of Sunset Boulevard adjacent to Cape May Point, that had been established in his name by the National Audubon Society, was turned over to the management of the New Jersey Audubon Society in 1945.

Another contribution of these "early birds" came in 1950, when Cape May Point resident, Dr. Ernest A. Choate, prepared *A Field List of Birds of Cape May County, New Jersey* that was published by The Cape May Geographic Society. Both Choate and Roger Tory Peterson had conducted season-long studies of migration at the Point. Peterson was first in 1936, and Choate followed with two: his first in 1965 and then again in 1970 with the assistance of Fred Tilly.

The most important ornithologist in documenting the south Jersey birds was Witmer Stone, curator of birds at the Academy of Natural Sciences.

(c.1940s) The most important ornithologist in documenting the south Jersey birds was Witmer Stone, curator of birds at the Academy of Natural Sciences. A wildlife sanctuary in Lower Township, on the south side of Sunset Boulevard adjacent to Cape May Point, which had been established in his name by the National Audubon Society, was turned over to the management of the New Jersey Audubon Society in 1945. *Courtesy of Marie G. Richards.*

Anne's Hideaway

Many non-profit organizations have almost indigent and sometimes zany beginnings. The Cape May Bird Observatory is no exception. At its founding in 1976, it had no home and few funds. Did it have a clear mission statement? That's doubtful too. What it did have was Bill Clark, who had been banding raptors at the Point each season since 1967, as its first director.

His first mission was to find some money to operate this new observatory. Two small federal grants carried him for the first six months. His entire staff was twenty-four-year-old Pete Dunne.

A home was found in 1979, when Pete Dunne took over as the new director. It was more than desk-space but not much more. It was free and often questionable space in Anne Ardrey Northwood's lakeside cottage, *Swan Sea Sanctuary*. Here is how Pete Dunne remembered it almost twenty years later:

> While Anne was alive she let the observatory use this room and a back room. The foyer was common ground. There was a large triptych which served as a door. Anne would hide behind the painting until someone would come in the front door. Then it would be flung back and Anne would walk out and try to sell her books.
>
> You would never know whether she would be wearing clothes or not. It's really hard to feel comfortable when a large-boned woman comes out stark naked and tries to sell you her books. It's a pretty formidable thing to people when they come into what they think is a bird observatory. They might find it difficult to accommodate that easily and react appropriately, and a lot of them decided that their best action was retreat. I saw far more of the backs of people than I did the fronts.

Anne had married d'Arcy Northwood when he was still the curator at Mill Grove, the Audubon Wildlife Sanctuary north of Philadelphia that had been John James Audubon's home for his first few years in America. Northwood retired in 1966, and he and Anne moved to Cape May Point. Before he died of cancer in 1973, Anne expressed her desire to leave their property to everyone in honor of d'Arcy's life spent in the cause of conservation. At her death in 1990, she willed the entire property to the New Jersey Audubon Society.

Her inclination to nudity was only one component of a personality that some might call eccentric. She was an artist by temperament, and some think all artists are eccentric. She painted in the manner of the impressionists; she wrote books of poetry and journals that she published herself under the imprint of the Swansea Press, and sold privately. Pete Dunne recalls her as "a warm, vulnerable, generous, and talented lady."

The deeding of her property to the Cape May Bird Observatory is a testament to that generosity. She has followed in the footsteps of another "lady of the lake," Annette Ferris, who owned Lake Lily and upon her death in the early 1940s, deeded it to the Borough of Cape May Point for the use of everyone.

(2002) A home was found in 1979 for the fledgling Cape May Bird Observatory. It was more than desk-space but not much more. It was free and often questionable space in Anne Ardrey Northwood's lakeside cottage, *Swan Sea Sanctuary*. Today the CMBO occupies the entire house for offices and a large gift shop. *Courtesy of the Author.*

Three's Not a Crowd

Considering its struggling start-up, the CMBO of today is an unbelievable success story. Scarcely a day goes by that there is not some engaging event scheduled for people of all ages and interests. Its focus is now on research, environmental education, bird conservation, and recreational birding activities.

The house that Anne Northwood donated is now known, in her honor, as the Northwood Center. Its rooms are tended by helpful staff and volunteers, and open everyday from nine to four-thirty, and filled to overflowing with nature books, as well as gifts and equipment for anyone interested in birding.

A fledgling organization, the Nature Center of Cape May, started in 1992 by a group of dedicated volunteers spearheaded by Charlotte Todd, was adopted by the New Jersey Audubon Society three years later. Located right on the banks of Cape May Harbor, its many volunteers work with the CMBO and other local organizations to deliver a variety of group educational programs, many of them directed to children.

To further its mission in Cape May County, the New Jersey Audubon Society, in 1997, opened a third and larger facility, the Cape May Bird Observatory Center for Education and Research, in the bay-area town of Goshen. The 8600 square-foot building on twenty-six acres of tidal marsh and upland is in a fine location close to the Delaware Bay shore.

A 170-seat lecture room provides adequate space for larger group education programs. Among its research activities are the continuation of the annual raptor counts that have been underway since 1967, coordination of the New Jersey Breeding Bird Atlas Project, North America's only full-season count of southbound seabirds, and butterfly surveys with emphasis on migrating monarchs.

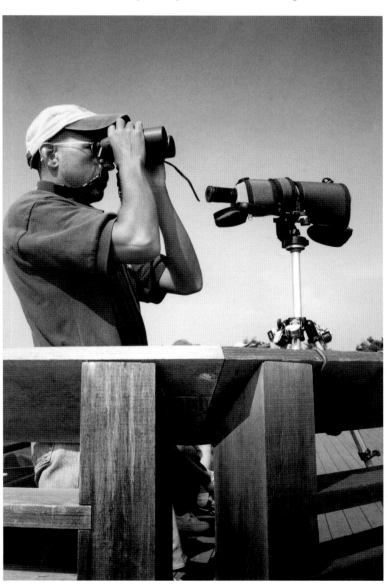

(2002) The Cape May Point Hawk Watch platform has been staffed each fall since 1976 by the Cape May Bird Observatory's official hawk counter from September 1st to the end of November. *Courtesy of the Author.*

(2002) Field trips are the Cape May Bird Observatory's most common offering to the public. Few days pass when one or more birding and nature walks are not underway, similar to this gathering at the nearby New Jersey State Park, being instructed by one of the park guides. *Courtesy of the Author.*

An Endless Quest

If the reader is really interested in birding, there is probably no better place in the world for you than the Cape May County peninsula. The dizzying array of activities that CMBO sponsors could keep the dedicated birder engaged for years. How a dozen and a half professional staff and volunteers, most with their own specialties, can keep up with the workload remains an elusive mystery.

Field trips are, of course, the most common offering. Few days pass when one or more birding and nature walks are not underway. For beginners, they may start at Lake Lily for its waterfowl and native flora, at Pavilion Circle for its butterflies, or at the nearby State Park for myriad bird watching.

At any season there is the Hawk Watch Platform, the Nature Conservancy Meadows, or the nearby Beanery, which is part of farmer George Rea's bayside spread. Further still, there are walks along the shores of Cape May Harbor, or at Two Mile Beach, just north of Cape May, or further up at Stone Harbor Point. Full days can be spent with CMBO experts visiting the many hotspots along the Delaware Bay National Wildlife Refuge.

Banding demonstrations, in the fall, of songbirds conducted by the CMBO as part of its research program are open to everyone. Groups meet at the Two Mile Beach National Wildlife Refuge. Another demonstration by the research team that attracts many fall visitors and butterfly lovers is the Monarch Monitoring Project that tracks the massive migration of these fascinating creatures through Cape May Point on there way to their wintering spot in the mountains of central Mexico.

All types of workshops are available, the most popular of which is the five-day Raptor Migration Peak Workshop conducted by Pete Dunne with Pat and Clay Sutton just before the highlight of the year's biggest blast – the historic Autumn Weekend and Bird Show. Another spectacular event is the 4-day Hawks, Owls, and Winter Waterfowl Workshop held in late January, where Pat and Clay are joined by Ward Dasey to check out all the action along the Delaware Bay shore and the salt marshes of the Atlantic Ocean. There are plenty more less-intense workshops for those interested in identifying hawks, owls, dragonflies, and wildlife food plants.

Of significant importance are the Group Education Programs for schools and other groups that are under the direction of the Nature Center of Cape May. They include habitat studies of New Jersey's pinelands, uplands, and domestic gardens; of the marine systems in the watersheds and wetlands; and of the botany, biology, and geology of the barrier island beaches.

One of the most pleasant and enlightening opportunities is a morning or sunset cruise through the vast salt marshes that lie between the Garden State Parkway and the Atlantic Ocean. Called the Skimmer, the comfortable catamaran glides through the shallow waterways of these timeless wetlands that seem so serene and mysterious. A CMBO naturalist is on board to reveal the many secrets of this enchanted maritime grassland.

For others who enjoy an adventure over the water there's the ferry ride to Delaware's bay shore with guided walks for birding and nature study on the beaches of Cape Henlopen and at the nearby Broadkill Marsh. A two-day trip is arranged for a look at a rare species, at Chincoteague, an uninhabited barrier island off the coast of Virginia. For the undaunted (and more affluent) birder the CMBO arranges a winter getaway to Costa Rica for a look at neo-tropical birding and local natural history.

The CMBO has brought the natural and historical delights of Cape May Point to a worldwide audience of birders and natural history enthusiasts. Many doubt that this all would have happened without the tireless enthusiasm of a very young Pete Dunne who had an image of what it could be, and who has once again, after an absence of sixteen years, become its director.

One of the most pleasant and enlightening opportunities is a morning or sunset cruise through the vast salt marshes that lie between the Garden State Parkway and the Atlantic Ocean.

(c.1990s) Hawk banding demonstrations, in the fall, conducted by the CMBO at the State Park, as part of its research program, are free and open to everyone. *Courtesy of the Cape May Star and Wave.*

Cape May Point Chronology

Before Sea Grove

1816 • Steamship travel to Cape Island opens with Captain Whilldin's *Delaware*
1823 • Cape May Point's first lighthouse is built
1835 • Oak Bluffs Camp Meeting Association is founded on Martha's Vineyard, Massachusetts
1847 • Cape May Point's second lighthouse is built
1849 • The first Life Saving Station, a simple unmanned boathouse, is built at Cape May Point
1854 • Atlantic City is founded and is accessible by the *Camden and Atlantic City Railroad*
1859 • Cape May Point's present lighthouse is built
1863 • The *Glassboro and Millville Railroad* opens service to Cape May City
1868 • The *Glassboro and Millville Railroad* becomes the *West Jersey Railroad*
1869 • Ocean Grove Camp Meeting Association is founded in northern New Jersey
1871 • Pitman Grove Camp Meeting Association is founded in southern New Jersey
• Sea Cliff Camp Meeting Association is founded in New York
1872 • The West Cape May Land Company is incorporated by Alexander Whilldin and others.

Part 1 – The Early Years
1875-1900

Sea Grove and the Sea Grove Association

1875 • The Sea Grove Association is incorporated by Alexander Whilldin and others
• The West Cape May Land Company transfers its holdings to the Sea Grove Association
• Sea Grove is founded by the Sea Grove Association
• The sand dunes are leveled and used as fill in the lower land areas on the Atlantic Ocean side
• The street system is laid out, woods are cut through, and the streets are graded and graveled
• The Sea Grove House hotel, the Signal Station, and the Pavilion are opened
• The cottages of Alexander Whilldin, John Wanamaker and others are completed
• The *Cape May City Passenger Railroad Company* offers horse-car service to Sea Grove
• A tornado strikes Sea Grove in late February
1876 • The Cape House and the Centennial House hotels are opened
• The Sea Grove House hotel adds a wing and expands its facilities
• Dr. J. Newton Walker's drug store opens next to the Sea Grove House hotel
• Alexander Whilldin sponsors a weeklong National Sunday School Conference in the Pavilion

• Gale force winds strike Sea Grove in September and November storms
1877 • John Wanamaker and Alexander Whilldin each conduct Sunday school services at the Pavilion
• A severe northeaster strikes Sea Grove
1878 • Sea Grove's name is changed to Cape May Point
• The Delaware Bay House opens at Sunset Beach as an excursion hotel

Cape May Point

1878 • Cape May Point becomes a borough within Lower Township
• The Sea Grove Association continues to sell lots with significant deed restrictions
• The steamship *Republic* opens service to Cape May Point
• The Cape May Point schoolhouse is under the direction of George Eldridge as schoolmaster
1879 • The *Delaware Bay and Cape May Railroad* offers steam locomotive service – replacing the horse-car rail service
• The Sea-Side Home opens as a summer vacation house for Presbyterian women and children
1880 • Saint Peters-by-the-Sea holds its first service
1881 • The Sea Grove Association sells all of its real estate holdings, including the Pavilion, Lake Lily, and three hotels at public auction
1882 • The Beadle Memorial Presbyterian Church holds its first service
1885 • The Union Chapel holds its first service as a Baptist church
• Saint Agnes Roman Catholic Church holds its first service
• The United Brethren in Christ opens the Sea Grove Camp Meeting Grounds between Knox and Stites Avenues
1886 • Quakers hold regular services in the Hilliard cottage – these continue until 1905
1888 • The African American Methodist Church opens on Alexander Avenue sometime after 1878 – it is destroyed by fire in the 1920s
• The Centennial House is destroyed in a fire that takes down many of the nearby cottages and stores.
• John Lankenau rents Walker's Ocean Cottage for the Lutheran Deaconesses of the Mary J. Drexel Home in Philadelphia
• The great blizzard of 1888 closes rail service to Cape May Point
1889 • Wanamaker entertains President and Mrs. Benjamin Harrison at his cottage
• A September storm destroys the steamboat landing pier at Sunset Beach
1890 • Wanamaker and others build a stately cottage and present it to President Benjamin Harrison's wife
• The Shoreham Hotel opens near the lighthouse
• The Lankenau Villa opens as a summer vacation home for the Lutheran Deaconesses

1891
- An October northeaster damages Beach Avenue and threatens the cottage of John Wanamaker
- The Lankenau Villa builds two additions

1892
- The *Cape May, Delaware Bay, and Sewells Point Railroad* opens electric trolley service to Cape May Point

1894
- The *South Jersey Railroad* opens service to Cape May City

1896
- Wanamaker closes his cottage at Ocean and Emerald Avenues and takes back the Harrison cottage for his summer home

1897
- Springer's Store opens where the Post Office currently is located

1899
- Wanamaker donates his cottage to the trustees of the Sea-Side Home — it becomes the Haddock Memorial
- Dr. Randall T. Hazzard opens the Cape May Point Social Club on West Lake Drive and builds the rustic bridge over Lake Lily
- A hurricane brings tides up to the foundations of the Carlton House hotel and many beachfront cottages are threatened

Part 2 – Through the Two World Wars 1900-1946

1903
- The steamship Republic ends service to Cape May Point and Cape May City

1905
- The Cape May Sand Company starts operations at Sunset Beach

1908
- A terrible fire destroys the Lankenau Villa and many of the surrounding cottages
- Cape May Point is incorporated as an independent borough separate from Lower Township

1909
- John Lankenau builds a new Lankenau Villa on the same site
- The Shoreham Hotel is purchased by the Sisters of Saint Joseph for a summer retreat house and renamed Saint Mary's-by-the-Sea

1910
- Durburrow swims across the Delaware Bay from Cape May Point to Lewes, Delaware in a fifteen hour feat

1911
- Two fire hose carts are acquired with 1,000 feet of hose and stored at the corner of Yale and Ocean Avenues

1913
- Saint Mary's-by-the-Sea purchases a large cottage to be used as a rectory for the priests on summer vacations
- The Sisters of the Immaculate Heart of Mary acquire the Carlton Hotel for a summer retreat house and rename it Villa Maria-by-the-Sea

1915
- The United States Coast Guard replaces the former Life Saving Service

1916
- The Wanamaker cottage is moved to the corner of Cape and Yale Avenues as the Presbyterian Orphanage

1917
- The *Delaware Bay, Cape May, and Sewells Point Trolley* goes out of business

1919
- Bus service opens between Cape May Point and Cape May

1920
- A fishing pier is constructed by the borough but demolished for its timber the following year

1922
- The Cape May Point Volunteer Fire Company Number 1 is authorized by the borough
- John Carmignano (John the Cop) is elected as Marshall and serves in that position for thirty-one years

1923
- Saint Mary's-by-the-Sea purchases the McAvoy cottage, *Queen of the Sea*

1924
- William C. Schwebel, a Philadelphia lawyer, sponsors regular Lutheran Sunday services in the Union Chapel
- An August hurricane strikes Cape May Point
- The Firehouse on Yale Avenue is completed and the first fire truck is purchased

1926
- The borough buys an American-LaFrance four hundred gallon pumper for the fire company
- Sunset Boulevard is paved in concrete, replacing the former gravel roadbed
- The *Atlantus*, a salvaged concrete cargo ship planned to be part of a ferry landing, runs aground at Sunset Beach

1927
- The borough buys a City Service hook and ladder truck for the fire company
- The jail is moved from Pearl Avenue to a lot behind the firehouse

1928
- The Edwin Gould cottage opens as an addition to the Presbyterian Orphanage

1930
- The Ferris family purchases Lake Lily

1931
- Twelve steel jetties are installed along the Cape May Point Beaches from Surf Street to Brainard Avenue
- The Point's schoolhouse is closed and children attend the consolidated school in Lower Township
- The borough permits Frank Hughes to build a fishing pier between Brainard and Central Avenues

1933
- A September hurricane strikes Cape May Point

1934
- The Coast Guard Station is moved back thirty feet from the shoreline and a bulkhead is built to protect it from further erosion

1935
- The New Jersey Department of Health threatens to shut down the borough's water system because of a high bacteria count
- The lighthouse installs an electric lamp, replacing the former kerosene lamp and original oil lamp

1936
- A savage northeaster with hurricane force winds strikes Cape May Point
- Villa Maria-by-the-Sea is closed and demolished
- The Sea-Side Home is closed and demolished
- Beachfront cottages are severely damaged or destroyed by the storm
- The first ordinance requiring a building permit is adopted
- The Taxpayers League of Cape May Point is formed to encourage the borough commissioners to increase the bonded debt

1937
- With WPA funding, the first concrete block jetty is installed in front of the Sea-Side Home

1938
- The Beach Front Property Owners Association is formed to lobby for more jetties and bulkheads from Ocean Avenue to Lighthouse Avenue
- A new sewage pumping station is constructed at the corner of Yale and Coral Avenues

1940
- Annette Ferris deeds Lake Lily to the borough for the free use of the public
- The borough starts selling building lots for twenty-five dollars

1941
- The New Jersey Department of Health demands that Cape May Point cease dumping its sewage into the South Cape May Meadows

1942
- Saint Mary's-by-the-Sea is leased as a military barracks for troops stationed in Cape May Point during World War II
- The WPA concrete block jetty projects at Cape and Alexander Avenues are halted and never resumed
- The Cape May Sand Company closes its beach mining operations
- The Northwest Magnesite Company plant is built at Sunset Beach

1943
- Garbage is collected for the first time in Cape May Point

1944
- A September hurricane delivers monumental destruction to Cape May and West Cape May but damage is relatively light in Cape May Point
- The Point sewers are connected to the Cape May City sewer line on Sunset Boulevard

1945 • The Harrison cottage, heavily damaged by the 1944 storm, is demolished by the borough

1946 • Saint Mary's-by-the-Sea is returned to the Sisters of Saint Joseph following the end of World War II

Part 3 – Peace and Prosperity 1947-Present Day

1950 • A November northeaster drives flood waters into Lake Lily, bringing in more oils, fertilizers, and pesticides which create excessive weed growth

1952 • The Lankenau Villa is sold and reopened as the Chelsea Hotel
• The Sunset Beach Sportsmen's Club opens at Crystal and Alexander Avenues

1954 • An ordinance is introduced to ban hunting, fishing, and boating on Lake Lily

1955 • The first Planning Board is established

1958 • After more than thirty years, Lutheran Services in the Union Chapel are discontinued

1959 • The Presbyterian Orphanage, Sunny Corner, closes as a summer home for the children of the Philadelphia institution
• The old Life Saving Station is destroyed by fire

1960 • A new sewage plant is constructed on the north side of Sunset Boulevard between Cape and Lighthouse Avenues

1962 • The Presbyterian Orphanage sells its property to the Marianist Society, Inc.
• A severe northeast storm, the worst in the Point's history, destroys many of the beachfront properties
• Lake Lily is flooded with sea water from the storm which eventually kills all of the water lilies that had given it its name
• The Army Corps of Engineers constructs an emergency dune system in Cape May Point and along the South Cape May Meadows

1964 • The Cape May Point Taxpayers' Association is formed to address beachfront protection following the 1962 storm

1968 • The first zoning ordinance is adopted
• The current dune system construction starts on the beaches to the west of Saint Mary's-by-the-Sea

1970 • The Point retires its wells and brings in domestic water service from Cape May

1971 • The current dune system, from one end of the Point to the other, is completed by the Army Corps of Engineers

1976 • The Cape May Bird Observatory is founded by the New Jersey Audubon Society

1979 • The Cape May Bird Observatory opens in Anne Northwood's cottage on East Lake Drive – it's known today as the CMBO Northwood Center

1980 • The Cape May Point Water and Sewer Utility is established as a separate entity from the borough government

1982 • The Taxpayers' Association sponsors the first annual garden awards program

1983 • The jailhouse is moved to Historic Cold Spring Village where it serves as a craft shop
• The Northwest Magnesite Company closes after forty-one years of operations

1984 • Major zoning changes are approved by the borough
• The Delaware County Aquarium Society surveys the water quality of Lake Lily

1986 • The Taxpayers' Association forms a Dune Committee and starts the first dune planting program
• West Cape May provides police service to Cape May Point under an inter-local agreement
• The Mid-Atlantic Center for the Arts leases the lighthouse to accommodate visitors and starts a twenty year improvement program

1989 • The Taxpayers' Association proposes improvements to Pavilion Circle
• The first annual Block Party is held at the Firehouse

1991 • The proposed Pavilion Circle improvements are approved by the taxpayers
• A heavy storm (the "Halloween Storm") strikes, flooding the eastern part of Cape May Point

1992 • A January storm brings more flooding – Lake Lily is filled almost to overflowing

1993 • Annual Rental Permits are required for all rental properties

1994 • The "Drainage East" project is completed
• Artificial reefs are installed on the two beaches between Lehigh and Coral Avenues

1995 • A new water tank is constructed on Sunset Boulevard just west of Cape Avenue
• The Delaware County Aquarium Society resurveys the water quality of Lake Lily

1998 • The "Drainage West" project is completed
• An environmental consultant is retained to design cleanup operations for Lake Lily

1999 • Three borough lots on Coral Avenue are sold at auction – an action opposed by the majority of taxpayers

2000 • The New Jersey Assembly appropriates funds for the cleanup of Lake Lily

2001 • Cape May Point's police service is provided by Cape May under an inter-local agreement

2002 • A second series of artificial reefs is installed on Cape Beach and Emerald Beach

2003 • Cape Avenue improvements and the dredging of Lake Lily are scheduled to begin

Bibliography

A Book of Cape May. Cape May, New Jersey: The Albert Hand Co., 1937.

Alexander, Robert Crozer. *Ho! For Cape Island*. Cape May, New Jersey, 1956.

Bailey, John. *Sentinel of the Jersey Cape*. Cape May, New Jersey: Cape Publishing, Inc., 2001.

Beesley, Maurice. *Early History of Cape May County*. Trenton, New Jersey: Office of the True American, 1857.

Biographical Dictionary of Philadelphia Architects. Philadelphia, Pennsylvania: Furness Library, University of Pennsylvania.

Black, Frederick Reeves. *The West Jersey Society, 1768-1784*. Philadelphia, Pennsylvania: The Pennsylvania Magazine.

Boyer, George F. *Cape May County Story*. Philadelphia, Pennsylvania: Historical Society of Pennsylvania.

Commissioners' Meeting Minutes, 1878-2002. Cape May Point, New Jersey: Borough Records, 2002.

Cape May Geographic Society, Annual Bulletins, 1956-1987. Cape May, New Jersey: Cape May Geographic Society.

Cress, J.A. *Guidebook and Directory of Cape May Point*. Cape May, New Jersey, 1881.

Cunningham, John T. *The New Jersey Shore*. New Brunswick, New Jersey: Rutgers University Press, 1958.

Directory of the Philanthropic, Educational, and Religious Associations and Churches of Philadelphia. Lancaster, Pennsylvania: The New Era Printing Co., 1903.

Dorwart, Jeffrey M. *Cape May County, New Jersey—The Making of an American Resort Community*. New Brunswick, New Jersey: Rutgers University Press, 1992.

Engerman, Stanley L. and Gallman, Robert E. *The Cambridge Economic History of the United States—Volume II*. Cambridge, United Kingdom: Cambridge University Press, 2000.

Geology of the County of Cape May, State of New Jersey. Trenton, New Jersey: Office of the True American, 1857.

Gibbons, Herbert Adams. *John Wanamaker*. Port Washington, New York: Kennikat Press, 1926.

Logue, Sr.Maria Kosta, *Sisters of Saint Joseph of Philadelphia*. Westminster, Maryland: The Newman Press, 1950.

MacCloskey, Jr., James E. *History of Harbison-Walker Refractories Company*. Pittsburgh, Pennsylvania, 1952.

Mather et al, *Tales of the Jersey Cape*. Cape May Court House: Cape May County Chamber of Commerce Bicentennial Celebration Commission, 1976.

Mather, Edith B.D. *The Gingerbread Church*. Lititz, Pennsylvania: Sutter House, 1985.

Map of Cape May County. New York, New York: F.W.Beers, 1872.

Richards, Horace. *A Book of Maps of Cape May*. Cape May, New Jersey: Cape May Geographic Society, 1954.

Salvini, Emil R. *The Summer City by the Sea*. New Brunswick, New Jersey: Rutgers University Press, 1995.

Sea Grove, Cape May Point, N.J., Philadelphia, Pennsylvania: Allen, Lane, and Scott, 1877.

Stevens, Lewis Townsend. *History of Cape May County*. Cape May, New Jersey: Star of the Cape, 1897.

Swain, R.B. *Atlas of Cape May County*. Cape May Court House, 1868.

The Biographical Encyclopedia of Pennsylvania of the Nineteenth Century. Philadelphia, Pennsylvania: Galaxy Publishing Company, 1874.

The Value of a Dollar, 1860-1999. Lakeville, Connecticut: Grey House Publishing, Inc., 1999.

The Seaside Resorts of New Jersey. Philadelphia, Pennsylvania: Allen, Lane, and Scott, 1887.

Thomas, George, and Doebly, Carl. *Cape May—Queen of the Seaside Resorts*. Cranberry, New Jersey: Associated University Presses,1976.

Timmons, Jean Totten. *This is Cape May*. 1979.

Toll, Jean Barth, and Gillam, Mildred S. *Invisible Philadelphia*. Philadelphia, Pennsylvania: Atwater Kent Museum, 1995.

Tomlin, Charles. *Cape May Spray*. Philadelphia, Pennsylvania: Bradley Brothers, 1913.

Weiser, Frederick S. *Loves Response—A Story of Lutheran Deaconesses in America*. Philadelphia, Pennsylvania: The Board of Publication of the United Lutheran Church in America, 1962.

Wheeler, Edward S., *Scheyichbi and the Strand*. Philadelphia, Pennsylvania: J.B. Lippincott, 1876.

Wilson, Ruth Swain. *The Tip of the Cape*. Cape May, New Jersey, 1976.

Woolman and Rose. *Historical and Biographical Atlas of the New Jersey Coast*, Philadelphia, Pennsylvania, 1878.

Zulker, William Allen. *John Wanamaker: King of Merchants*. Wayne, Pennsylvania: Eaglecrest Press, 1993.

Index

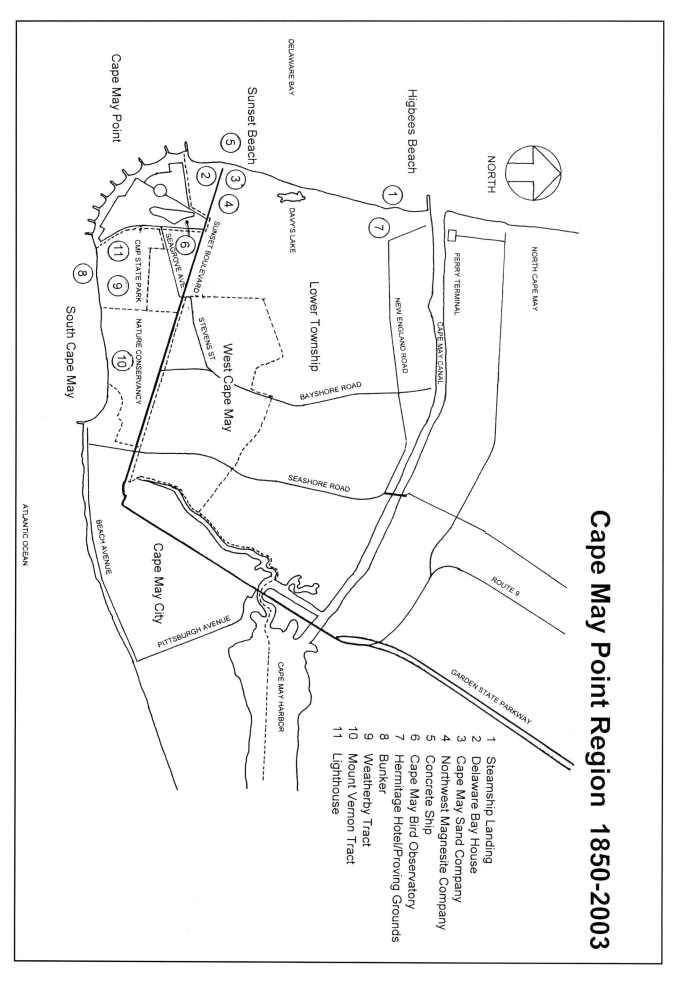

Cape May Point Region 1850-2003

NORTH

NORTH CAPE MAY

FERRY TERMINAL

CAPE MAY CANAL

NEW ENGLAND ROAD

Higbees Beach

DELAWARE BAY

DAVY'S LAKE

Lower Township

BAYSHORE ROAD

SEASHORE ROAD

ROUTE 9

GARDEN STATE PARKWAY

Sunset Beach

Cape May Point

SUNSET BOULEVARD

SEAGROVE AVE.

CMP STATE PARK

NATURE CONSERVANCY

STEVENS ST.

West Cape May

South Cape May

ATLANTIC OCEAN

BEACH AVENUE

Cape May City

PITTSBURGH AVENUE

CAPE MAY HARBOR

1 Steamship Landing
2 Delaware Bay House
3 Cape May Sand Company
4 Northwest Magnesite Company
5 Concrete Ship
6 Cape May Bird Observatory
7 Hermitage Hotel/Proving Grounds
8 Bunker
9 Weatherby Tract
10 Mount Vernon Tract
11 Lighthouse

176